The Jewish Information Source Book

THE
JEWISH
INFORMATION
SOURCE BOOK

A Dictionary and Almanac

Ronald H. Isaacs

JASON ARONSON INC.
Northvale, New Jersey
London

The author gratefully acknowledges permission to quote from the following sources:

From the *Encyclopaedia Judaica*, copyright © 1972 by Keter Publishing House Ltd. Used by permission.

From *A Dictionary of Jewish Names and Their History* by Benzion C. Kaganoff. Copyright © 1977 by Schocken Books, Inc. Used by permission of the author.

From *Gateway to Judaism*, Volume I, by Albert M. Shulman. Copyright © 1971 by A. S. Barnes and Company, Inc. Used by permission of Associated University Presses.

Population figures for cities and counties in the United States adapted from the *American Jewish Year Book*, copyright © 1992 by the American Jewish Committee and Jewish Publication Society. Used by permission.

Population figures for foreign cities from 1991 *Jewish Yearbook*, copyright © 1991 by Jewish Chronicle Publications. Published by Vallentine Mitchell & Co., London. Used by permission.

This book was set in 10 pt. Garamond by Lind Graphics of Upper Saddle River, New Jersey, and printed by Haddon Craftsmen in Scranton, Pennsylvania.

Ref
BM
50
I78
1993

Library of Congress Cataloging-in-Publication Data

Isaacs, Ronald H.
    The Jewish information source book : a dictionary and almanac / by Ronald H. Isaacs.
        p.   cm.
    Includes index.
    ISBN 0-87668-354-5
    1. Judaism—Dictionaries.   2. Jews—Dictionaries.   3. Judaism—Miscellanea.   4. Jews—Miscellanea.   I. Title.
    BM50.I78   1993
    296.'.03—dc20   92-39645

Manufactured in the United States of America. Jason Aronson Inc. offers books and cassettes. For information and catalog write to Jason Aronson Inc., 230 Livingston Street, Northvale, New Jersey 07647.

To my brothers,
Mendy and Barry,
with love

CONTENTS

PREFACE

The words, concepts, and body of knowledge that enable any person to truly understand Judaism and the history of the Jewish people are many and perhaps beyond counting. These concepts continue to change and evolve as each new generation brings to them its own experiences and responses.

This *Jewish Information Source Book* is intended to present a ready reference of terms that are essential to an understanding of the language of Judaism. The first part of the book, the dictionary, contains concise definitions of terms, concepts, vocabulary, places, and people that have shaped the Jewish people throughout their history.

The second part of the book is a mini Jewish almanac, which presents some fascinating facts related to Jewish experience, life, culture, and history. I hope that my selections and definitions will have practical value for the person engaged in Jewish study. It is my desire that the knowledge gained from the dictionary and almanac will stimulate the reader to explore the great Jewish books, sacred and secular, past and present, which reveal and make vivid the rich and wondrous life and beliefs of the Jewish people.

Using the Dictionary and the Almanac

The terms in the dictionary are listed in alphabetical order. Words have been transliterated according to the preferred spelling, unless the well-known spelling is more readily recognized and accepted.

The almanac is a celebration of Jewish life and the Jewish people—a fact-filled treasury of information related to Jewish history, religion, and tradition. It is not intended to be read all at once. Rather, you, the reader, should feel free to flip through the book, each time finding something new to suit your mood or interest.

PART I

THE JEWISH DICTIONARY

A

Aaron (13th century B.C.E.) Elder brother of Moses and a leading figure in the exodus from Egypt.

Abba Literally, "father." Honorary title given to some scholars during the time of the Talmud.

Abel Second son of Adam and Eve and brother of Cain. Cain killed Abel because he was envious of Abel's sacrifice to God.

Abrabanel, Isaac (1437–1509) Statesman, philosopher, and biblical commentator. His works of philosophy are essentially antirationalist. His general religious writings stress the importance of divine revelation and the Messiah.

Abraham First patriarch and founder of the Hebrew nation.

Absorption Process of acculturating new immigrants to Israel. In modern times this especially refers to Russian and Ethiopian Jews who, when immigrating to Israel, need assistance in learning Hebrew, obtaining housing, finding jobs, and so forth.

Academies Schools of higher learning established by the rabbis during talmudic times. Two of the most well known academies were Sura and Pumpedita.

Acculturation Process of adopting the traits of another culture, such as when the immigrant Jews adopted the ways of American society and became "Americanized."

Acre (Hebrew *Akko*) Israeli town located in the northern part of Haifa bay. It was the most important seaport in Israel from ancient times until the 19th century. Today a large Jewish residential area has developed outside the Old City of Acre.

Adam and Eve First man and woman in the Bible. They were placed in the Garden of Eden, where they ate of the forbidden Tree of Knowledge, resulting in expulsion from the Garden.

Adar Twelfth month of the Jewish religious year, approximating to February or March. In the event of a Jewish leap year, a 13th month, called Adar II, is added. Adar is a happy month, primarily because of the celebration of the Purim holiday on the 14th of Adar.

Adler, Cyrus (1863–1940) Scholar and social worker, he was active in founding the Jewish Publication Society and helped to reorganize the Jewish Theological Seminary of America.

Adloyada Literally,"until he does not know . . . the difference between Haman and Mordecai." This refers to a practice of drinking on Purim until one cannot tell the difference between "Cursed be Haman" and "Blessed be Mordecai."

Adonai The name of God is written in the Bible with the four consonants YHWH (known as the tetragrammaton). By the 3rd century B.C.E., the pronunciation of YHWH was avoided and *Adonai*, "the Lord," was substituted for it.

Afikomen (Greek, meaning "dessert") The piece of *matzah*, hidden during the early part of the *Seder* meal, which is searched for and found. It is then shared by all of the *Seder* participants.

Aggadah The part of the Talmud that includes things not of a legal nature, such as descriptions of historical events, legends, and proverbs. About 30 percent of the Talmud is made up of *aggadah*.

Agnon, S. Y. (1888–1970) Twentieth-century Israeli novelist and Nobel Prize winner for literature. His writing is highly symbolic and his stories often contain biblical and talmudic elements.

Agudat Israel (Hebrew, meaning "Union of Israel") World organization of Orthodox Jews founded in 1912, which today has representation in Israel's Knesset.

Ahad Ha-Am (Asher Ginzberg) (1856–1927) One of the foremost thinkers and essayists in Hebrew literature, and the philosopher of cultural Zionism. He insisted that a spiritual and national revival must come before the return to Zion.

Ahasuerus King of Persia, who was an important figure in the Book of Esther. Biblical scholars often identify him with Xerxes (486–465 B.C.E.). Ahasuerus first married Vashti and later took Esther as his wife and queen.

Akdamut Mystical poem in honor of the Torah, which is recited by Ashkenazic Jews before the Torah reading on the festival of Shavuot. It was written in Aramaic by Meir ben Isaac in the 11th century.

Akiva (*c.* 40–135 C.E.) Talmudic scholar and leader of his people. According to legend, he started his Jewish education at age 40, and his editing of the many teachings of previous scholars laid the foundation for the editing of the Mishnah.

Al Chet Prayer said on the High Holidays that alphabetically enumerates various types of sins. It is a chief element in the liturgy for Yom Kippur.

Al HaNissim Literally, "for the miracles" that God brought for us, this prayer is part of the liturgy included in festival observances that proclaim God's miraculous power in saving the Jewish people.

Alav HaShalom/Aleha HaShalom When speaking of the deceased, these terms are customarily used, meaning "may peace be with him/her."

Aleikhem, Shalom (Shalom Rabinovitz) (1859–1916) Yiddish author and humorist whose sketches often afforded penetrating insight into the immigrant generation in America.

Alenu Prayer proclaiming the sovereignty and unity of God, possibly composed by Rav of Babylonia for the New Year. Today it is recited at the conclusion of every synagogue service.

Alexander the Great (356–323 B.C.E.) King of Macedonia, who introduced Greek language and customs wherever he went. As a result, the Greek and oriental cultures mixed and created a new civilization—Hellenism—that spread over Alexander's empire.

Alexandria City in northern Egypt founded by Alexander the Great. It was the first city to give citizenship to the Jews.

Al-Fatah Arab terrorist movement founded in 1965 to carry on the struggle for the "liberation of Palestine."

Aliyah (Hebrew, meaning "ascent") 1. Term referring to the immigration of Jews to Israel. The first *aliyah* (1882–1903) consisted of 25,000 Jews who established agricultural settlements as they arrived. Subsequently there was a second *aliyah* (1904–1914), a third *aliyah* (1919–1923), a fourth *aliyah* (1924–1928), and a fifth *aliyah* (1933–1939). 2. A calling up to read the Torah in the synagogue during worship. Originally each person read his particular Torah section. Today a Torah reader, often a cantor, may read on behalf of the person.

Allen, Woody (1935–   ) Well-known American writer and director of, and actor in, a variety of films.

Altar Place of sacrificial offerings to a deity.

Am HaAretz Term denoting a person ignorant of Jewish law and custom. Originally it was used as a collective noun signifying "the people of the land" or the masses of people.

Amalekite Ancient biblical people know for their extreme hostility to the Israelites. Haman, the archenemy of the Jews in the Book of Esther, is regarded as a descendant of Agag, king of the Amalekites.

Amen (Hebrew, meaning "so be it") Expression of affirmation used as a response to prayers and benedictions. It is also used by Christians and Moslems.

American Israelite Anglo-Jewish weekly newspaper established in 1854 by Isaac M. Wise as a forum for his ideas.

American Jewish Committee (AJC) Nationwide American Jewish organization founded in 1906. Its objectives, stated in its charter, are: "to prevent the violation of the civil and religious rights of Jews everywhere; to secure for Jews equality of economic, social, and education opportunity; and to relieve Jews who suffer from persecution and other disasters."

American Jewish Congress Founded in 1918, its goals include the securing of full rights for Jews of all lands and the abolishment of all laws discriminating against Jews.

American Jewish Year Book A handbook of information on Jews the world over, published annually since 1909 by the American Jewish Committee and the Jewish Publication Society.

American Nusach A relatively new term that refers to contemporary popular Jewish music, which combines a

Jewish theme with a contemporary musical mode such as folk rock or country and western.

Amidah Principal prayer, also known as *HaTefillah* (the prayer) or the *Shmoneh Esrei* (eighteen) because the early compilation of the prayer had eighteen benedictions in it.

Amora Title given to a talmudic sage who was active from the 3rd through the 6th centuries. The *amoraim* continued the work of the *tannaim*, the creators of the Mishnah.

Amos Eighteenth-century Judean prophet. In his book (the third of the twelve Minor Prophets) he warns Israel of the danger from Assyria.

Amram Gaon Teacher and intellectual leader, head of the Sura Academy.

Angel Referring to numerous types of supernatural beings in the Bible, including cherubim and seraphim. Angels are often sent to Earth, sometimes with a human appearance, to bring the message of God to the people.

Ani Maamin "I believe . . . with perfect faith," a statement based on Maimonides'principles of faith, became the badge of courage for the Jews of the Holocaust who marched into the gas chambers chanting, "I believe with perfect faith in the coming of the Messiah, and though he may tarry, I still continue to believe."

Aninut Refers to the period of initial grief between death and burial. The individual mourner is called an *onen*.

Anos Within the Sephardic community, the commemoration of the anniversary of a person's death. It is similar to a *yahrzeit* in the Ashkenazic tradition.

Anti-Defamation League (ADL) Founded by B'nai B'rith in 1913, this organization's purpose is to stamp out prejudice in America by exposing the motives and methods of anti-Semites.

Antiochus Name of thirteen Greek kings who ruled Syria in the Hellenistic Period. Antiochus IV (175 B.C.E.) is believed to be the Antiochus referred to in the story of Chanukah.

Anti-Semitism Term referring to the hatred of all Jews. The term appears to have been first used in Germany in 1879 in a pamphlet by Wilhelm Marr, founder of the Anti-Semitic League.

Apocrypha Religious writings that are noncanonical, written during the period of the Second Temple and sometime after its destruction. The Book of Judith is one of the oldest apocryphal books.

Aqaba, Gulf of Gulf at the northeastern end of the Red Sea, which provided a port for King Solomon's ships. Today it provides Jordan with its only harbor.

Arab League Political organization founded in 1945 by Egypt, Syria, Lebanon, Iraq, Jordan, Saudi Arabia, and Yemen. Hatred of Israel is the common thread that unites the members of the Arab League.

Arabic Language Semitic language that borrowed many Hebrew-Aramaic words. It is the official language of the Arabs.

Arabs Semitic people who trace their origin to Ishmael, son of Abraham and Hagar. They live in Egypt, Saudi Arabia, Yemen, Syria, Iraq, Jordan, Lebanon, and Israel.

Arabs, Palestinian Arabs living in Israel before its statehood in 1948. Israel was previously called Palestine, and its Arab population were called Palestinian Arabs.

Arad Town in the Negev (southern Israel) that was captured by Joshua in biblical times. Modern Arad was founded in 1961 and is located 32 miles east of Beersheba. It is the first Israeli development town to be planned by architects and engineers living on the site.

Arafat, Yassir (1929–   ) Leader of the Palestinian Liberation Organization (P.L.O.), a terrorist group whose mission is to destroy the State of Israel.

Aramaic A group of Semitic languages dating roughly from 900 B.C.E. It was the language of the Jewish exiles in Babylon and is the language of the Talmud.

Aravit Refers to the evening worship service.

Aravot Willow leaves of the brook, placed on the *lulav* for the festival of Sukkot, opposite the myrtle *(hadassim)*. The willow leaves are symbolic of a person's mouth.

Arba Minim Literally, the "four species," it refers to the four items that are used during the festival of Sukkot, namely the *lulav* (palm), *aravot* (willow), *etrog* (citron) and the *hadassim* (myrtle).

Arbaah Turim Important legal code written in the 13th century by Jacob ben Asher. The book is divided into four parts: *Orach Chayyim*, dealing with daily conduct; *Yoreh De'ah*, including dietary laws; *Even HaEzer*, dealing with personal and family matters; and *Choshen Mishpat*, dealing with civil law.

Archaeology The scientific investigation of ancient cultures through their material remains. Bible study is often illumined by discoveries made through archaeological digs.

Ark of the Covenant The chest in which the Ten Commandments were kept. Its exact description is provided by Exodus 25:1–22.

Armageddon According to Christian tradition, the place of the final battle between good and evil (Revelation 16:16).

Aron HaKodesh Holy Ark used to house the Torah scrolls in the synagogue.

Articles of Faith, Thirteen Referring to the creed of faith as articulated by the philosopher Maimonides, these truths of religion include the following: (1) the existence of God; (2) God's unity; (3) God's incorporeality; (4) God's eternity; (5) obligation to worship only God; (6) there is prophecy; (7) Moses is the greatest of all the prophets; (8) The Torah, delivered by Moses, is of divine origin; (9) the eternal validity of the Torah; (10) God knows the deeds of all people; (11) God metes out reward and punishment; (12) God will send a messianic redeemer; (13) God will resurrect the dead.

Arukh HaShulchan Important law code written by Jehiel Epstein, a 19th-century rabbi. This law code deals only with laws that have practical importance.

ARZA (Hebrew, meaning "to the land") The Reform movement's official party in the World Zionist Organization. Its

English acronym stands for "Association of Reform Zionists in America."

Asch, Sholem (1880–1957) Outstanding Yiddish novelist and dramatist whose plays and novels revealed his keen observation and vivid portrayal of Jewish life the world over.

Ashamnu Literally, "we have sinned," it refers to the alphabetical confessional prayer recited on Yom Kippur.

Ashdod One of a number of Philistine cities in ancient Palestine. Modern Ashdod is located 24 miles south of Tel Aviv and serves as a port for cruise liners.

Ashkelon Ancient Mediterranean seaport and an important Philistine city in biblical times. Today modern Ashkelon is located 35 miles south of Tel Aviv and is a popular tourist resort.

Ashkenazim (Hebrew, meaning "Germans") Name applied to the Jews of Germany and Northern France from the 10th century on. In the 16th century, the term Ashkenazim also came to include Jews of Eastern Europe.

Ashray Initial word of Psalm 84:5 ("Happy are they who dwell in Your house"). This verse (ie., Psalm 84:5) is prefixed (with Psalm 144:15) to the verses of Psalm 145 and recited in both the morning and afternoon Jewish worship services.

Asser, Levy (1628–1682) One of the original band of twenty-three pilgrims who came to New York in 1654. A butcher, he built New York's first slaughterhouse.

Assimilation Term referring to the adoption of language, manners, and customs of one's neighbors. Throughout Jewish history, Jews have tended to assimilate the customs of their neighbors wherever they lived.

Attarah Neckpiece of the *tallit* (prayer shawl) on which is usually written the prayer shawl blessing.

Auschwitz Largest death camp established by the Nazis.

Auto-da-fé (Portuguese, meaning "act of faith") Public spectacle to which Jews and other heretics were sentenced during the Inquisition in Spain.

Av Fifth month of the Jewish religious year and approximating the 11th month of the civil year. The commemoration of Tisha B'Av, which remembers the destruction of the Jerusalem Temple, occurs on the 9th of the month of Av.

Av Bet Din (Hebrew, meaning "Father of the Court") Vice-president of the Supreme Court in Jerusalem during the Second Temple. The *Av Bet Din* handled court procedure. In modern times the *Av Bet Din* often refers to the head of a Jewish religious court, called a *Bet Din* in Hebrew.

Avdat Ancient Nabatean city (3rd century B.C.E.). Its archaeological ruins lie 40 miles south of Beersheba and are a popular tourist attraction.

Avelut The period of mourning following a burial.

Averah Literally, "transgression," this Hebrew term refers to a breach of a religious law.

Avinu Malkenu Literally, "our Father our King," it is a well-known selection from the High Holiday liturgy that is recited during the Ten days of Repentance and on public fast days. This prayer acknowledges God's sovereignty in the world.

Avnet Belt that is wrapped around the Torah scroll to hold it together when stored in the *aron hakodesh*.

Avodah Literally, "service," it refers to the Temple sacrificial service and to the Day of Atonement ritual of the high priest. It also refers to the section of the additional *Musaf* service on the Day of Atonement describing the Temple service on that day with its repeated confession of sins.

Avot (Hebrew, meaning "Fathers") Tractate of the Mishnah in the order *Nezikin* having no Gemara . It contains ethical teachings of the rabbis from the 3rd century B.C.E to the 3rd century C.E. The tractate is alternately called *Pirke Avot*, (Ethics of the Fathers).

Avot Literally, "fathers," it refers to the ancestors of the Jewish people and particularly to the patriarchs. It also refers to the first paragraph of the *Amidah* prayer.

B

B'ezrat HaShem Literally, "With the help of God," it is often used today as an expression in speech that demonstrates one's total reliance on God for guidance.

B'nai B'rith Jewish service organization founded in New York in 1843. Its objectives are moral, social, philanthropic, and educational. Its programs today include the Hillel Foundations and Anti-Defamation League.

B'nai Yisrael Literally, "children of Israel," it is a reference today to the Jewish people in general.

Baal (Hebrew, meaning "husband," "owner," or "lord") Foremost among the Canaanite gods, Baal was the presiding deity of a given locality. The Bible often records how the prophets fought Baal worship among the Israelites.

Baal Koreh Person who reads publicly from the Torah during synagogue prayer services.

Baal Shem Tov Literally, "master of the Good Name," also called the Besht, the Baal Shem Tov was the founder of the chasidic movement. His real name was Israel ben Eliezer.

Baal Tefillah Person who reads the liturgy during synagogue prayer services, sometimes called the *shaliach tzibbur*.

Baal Tekiah Person who sounds the *shofar* in the synagogue during services on the New Year and during the penitential period.

Baal Teshuvah Historically, this term referred to a person who had abandoned Judaism and then returned to embrace it. Today the term refers to a Jew by birth who has actively embraced Judaism through positive Jewish ritual acts.

Baalzebub Canaanite deity adopted by the Philistines. In the New Testament Baalzebub is transformed into Beelzebub, chief of all the demons.

Babi Yar Place in German-occupied Russia where in 1941 34,000 Jews were machine-gunned by local anti-Semites.

Babylon Ancient land lying between the Tigris and Euphrates rivers. It is the scene of the biblical story of the Tower of Babel.

Babylonian Exile Between the years 587–538 B.C.E.., the Jews were dispersed from Jerusalem by King Nebuchadnezzar and forced to live in Babylon.

Babylonian Talmud First sourcebook of Jewish law with over 2,000 rabbinic contributors. It is composed of the Mishnah, a 6-volume work edited by Judah the Prince (200 C.E.) and the Gemara, which explains the Mishnah, completed in approximately 500 C.E.

Baeck, Leo (1873–1956) Rabbi and theologian, Baeck wrote on Jewish philosophy and theology, contending that evil was the misuse of human freedom. Among his well-known works is *The Essence of Judaism*.

Bahya ben Joseph ibn Pakuda Spanish philosopher who lived in the latter part of the 11th century. His best-known work, *Duties of the Heart*, focuses on the obligation of the individual regarding his inner life rather than his actions.

Balaam Heathen prophet invited by Balak, king of Moab, to curse the Israelites. Divinely inspired, Balaam uttered a blessing instead of a curse (Numbers 22:5).

Balak Thirteenth-century king of Moab.

Balfour, Arthur (1848–1930) British philosopher and statesman, he headed the government with which Theodor Herzl negotiated in 1902. In 1917 he issued the Balfour Declaration and in 1925 he opened Hebrew University.

Bank Leumi Bank established in 1903 by the Jewish Colonial Trust as the Anglo-Palestine Company. It later became the central bank of Palestinian Jewry.

Banyas Located in the northern Golan region of Israel on a tributary of the Jordan River, Banyas is a popular tourist attraction because of its beautiful setting.

Bar Kochba Revolutionary leader who in 135 C.E. made a final stand against the Romans at Betar. As a result of the revolt, Judea fell into dissolution.

Bar/Bat Mitzvah (Hebrew, meaning "son or daughter of the commandment") Ceremony marking the initiation of a child into the Jewish religious community and into observance of the precepts of the Torah. A boy customarily becomes a *Bar Mitzvah* at age 13, whereas a girl may become a *Bat Mitzvah* on her 12th birthday.

Baraita Term signifying all tannaitic statements that were not included in the Mishnah by Judah the Prince.

Baron, Salo (1895–1990) Jewish historian, best known for his multivolume work *A Social and Religious History of the Jews*.

Barukh HaShem Literally, "may God be blessed," it is often used in response to polite inquiries such as "How are you?"

Barukh tihiyeh Hebrew for "may you be blessed," it is a response to *Yasher Koach*, which is traditionally expressed to any individual who has completed an *aliyah* to the Torah.

Bat Kol A mysterious voice by which God on occasion communicated to an individual or a group after the end of prophecy. The *bat kol* often offered guidance in human affairs.

Bathsheba Wife of King David. In order to marry her, David engineered the death in battle of her husband, Uriah the Hittite.

Bava Batra (Hebrew, meaning "last gate") A talmudic tractate in the order *Nezikin*, dealing with real estate and laws of inheritance.

Bava Kamma (Hebrew, meaning "first gate") A talmudic tractate in the order *Nezikin* dealing with damages caused by property or agents (e.g., by an ox or fire).

Bava Metzia (Hebrew, meaning "middle gate") Talmudic tractate in the order *Nezikin* dealing with the laws of lost and found property, fraud, usury, and rights of hired laborers.

Be fruitful and multiply The first of Judaism's commandments, found in the Book of Genesis.

Bedikat Chametz Literally, "searching for the leaven." Ritual ceremony held on the eve of Passover whose purpose is to search for any existing leaven, which is burned the next morning. This ceremony is usually performed using a wooden spoon as a dustpan and a candle to light the way.

Bedouins Nomadic Arabs, the Bedouins still live in tents. Their main occupation is breeding sheep and goats in the Negev.

Beersheba Once a biblical town serving southern Palestine as a religious and administrative center, today Beersheba is a thriving, modern city. Its important sites include Ben-Gurion University and the Desert Research Institute.

Begin, Menachem (1913–1992) Writer and militant Zionist, Begin became the commander in chief of the Israeli underground (known as the Irgun), which led the fight against the British. In 1977 he became prime minister of Israel.

Bellow, Saul (1915–   ) American novelist raised in Canada and Chicago, best known for his novels *Herzog* and *The Adventures of Augie March*.

Benny, Jack (1894–1974): Comedian, radio, and television entertainer.

Ben-Gurion, David (1886–1973) Pioneer builder of the State of Israel and Israel's first prime minister (1948–1954).

Ben/Bat Avraham (V'Sarah) When a person converts to Judaism, he or she is given the name of the father of the Jewish people as his or her father. In Conservative, Reform, and Reconstructionist Judaism, the name of the mother, Sarah, is also added to the convert's name.

Ben Yehudah, Eliezer (1858–1922) Known as the "Father of spoken Hebrew," Ben Yehudah's major work was the *Dictionary of the Hebrew Language, Old and New*.

Bene Israel Refers to the Jewish community in India.

Benjamin Twelfth and youngest son of Jacob and second son of Rachel.

Benjamin of Tudela Greatest medieval Jewish traveler, who recorded his travels, thereby leaving us with a full account of the cities and people he encountered.

Berakhah A formula of praise and thanks established by the Men of the Great Assembly. Sometimes called a "blessing," it begins with the Hebrew words, *Barukh atah Adonai*.

Berakhot (Hebrew, meaning "blessings") First tractate of the Mishnah order *Zeraim*, dealing with the reciting of the prayer *Shema*, blessings, and prayer in general.

Bergen-Belsen Nazi concentration camp near Hanover, Germany. Thirty thousand Jews perished here.

Berit Trumpeldor Youth organization of the Zionist Revisionist Movement, originally a scouting movement. Members of Berit Trumpeldor (known as Betar) have played an important role in the Irgun underground movement.

Berkovits, Eliezer (1900–   ) Orthodox rabbi whose contribution lies in his understanding of the Holocaust. He maintains that those who were not in the Nazi death camps do not have the right to say whether or not God was there.

Berle, Milton (1908–   ) Actor and comedian, known as "Uncle Miltie."

Berlin, Irving (1888–1989) Composer and writer of popular songs and musical comedies. He wrote "God Bless America."

Bernstein, Leonard (1918–1990) American conductor and composer who conducted the New York Philharmonic Orchestra.

Besamim Spices, particularly those used during the observance of the *Havdalah* ceremony.

Bet Chaim Literally, "house of life," euphemistically it refers to a Jewish cemetery.

Bet Din (Hebrew, meaning "house of judgment") Rabbinic court of law with jurisdiction in civil, criminal, and religious matters. During Temple times the Sanhedrin was the High Court. Today a *Bet Din* consists of three persons who have power that is limited to voluntary arbitration and jurisdiction in ritual matters.

Bet HaKnesset Literally, "a house of gathering," today it refers to a synagogue.

Bet HaMidrash (Hebrew, meaning "house of study") 1. School for higher rabbinic learning. Here students gathered for study, discussion, and prayer. 2. In the Talmud, *Bet HaMidrash* refers to an academy of learning headed by an important rabbinic leader.

Bet HaMikdash Refers to the ancient Temple in Jerusalem.

Bet Sefer Literally "house of the book," it means a school.

Bethel Ancient Israelite city 10 miles north of Jerusalem. Abraham erected an altar near the site, which was formerly called Luz (Genesis 12:8). Because *Bethel* means "house of God," many synagogues are named Bethel.

Bethlehem Ancient Palestinian town south of Jerusalem and birthplace of King David. Christians ascribe special sanctity to Bethlehem as the town of Jesus' birth. Called Ephrat in the Bible, Bethlehem is also the setting for the Book of Ruth.

Betzah (Hebrew, meaning "egg") Seventh tractate in the Mishnah order *Moed*, dealing with laws related to the Jewish festivals.

Bialik, Chaim Nachman (1873–1934) One of the most important Hebrew poets of modern times. The Bialik home in Tel Aviv has been preserved as a cultural center.

Bible accents (Hebrew *taamei hamikra*) Special signs of cantillation or accents, which are placed both above and below the words of the Hebrew Bible. Tradition ascribes the origin of these accents to Ezra and the Men of the Great Assembly.

Bikkur Cholim (Hebrew, meaning "visiting the sick") One of the most important commandments in Judaism, derived from God's visit to Abraham after Abraham's having been circumcised.

Bikkurim (Hebrew, meaning "firstfruits") Eleventh and final tractate in the Mishnah order *Zeraim*, dealing with the offerings of first fruits during Temple times (See Exodus 23:19).

Bimah Among the Ashkenazim, the dais or platform in the synagogue where the reading of the Torah takes place.

Bintel Brief Advice and letters column in *The (Jewish Daily) Forward*, a Yiddish socialist newspaper.

Birkat HaGomel Blessing said by men and women who have recovered from a great illness or escaped grave danger.

Birkat HaMazon The grace or blessings customarily recited after one has eaten a meal.

Birkot Hanehenin Blessings said in gratitude for the pleasure one derives from eating, drinking, seeing wonders of nature, and so forth.

Black Death, the Epidemic that killed a great part of the population of Europe and led to murderous attacks on many Jewish communities, particularly in Germany.

Bloch Publishing Company Founded in Cincinnati in 1854 by Isaac M. Wise and Edward Bloch. It has published books on a variety of Jewish subjects in New York since 1901.

Blue Laws Laws that prevented commercial establishments from being open on Sundays.

B'nai Brak An important Jewish center in the first and second centuries, and home to Rabbi Akiva's academy. In 1924 it was founded as an agricultural colony by religious Polish Jews, and today it is home to a large number of *yeshivot* and chasidic sects.

Boaz Husband of Ruth and great-grandfather of King David.

Booths (Hebrew *sukkot*, meaning "tabernacles") Small huts erected for the Feast of Tabernacles when for 7 days Jews "dwell," or at least eat, in them (Leviticus 23:42).

Borowitz, Eugene A. (1924–   ) Leading Reform rabbi and theologian whose work focuses on an exploration of autonomy in decision making and a covenant theology in explaining the relationship between God and the individual.

Brandeis, Louis (1856–1941) Justice of the United States Supreme Court and Zionist leader, he came to be known as the "people's lawyer" and a leader of the liberal forces in America. Brandeis University in Boston is named after him.

Bread of Affliction Unleavened flat bread (*matzah*) symbolizing the haste with which the people of Israel had to leave Egypt, with no time to allow for the rising of their bread.

Breaking of the Vessels Kabbalistic term referring to a primordial catastrophe that occurred in the early stages of creation. According to Isaac Luria, the divine light emanating from Adam Kadmon into creation, burst the vessels which were to contain it and many of the divine sparks fell into chaos. Since then the entire universe is in need of restoration and repair (*tikkun* in Hebrew).

Brit Milah The covenant of circumcision performed on male Jewish children on the eighth day after birth.

British Mandate In 1922, the League of Nations entrusted Britain with a mandate that incorporated the Balfour Declaration and recognized the historical connection between the Jewish people and the land. The mandate called upon Britain to pave the way for the creation of a national home for the Jews.

Bruria Wife of Rabbi Meir (2nd century C.E.), known as one of the few women in the Talmud who participated in legal discussions.

Buber, Martin (1878–1965) Religious philosopher who conceived of religious faith as a dialogue between man and God. This conception (''I and Thou'') has deeply influenced contemporary Christian theology.

Bund, The Jewish Socialist Party, founded at a conference in Vilna in 1897. It served both as a trade union and a political party, and was especially influential in journalism and the labor movement.

Bureaus of Jewish Education First established in New York City, these bureaus serve as the central coordinating bodies for Jewish education in individual communities.

Burning bush Desert shrub from which the angel of God appeared to Moses. The bush burned but miraculously was not consumed (Exodus 3:2–4).

Burnt offering A type of biblical sacrifice in which an entire animal was placed upon the altar to be burnt.

C

Cabinet Headed by a prime minister, the cabinet is the main policy-making body of the State of Israel.

Caesarea Originally an ancient Mediterranean coastal town. Today its excavated Roman amphitheater had been reconstructed and is both a tourist site and a place for outdoor concerts.

Cain Eldest son of Adam and Eve. After killing his brother, Abel, he was condemned by God to wander through the land of Nod, east of the Garden of Eden.

Calf, golden Golden idol constructed by Aaron at the demand of the Israelites, who had become impatient due to the long absence of Moses on Mount Sinai.

Camp David Accord Agreement signed in 1978 at Camp David (United States presidential retreat) between Menachem Begin, prime minister of Israel; Anwar Sadat, president of Egypt; and President Jimmy Carter. The agreement called for Israel to leave the Sinai desert and return it to Egypt. Egypt agreed to open the Suez Canal and the Straits of Tiran.

Canaan Name for the territory that in biblical times was principally Phoenicia. It is the land God originally promised to Abraham.

Canon The authoritative collection of biblical books that became closed forever to the subtraction or addition of other sacred books to the Hebrew Bible.

Cantor In Hebrew, *Chazzan*, the person who sings and chants the liturgy during worship services. He is the emissary for the congregation.

Cantor, Eddie (1892–1964) American comedian, prominent in every medium of entertainment. He was president of the Jewish Theatre Guild and the Screen Actors Guild.

Capernaum Ancient town on the northwest shore of the Sea of Galilee. Jesus visited Capernaum and preached in its synagogue. In the late 19th century, Franciscan monks built a monastery there and restored part of the synagogue, which today is a popular attraction for tourists.

Cardozo, Benjamin (1870–1938) Associate justice of the United States Supreme Court and a fine interpreter of common law.

Carmel Mountains Mountain range in Israel between the Valley of Jezreel, the Haifa coastal plain, and the Mediterranean Sea. Haifa's suburbs extend up its slopes, which are also traveled by Israel's only underground cable car, called the "Carmelite."

Caro, Yosef Sixteenth-Century Spanish codifier known for editing Judaism's most authoritative law code, called the *Shulchan Arukh*, also known as the Code of Jewish Law.

Central Conference of American Rabbis (CCAR) Established in 1889, it is the professional association of Reform rabbis.

Chabad The intellectual brand of Chasidism. The name is an acronym for the Hebrew words meaning wisdom, understanding, and knowledge. Chabad is also known as Lubavitch.

Chagall Windows Stained-glass windows featured in the Hadassah Medical Center in Jerusalem, depicting the twelve Israelite tribes. Created by the famous artist Marc Chagall, they are one of Israel's most important and popular tourist sites.

Chai (Hebrew, meaning "life") In *gematria* its number value is eighteen. Because of this, Jewish people often give charitable contributions in denominations of eighteen, symbolizing good luck and good life.

Chaim Yankel Today it means "so-and-so." In rabbinic literature the term meaning "so-and-so" was *Plony ben Plony*.

Chakham Originally a term referring to an officer of the ancient rabbinic courts in Palestine or Babylonia. Today it means a wise scholar. In Yiddish the term is used to mean "wise guy."

Challah Literally, "dough offering," it refers to the egg bread used on the Sabbath and festivals.

Chalutzim (Hebrew, meaning "pioneers") These pioneers made up the bulk of the third *Aliyah* to Palestine from 1918–1924. Their difficult task included building roads and draining the insect-infested swamps.

Chametz Any food containing leaven. All leaven is forbidden to be eaten during Passover.

Chamsah From the Arabic word for five, an amulet shaped like a hand, often used to ward off the so-called evil eye.

Chanaton This *kibbutz* was established in 1984 by twenty-five American and Israeli settlers. It is located on the site of the biblical Chanaton in the Lower Galilee and is Israel's only *kibbutz* to be established by Jews of the Conservative movement.

Chanukah Sometimes called the festival of lights, this 8-day celebration commemorates the victory of Judah Maccabee over the Syrian-Greeks in 165 B.C.E. and the rededication of the Jerusalem Temple.

Chanukat HaBayit Dedication of a new home. This ceremony generally includes the affixing of a *mezuzah* to one's doorpost.

Charoset Food made out of cinnamon, apples, and nuts that is eaten at the Passover *Seder*. It symbolizes the mortar with which the Israelites worked in Egypt.

Chasidism Religious and social movement founded by the Baal Shem Tov in the eighteenth century. Its philosophic basis is the Kabbalah.

Chattan (Hebrew, meaning "bridegroom") The term is also used in reference to the reading of the Torah. For example, when one is given the privilege of reading the final paragraph of the Torah on Simchat Torah, that person is referred to as a *chattan Torah*, a bridegroom of the Torah.

Chavurah A group of people who gather together regularly for a common purpose. For example, people in a Bible *chavurah* might meet and study Bible together, either in a home or in the synagogue.

Chazak, Chazak venetchazek "Be strong, be strong, and may we be strengthened"—a traditional recitation at the conclusion of the public reading of one of the five books of the Torah.

Chazakah (Hebrew, meaning "taking hold") In general, a talmudic term that refers to the act of taking possession of property. It can also mean a presumption based on facts, or custom that we accept as true.

Chazal (acronym) Term that refers to the talmudic sages.

Cheder Literally, "a room," today a *cheder* refers to an elementary religious school.

Chelm A fictitious European community whose citizens are mocked for their lack of common sense. They have figured in many anecdotes and stories of Jewish folk-humor.

Cherubim Winged figures, usually with human, animal, or bird's head and body. Frequently mentioned in the Bible, cherubim guarded the gates to the Garden of Eden. Their images were also place on either side of the Ark of the Covenant.

Cherut Party Israeli political party founded in 1948 by veterans of the Irgun and members of the Revisionist party and Betar. Among its objectives is the ingathering of the exiles.

Cheshvan Second month of the Jewish religious year and approximating the eighth of the civil year. It is sometimes called Marcheshvan (the bitter month of Cheshvan), because it is the only month without a Jewish holiday.

Chevrah A group of friends.

Chevrah Kaddisha Known as the Holy Burial Society, this group of people is responsible for the preparation of the deceased for Jewish burial.

Chewing of the cud According to the Bible, one of the characteristics an animal had to possess in order for it to be eaten by an Israelite was that it chew its cud. The other characteristic was that the animal possess split hooves.

Chidush An invention or a new way of looking at something in life.

Chief Rabbinate Israel's final religious authority, an Ashkenazic and a Sephardic chief rabbi preside over it jointly.

Chokhmah (Hebrew, meaning "wisdom") Also the second level of the Kabbalah notion of *sefirot*.

Chol HaMoed Refers to the intermediate day of a Jewish festival.

Chosen, The Novel by Chaim Potok, and later a film, it describes the relationship of a modern Orthodox boy and his friend, who is the son of the local leader of the *chasidim*.

Chosen People Concept that Israel has been elected by God to carry the message of His law to the world. It is based on the original covenant between God and Abraham (Genesis 15).

Choshen Breastplate placed over the Torah reminiscent of the breastplate worn by the priest during Temple times.

Chronicles Name of the last two books of the Hebrew Bible. These books, which stress priestly duties and Temple ritual, retell the history of the Jewish people from the creation to the end of the Babylonian exile.

Chullin (Hebrew, meaning "profane matters") Third tractate in the Mishnah order *Kodashim*, dealing with laws of ritual slaughtering and preparation of animal food.

Chumash Refers to the first five books of the Bible, sometimes called the Five Books of Moses. The books of the *Chumash* include Genesis, Exodus, Leviticus, Numbers, and Deuteronomy.

Chuppah Refers to the Jewish wedding ceremony as well as the portable canopy under which the bride and groom stand during the ceremony. Originally the word referred to the bridal chamber itself, of which the modern canopy is considered a symbolic representation.

Chutzpah Daring or boldness.

Coalition government Refers to the ruling Israeli political party and other parliamentary systems having to invite other political parties to join them, in order to maintain a majority of party seats in the cabinet.

Coat of many colors Special garment Jacob gave to his son Joseph. The coat caused great jealousy among Jacob's other sons.

Cohen, Gerson (1924–1991) Historian and chancellor of the Jewish Theological Seminary during the latter part of the 20th century.

Cohen, Hermann (1842–1918) German philosopher and founder of the Marburg School of Neo-Kantianism. He emphasized the importance of ethics.

Concentration camp Camp built by the Nazis to bring together all of the Jews, put them into forced labor, and put them to death. The greatest number of Jews perished in Auschwitz.

Concubine A marital companion of inferior status to a wife. Concubines in the Bible include Hagar, the concubine of Abraham, who bore him Ishmael.

Confirmation Religious ceremony that generally takes place on Shavuot and was first introduced by the Reform movement. Today it usually refers to the the graduation of 10th-grade Hebrew high-school students.

Consecration Ceremony introduced by the Reform movement as the time when a young child marks the beginning of his or her formal Jewish education.

Conservative Judaism One of four major streams of American Judaism, Conservative Judaism emphasizes both tradition and change.

Copland, Aaron (1900–1990) American composer whose compositions include symphonies, ballets, and operas.

Council of the Four Lands Central institutions of Jewish self-government in Poland and Lithuania from the middle of the 16th century until 1764.

Council of Jewish Federations (CJF) Established in 1953, it is the national body that coordinates the work of all of its member Jewish Federations.

Court Jews Jews who served as financial or other agents of rulers in Central and Eastern Europe during the 17th and 18th centuries.

Covenant A mutually binding agreement between persons or nations. In the Hebrew Bible, God made a covenant with Noah, Abraham, and Moses. To Noah, the sign of the covenant was a rainbow. God promised Abraham that he would become the father of a great nation, sealing the covenant with the requirement of circumcision of all Israelite males. To Moses, God said that the Israelites would reach the Promised Land but must obey the Mosaic Law.

Creatio ex nihilo Creation from nothing; the theological notion that God created the world out of nothing.

Crown Usually refers to the *keter Torah*, the crown of the Torah, placed on the top of the Torah as an adornment. The crown may also refer to the special scribal markings placed on several of the Hebrew letters in a Torah scroll in order to adorn them.

Cubit A biblical measurement equivalent to the length of the forearm from the elbow to the tip of the middle finger (approximately 18 inches).

Cutting keriah Refers to the practice of cutting one's garment as a sign of mourning. Today some Jewish mourners wear a black ribbon and cut or tear it as a symbol of their mourning.

Cyrus, King King of Persia who reigned from 559–529 B.C.E. He ended the Babylonian exile and allowed the Jews to return to Jerusalem.

D

D Source The projects of gathering the biblical stories and traditions were believed by some biblical scholars to be carried out by various groups of people, called schools or writers or editors. The D Source, or School, derives its name from the Book of Deuteronomy.

Dachau Town near Munich, Germany, and site of a concentration camp built in 1933. It served as a model for all of the other camps.

Dan Fifth son of Jacob and Bilhah. The tribe of Dan settled in south Canaan and up along the coast north of Jaffa.

Daniel The main character in the section of the Bible called Writings, whose history comprises the book's contents. Daniel was cast into a lion's den and miraculously saved from death.

Dati Literally, "religious," used to refer to the Israeli Orthodox.

Davar An early 20th-century labor newspaper. Today it is one of a number of Israeli daily newspapers.

Daven Yiddish term, meaning "to pray."

David Second king of Israel (*c*. 1000–*c*. 960 B.C.E..) Under David's reign the tribes of Israel were united and Jerusalem became the capital of Israel. A luxury hotel in Jerusalem is named after King David and is a popular tourist site.

Davka (Aramaic term, meaning "exactness") Today it is often used to emphasize the accuracy of a fact or to draw attention to something unexpected.

Day school Any school whose curriculum includes the study of Jewish and secular subjects.

Dayan Judge of a rabbinical court.

Dayan, Moshe (1915–1981) Founder of the Palmach, he lost an eye in 1941 while serving in the British army. In 1967 he became Israel's minister of defense.

Dead Sea The southernmost and largest lake in Israel, the Dead Sea, at 1,300 feet below sea level, is the lowest point on earth. The rich minerals of the Dead Sea have become an important Israeli export. Many health spas have located themselves in this area and are annually attracting a flock of new tourists.

Dead Sea Scrolls Ancient manuscripts found in the caves of Qumran near Jericho. The study of these scrolls (generally believed to date from the 1st century B.C.E..) have advanced the study of the Hebrew text of the Bible.

Deborah A female prophet (*c*. 1150 B.C.E.), Deborah roused the Israelite tribes to revolt against the Canaanite king Jabine and Sisera, his ally (Judges, chap. 4). Her song of victory in the fifth chapter of the Book of Judges is regarded as one of the oldest Hebrew compositions.

Declaration of Independence, Israeli Official document read by Prime Minister Ben-Gurion on May 14, 1948, proclaiming the official statehood of Israel.

Deganyah First *kibbutz* in Israel, established in 1948 in an area south of the Sea of Galilee. One of its most famous settlers was Moshe Dayan.

Demai Third tracate in the Mishnah order *Zeraim*, dealing with the requirements for tithing produce when there is doubt regarding whether the proper tithes have been given.

Deuteronomy Fifth and last book of the Five Books of Moses.

Devar Torah Literally, "a word of Torah," it refers to the teaching of a text, usually a sacred one.

Devekut Mystical concept referring to a person's attempt to cling to God.

Diaspora Greek word meaning "dispersion," applied to the Jewish community outside of Israel.

Diaspora Yeshiva Traditional Judaic school of higher learning located in Jerusalem for foreign students with little or no background in Judaism.

Dimont, Max (1912–　　) 20th-century writer of popular Jewish history, including his well-known *Jews, God, and History*.

Din (Hebrew, meaning "judgment") Refers to a law, legal decision, or a lawsuit.

Dinah Daughter of Jacob and Leah. Her rape by Shechem was avenged by her brothers, Simeon and Levi, who annihilated the inhabitants of the town of Shechem (Genesis 34).

Divine attributes Characteristics of God.

Divine revelation The act of communication from God to man and the content of such a communication. The most famous occurrence of divine revelation was God's revelation to Moses atop Mount Sinai.

Documentary Hypothesis Theory that holds that the Bible was the product of various groups of people who gathered and edited collections of material.

Dome of the Rock Also known as the Mosque of Omar, this Moslem mosque was built in the center of the Temple area in Jerusalem in 738 C.E.. It is situated on what is believed to be the traditional site of Mount Moriah, the place where Abraham was told to sacrifice his son Isaac.

Downtown Jews Eastern European Jews immigrating to the United States in the first quarter of the 20th century who lived on the Lower East Side of New York City upon their arrival.

Dreidl A spinning top, called a *sevivon* in Hebrew, that is used as a game during the festival of Chanukah.

Dreyfus, Alfred (1859–1935) French soldier, falsely accused and convicted of selling secret documents to Germany. He was finally pardoned in 1906.

Druze Followers of a religious sect that split from Islam in the 11th century. Druze live throughout the Galilee and on Mount Carmel. They have their own spiritual leadership and courts of law, and some have been known to serve in the Israeli army.

Dry Bones Refers to the story in Chapter 37 of the Book of Ezekiel where bones knit together and are covered with flesh. The story has come to symbolize the regeneration of the nation of Israel.

Duchanan During a worship service (usually in Orthodox synagogues), those of the priestly lineage gather in front of the congregation and in front of the Holy Ark to bless the people.

Dutch West Indies Company Founded in Amsterdam in 1621 with a representative number of Jews as shareholders, it overrode Governor Peter Stuyvesant's discrimination against the first Jewish settlers in 1654.

Dybbuk Soul of a dead person that is believed to enter a living person, usually causing a change in personality.

E

Eban, Abba (1915–   ) Former chief of Israel's delegation to the United Nations, and ambassador to Washington. He is a popular speaker on the American lecture circuit. His book, *My People*, a history of the Jewish people, has become a classic.

Ecclesiastes One of the five scrolls in the Hagiographa section of the Bible. The author, called *Kohelet* in Hebrew, and traditionally identified as King Solomon, seeks to discern the purpose of human life. One famous line from the book is "vanity of vanities, all is vanity."

Eden, Garden of Original dwelling place of Adam and Eve, containing the Tree of Life and the Tree of Knowledge, from which Adam and Eve were forbidden to eat. In later Jewish literature, the Garden of Eden often refers to the abode of righteous people after death.

Educational Alliance Well-known Americanization center located in New York City.

Educator's Assembly (EA) Professional association of Jewish educators affiliated with Conservative Judaism.

Eduyyot (Hebrew, meaning "testimonies") Seventh tractate in the Mishnah order *Nezikin*, consisting of personal testimonies of sages regarding legal rulings they had received from their teachers.

Egypt (Hebrew *Mitzrayim*) Country in Northeast Africa. Ruled in ancient times by a Pharaoh, Egypt figures prominently in a variety of biblical events, including the story of Moses and the exodus from Egypt.

Eichmann, Adolf (1906–1962) Nazi functionary who was responsible for implementing the scheme to exterminate all of European Jewry. In 1960 he was discovered living in Argentina. He was later brought to trial in Israel and executed.

Eilat Southernmost town in Israel, situated on the northern end of the Red Sea. Today modern Eilat is a popular European and American tourist attraction.

Ein Sof Literally, "without end," it is the name for God in the mystical tradition.

Einhorn, David (1809–1879) Reform rabbi who led the extreme Reform wing of American Jewry. He was prominent in the antislavery movement and was an eloquent preacher in Germany.

Eishes Chayil Refers to the "woman of valor" in Proverbs 31. Today it is often used to refer to any woman of extraordinary goodness and righteousness.

El A word denoting God, occurring in all Semitic languages.

El Al Israel's national airline, established in 1949.

El Malei Rachamim Literally, "God who is full of mercy," it refers to a memorial prayer that asks God to make souls rest in peace. It is chanted during funerals as well as *Yizkor* memorial services.

Elders (Hebrew *zakenim*) In biblical times, members of the authoritative group of the nation, influential in shaping the form of government and often serving as judges.

Eliyahu HaNavi Elijah the Prophet (9th Century B.C.E.) who is popularly believed to herald the coming of the Messiah. He is invited into Jewish homes during the *Seder* meal on Passover.

Elohim One of God's biblical names, *Elohim* (plural of *El*) is also used to denote "gods" and idols.

Elul Sixth month of the Jewish religious calendar and last of the civil. It is the month that precedes the festival of Rosh HaShanah and a time to contemplate the meaning of repentance.

Emancipation Term applied to the removal of discrimination against the Jews.

Emunah (Hebrew, meaning "faith") One of the levels of the *sefirot,* according to the Kabbalah.

Encyclopaedia Judaica The newest full-scale English-language encyclopedia of Judaism, issued from Jerusalem in the 1970s.

Enlightenment Also known as the *Haskalah,* it refers to the 18th-century movement for spreading modern European culture among the Jews. Perhaps the first representative philosophy of this type was that of Moses Mendelssohn.

Enoch Eldest son of Cain and grandson of Adam and Eve.

Entebbe In 1976, Palestinian terrorists skyjacked a plane on its way from Israel and flew it to Uganda. There the terrorists announced they would kill all the hostages unless Israel released more terrorists from prison. A daring rescue of the hostages followed, known as "Operation Entebbe."

Ephraim Younger son of Joseph. Also the name of an Israelite tribe and a term that refers to the northern kingdom of Israel.

Epic of Gilgamesh Babylonian creation story containing several parallels with the biblical narrative, especially the story of the flood.

Erev Shabbat The eve of the Sabbath (i.e., Friday).

Eruv Technical term for the rabbinical provision that permits the alleviation of certain Sabbath restrictions. These include carrying on the Sabbath and cooking for the holiday.

Eruvin Second tractate in the Mishnah order *Moed,* dealing with the laws of the *eruv* (a technical term referring to a symbolic act of combining several domains for the purpose of making it permissible to transport things on the Sabbath).

Esau Son of Isaac and elder twin brother of Jacob. He had his birthright stolen by Jacob.

Eshkol, Levi (1895–1969) Third prime minister of Israel. During his time in office, diplomatic relations were established with West Germany and the labor parties united to form the Israel Labor Party.

Esnoga Sephardic term for synagogue.

Essenes Religious sect in ancient Israel at the end of the Second Temple period. They lived an ascetic life, their chief occupation being farming. The Essenes may have been responsible for writing some of the Dead Sea Scrolls.

Esther Central character of the biblical Book of Esther. King Ahasueras chose her to be queen and she used her influence to save the Jewish people from Haman.

Ethical monotheism Refers to the belief in one God that is the standard for ethics in the world.

Ethical will Testament expressing the moral and ethical instructions of the deceased to his or her family.

Etrog A citron, a lemonlike fruit used on the festival of Sukkot. It is one of the Four Species.

Everything is foreseen, yet permission is given Classic statement of Rabbi Akiva from *Ethics of the Fathers*, from which we learn that the individual is free to do what he or she wishes, but God already knows what the choice will be.

Exilarch (In Aramaic, *resh galuta*, head of the exile) Title given to the head of Babylonian Jewry. Believed to be a direct descendant of the royal house of David, he was responsible for the internal government of the Jewish people.

Exodus (1947) Ship that carried 4,554 Jewish refugees to Palestine under Haganah auspices in 1947. It was seized by the British and the ship was forcibly returned to France.

Exodus Name of the second book of the Five Books of Moses. Exodus tells the story of the slavery of the Jewish people in Egypt, the exodus from Egypt, and the giving of the Ten Commandments.

"Eye for an eye" Biblical principle of justice that requires a punishment equal in kind to the offense.

Eytz Chayyim Literally, "tree of life," it refers to the wooden rollers around which the parchment of a Torah scroll is wrapped.

Ezekiel Third of the Major Prophets, Ezekiel witnessed the destruction of the First Temple and went into exile in Babylon. One of his most famous visions was the resurrection of the dry bones in the valley (Chapter 37).

Ezra One of the two leaders of the return from the Babylonian captivity and author of the Book of Ezra. Among his achievements was the custom of reading portions of the Torah on Sabbaths and market days (Mondays and Thursdays).

F

Fackenheim, Emil (1916–   ) Reform Jewish theologian and philosopher, known for his writings related to the Holocaust. He argues that the Holocaust marked a new level of human evil and the Jewish response to it is a new revelation.

Falasha Meaning "stranger," also used to refer to an Ethiopian Jew.

False Messiah Individual who claims to be the Messiah. There have been many throughout Jewish history.

Fast of Esther Minor fast lasting from sunrise to sundown on the day before the reading of the Purim *Megillah*. It commemorates Esther's fast in the Scroll of Esther.

Fast of the Firstborn Required of firstborn male children, prior to the festival of Passover, in recognition of the saving of their lives during the period of the Ten Plagues of Egypt.

Fast of Gedaliah Immediately after Rosh HaShanah, this minor fast is observed in commemoration of the murder of Gedaliah, the Jewish governor appointed by Nebuchadnezzar.

Fast of the Seventeenth of Tammuz Fast in the month of Tammuz commemorating a number of sad events in Jewish history, including the breaking down of the Temple walls by the Romans in the year 70 C.E.. This fast ushers in the 3 weeks of mourning until the end of Tisha B'Av.

Fatah A terrorist organization founded in 1965 to carry on the struggle for the so-called liberation of Palestine.

Fedayin Terrorist raiders in the Arab refugee camps of Gaza and Sinai that were trained by Egyptians and sent into Israel to murder.

Feinstein, Moshe (1895–1989) Orthodox rabbi and leader of Orthodox Jewry, he became the leading halakhic authority of his time.

Felafel Ground chick-peas, shaped into balls and fried in oil, often served with diced salad in a Middle Eastern sandwich called "pita."

Fence around the Torah A Jewish legal concept that refers to the layers of regulations that have been placed around a Jewish law in order to safeguard the law and prevent its transgression.

Fertile Crescent Area in the Middle East consisting of a narrow belt of land shaped like a huge horseshoe. Its valuable land has been settled for more than 6,000 years and is one of the earliest homes of civilized people.

Festivals Term usually referring to the three major pilgrimage festivals of Sukkot, Pesach, and Shavuot.

Final Solution, The Refers to the Nazi plan to exterminate the Jews.

Finkelstein, Louis (1895–1991) Scholar and chancellor of the Jewish Theological Seminary of America, succeeding Cyrus Adler.

Firstfruits Biblical law that calls for bringing the first choice fruits of one's field to the Temple. (Deuteronomy 26:5–10). The firstfruits could be brought any time between Shavuot and the festival of Sukkot.

Five Books of Moses The first five books of the Hebrew Bible, traditionally ascribed to the authorship of Moses. They include Genesis, Exodus, Leviticus, Numbers, and Deuteronomy. Other names for the five books include the Torah and the *Chumash*.

Fleishig Yiddish, referring to a meat meal. According to Jewish dietary laws, milk and milk-derived (*milchig*) products may not be eaten at the same meal as meat.

Flood Deluge brought by God to destroy the whole world because of its wickedness (Genesis 6–9). Noah, the central character of the story, builds an ark that shelters his family and all living creatures.

Forbidden foods Foods expressly forbidden by the Bible. Included in this list are animals that die naturally or are killed by another animal, animals that do not chew their cuds and have split hooves, and fish that do not have both fins and scales.

Former Prophets The second major part of the Hebrew Bible is called the Prophets and is divided into the Former Prophets and the Latter Prophets. The Former Prophets include the books of Joshua, Judges, 1 Samuel, 2 Samuel, 1 Kings, and 2 Kings. The narratives of these books open with the Hebrew tribes moving into Canaan under the leadership of Joshua.

Forward, The (Jewish Daily) Yiddish socialist newspaper that served as a powerful force of acculturation.

Frank, Anne (1929–1945) Dutch child and writer who wrote a diary during the Nazi occupation of Holland. The diary was discovered after her death and has been published in many languages.

Frank, Jacob (1726–1791) False Messiah and founder of a sect called the Frankists.

Frank, Leo M. (1884–1915) Factory manager in Georgia wrongly accused of murder just prior to World War I. He was lynched in 1915, and 10 years later the real murderer confessed to the crime.

Frankel, Zecharias (1801–1875) Rabbi and scholar who directed the Breslau Rabbinical Seminary from 1854 until his death in 1875. He endeavored to combine religious tradition with the European enlightenment.

Frankfurter, Felix (1882–1965) Jurist and professor at Harvard Law School, he was appointed to the U.S. Supreme Court in 1939.

Free Loan Society Organization established in the second half of the 19th century to help the needy move toward being self-supporting by advancing interest-free loans.

Freehof, Solomon B. (1892–1990) Reform rabbi of Rodef Shalom Congregation in Pittsburgh, he was the foremost authority on Jewish *responsa* in his generation.

Frontlets A band or phylactery worn on the forehead in biblical times as a reminder of God's dependability as a liberator from slavery to freedom.

Frum Yiddish for a very observant Jewish person.

G

Gabbai Originally a collector of dues and charitable contributions. Today it usually refers to an official of a synagogue service who assists during the reading of the Torah.

Gabirol, Solomon ibn (*c.* 1020–*c.* 1057) Spanish poet and philosopher whose writings reflect mystical tendencies and scientific knowledge.

Gad Seventh son of Jacob and head of the tribe of Gad. The tribe of Gad supplied King David with some of his most outstanding warriors.

Gadna Israel movement for the preliminary training of youth ages 14 through 18. Today Gadna operates pioneer farms and occupational training projects.

Galilee Northern district of Israel. Among its famous sites are Deganyah Israel's first *kibbutz*, and Safed, one of Israel's famous mystical holy cities.

Gaon Title applied to the heads of the two major Babylonian academies at Sura and Pumbedita who were looked upon as the spiritual guides of the Jewish people between the 6th and 11th centuries.

Garment center Located in New York City, it was the leading location for the production of ready-made garments from 1880 onward.

Gaza Ancient Palestinian city on the south coastal plain of Israel along the Mediterranean Sea. It was an important

Philistine city. In 1967 it again became part of Israel after the Six Day War.

Gaza Strip Tongue of land including the town of Gaza stretching along coastal Israel for twenty-two miles.

Gefilte fish Ground-up whitefish that is often served as part of the Friday-evening Sabbath meal.

Geiger, Abraham (1810–1874) German scholar and religious reformer, he convened the first conference of Reform rabbis in 1837.

Gelilah Refers to the honor of rolling up the Torah after its reading in the synagogue.

Gelt Yiddish term for money.

Gemara A commentary on the Mishnah by a group of later scholars, called *amoraim*, who attempted to reconcile the various conflicting opinions in the Mishnah. The Gemara was edited in the year 500 C.E..

Gematria Method of biblical interpretation based on the interpretation of words according to the numerical values of their letters in the Hebrew alphabet.

Genesis First of the Five Books of Moses. Genesis tells the story of the creation of the world, the flood, and the patriarchs.

Genizah Depository for used holy books.

Geonim Intellectual rabbinic leaders of the Babylonian Jewish community in the posttalmudic period (6th–11th centuries).

Gershon Sometimes called Gershom, he was the eldest of Levi's three sons. Gershon is also the name of Moses' first child born to his wife Zipporah.

Gershwin, George (1898–1937) American composer who introduced jazz and blues styles into symphonic music.

Get Hebrew for Jewish divorce, traditionally given by a man to a woman in the presence of a *Bet Din*.

Gezerah A decree of regulation by the sages that prohibits something that was once permitted.

Ghetto Jewish quarter, set up by law to be inhabited only by Jews. The name derives from the ghetto in Venice, Italy, where the Jews were segregated in 1517.

Ginzburg, Louis (1873–1953) Scholar and professor of Bible at the Jewish Theological Seminary of America. He was one of the founders of the American Academy for Jewish Research.

Gittin (Hebrew, meaning "bills of divorce") Fifth tractate in the Mishnah order *Nashim*, dealing with the laws of divorce.

Gleanings The remains of the crop after the harvest, which are supposed to be left for the poor (Leviticus 19:9–10). The Book of Ruth described the gathering of the gleanings by the poor.

G'mar chatimah tovah Literally, "may your stamp of approval by God be completed favorably," this phrase is a traditional greeting used during the High Holidays.

Gnosticism Reflecting a dualism in the world between light (good) and darkness (evil). Primarily a Christian movement, Judaism influenced it primarily through the Bible.

Golan Heights Hilly area located north of the Upper Galilee. It was captured by Israel during the Six Day War and remains a strategic defense point to this day.

Golden Age of Spain Period from the 11th through the 13th centuries, when Jews and Jewish scholarship flourished.

Goldeneh Medinah Literally, "land of gold," a reference to the United States as a country whose streets are metaphorically paved with gold.

Goldwyn, Samuel (1882–1974) American film producer and an original partner in Metro-Goldwyn-Mayer (MGM), he introduced many leading stars to the screen.

Golem An automaton, especially in the form of a human, usually created by magical means. The *golem* has been a favorite topic in Jewish literature. In Yiddish, *golem* generally refers to a "stupid person."

Goliath Philistine giant slain by King David (1 Samuel 17; 21:10).

Gomarrah One of the five cities of the Jordan plain destroyed by God in the time of Abraham. The chief of the five cities was Sodom.

Good Fence Established as a point of exchange between Lebanon and Israel.

Gordis, Robert (1908–1992) Bible scholar, author, and rabbi. His portfolio includes professorships at Columbia University and the Jewish Theological Seminary.

Gratz College First Jewish teachers' training college in the United States. It was founded in Philadelphia in 1893.

Graven image A sculptured image meant to be worshiped as a real god. The prohibition of the creation of graven images is described in the third of the Ten Commandments (Exodus 20:4).

Greenberg, Henry Benjamin ("Hank") (1911–1986) Baseball player voted the most valuable player of the year in 1935. During his career he played for the Detroit Tigers and Pittsburgh Pirates and was later a manager and owner.

Greenhorn Refers to a newly arrived immigrant.

Greggar Noisemaker used to drown out Haman's name during the reading of the *Megillah* on Purim. In Hebrew it is called a *raashan*.

Guggenheim, Simon (1867–1941) American senator in the early 20th century. In 1925 he set up a foundation to award fellowships for research and creative work.

Guide for the Perplexed Philosophical work written by Maimonides in which he reveals the hidden philosophic truths inherent in the Bible.

H

Habakkuk The prophet whose book is the eighth of the Minor Prophets. The three-chapter book contains an outcry against the rule of sin in the world.

Habimah Theatre Israel's national theater since 1958, located in modern Tel Aviv.

Hachnasat orchim Literally, "greeting the stranger," this term refers to the important Jewish value of being hospitable to strangers.

Had Gadya (Aramaic, meaning "one kid") The song that concludes the Passover *Haggadah* and builds in the style of "The House that Jack Built."

Hadassah 1. Another name for Esther, heroine of the Book of Esther. 2. The Women's Zionist Organization of America, founded in 1912 by Henrietta Szold. In 1949 Hadassah opened Israel's first medical school. Its hospital is located on Mount Scopus and its famous Chagall windows have made it a popular tourist site.

Hadassim Myrtle leaves, placed to the right of the *lulav*, which is used on the festival of Sukkot.

Hadlakat haneirot Literally, "the lighting of the candles," it refers the lighting of candles to usher in Jewish festivals.

Haftarah Meaning "conclusion," it refers to the concluding prophetic Bible portion that is read on the Sabbath and festivals.

Haganah Secret organization for Jewish self-defense in Palestine. After World War II the Haganah established an "illegal" underground immigration system through which European Jews came to Palestine.

Hagar Egyptian handmaid of Sarah and the mother of Ishmael.

Hagbah Refers to the honor of lifting the Torah at the conclusion of the Torah reading.

Haggadah Passover book used during the Passover *Seder* that tells the story of the exodus of the Jews from Egypt.

Haggai Postexilic prophet (*c.* 520 B.C.E.) whose book is the tenth of the Minor Prophets.

Hagigah (Hebrew, meaning "festival offering") Twelfth tractate in the Mishnah order *Moed* dealing with Temple sacrificial offerings during the three pilgrimage festivals.

Hagiographa Meaning "holy writings," Hagiographa is the Greek word used to designate the Hebrew Bible's third division, called *Ketuvim* in Hebrew. Books in the Hagiographa include: Psalms, Proverbs, Job, Song of Songs, Ruth, Lamentations, Ecclesiastes, Esther, Daniel, Ezra, Nehemiah, and 1 and 2 Chronicles.

Hai Gaon *Gaon* in Pumbedita and last of the Babylonian *Geonim*, noted for his talmudic scholarship.

Haifa Israel's chief seaport, located on the northern slopes of Mount Carmel. Among its attractions today are the University of Haifa and the Bahai Temple.

HaKadosh Barukh Hu Literally, "the Holy One, Blessed be He," used as one of the many different terms for God.

Hakafot Literally, "circuits," it refers to the processional of circuits during Jewish festivals when the Torah scroll is paraded around the synagogue.

Halakhah The legal part of the Talmud, in contrast to the *aggadah*, the nonlegal part.

Half shekel The *shekel* is a silver unit of weight that became an official coin in the time of the Maccabees. In biblical times the Israelites were asked to pay a fee of one-half *shekel* for the maintenance of the sanctuary (Exodus 30:13).

Hallel Psalms of praise to God that are recited on Jewish holidays. The specific psalms in the Hallel are numbers 113 to 118.

Halleluyah Hebrew word meaning "praise the Lord," *Halleluyah* is often used as a refrain at the beginning and end of certain psalms.

Ham Son of Noah whose unseemly behavior toward his father led to the curse of the Canaanites (Genesis 9:20).

Haman Chief minister of Ahasuerus, king of Persia. He attempted to destroy the Jews. Instead he was hanged on his own gallows.

Hamantaschen Triangular pastries served during the festival of Purim, said to be reminiscent of Haman's three-cornered hat.

Hammerstein, Oscar (1847–1919) Builder of theaters and opera houses. His grandson, Oscar Hammerstein II (1895–1960), composed and produced many musical comedies and operas.

Hammurabi Semitic king who ruled in Babylon (1728–1686 B.C.E.). He was known for his legal code, which in many respects resembles the laws in the Bible.

Hannah Mother of Samuel the prophet and wife of Elkanah.

HaShem Literally, "the Name," today it is a euphemism for God as a referent so that one does not say God's name in vain.

Hasmoneans Title for the Maccabees, whose successful rebellions assured the continued existence of Judaism.

Hatafat dam brit Refers to the spilling of a drop of blood as part of a symbolic circumcision. This ceremony is observed when a male had a prior circumcision that was not done according to prescribed Jewish law.

HaTikvah National anthem of the State of Israel.

HaTzofim Israeli scouting organization. Its graduates have founded several *kibbutzim*.

Havdalah Literally, "separation," this ceremony bids farewell to the Sabbath. It consists of blessings over wine, spices, and fire.

Hebrew *Ivri* in Hebrew, denoting either a descendant of Eber, grandson of Shem (Genesis 10:24), or one who comes from the other side of the Euphrates river. Abraham is called "the Hebrew" (Genesis 14:13).

Hebrew Bible The authorized Bible of the Jewish people, it consists of thirty-nine books with three main sections: Five Books of Moses, Prophets, and Writings. The Hebrew Bible is also known as the Old Testament or the Tanach.

Hebrew Immigrant Aid Society (HIAS) Philanthropic organization established to provide aid of Jewish immigrants in the United States and abroad.

Hebrew language Belonging to the Canaanite branch of Semitic languages, Hebrew, along with Arabic, is one of the official languages of Israel.

Hebrew Union College-Jewish Institute of Religion Institution to train rabbis, cantors, and educators under the auspices of the Reform movement. Campuses are located in New York, Cincinnati, Los Angeles, and Jerusalem.

Hebrew University A teaching and research institution that opened in 1925 on Mount Scopus.

Hebron Ancient city of Judah, situated 18 miles south of Jerusalem. The modern city of Hebron is one of Israel's four sacred cities. It was there that Abraham purchased a burial plot for his wife, Sarah. In the Bible, Hebron was called Kiryat Arba.

Hellenism Form of Greek civilization that was spread over the Mediterranean and the Middle East after the end of the 4th century B.C.E. as a result of the conquests of Alexander the Great.

Herberg, Will (1909–1977) Contemporary American theologian and writer, best known for his volume *Judaism and Modern Man*.

Hermon, Mount Mountain range in the Upper Galilee. The highest point is always snowcapped and provides Israel with a popular ski resort.

Herod the Great (*c.* 73–4 B.C.E.) King of Judea, he rebuilt the Second Temple.

Herzl, Theodor (1860–1904) Founder of modern political Zionism. He presided over five Zionist congresses and his novel *Altneuland* portrayed a utopian vision of the Zionist state. He is often remembered for his optimistic proverb, "If you will it, it will be no legend."

Herzog, Chaim Head of the Israel Military Intelligence from 1948 to 1950, and again from 1959 to 1962. In 1967 he became the leading military commentator of the Israel Broadcasting Services. In 1983 he became President of the State of Israel.

Heschel, Abraham Joshua (1907–1972) Philosopher who served as professor of Jewish ethics and mysticism at the Jewish Theological Seminary of America. In his works he attempts to trace the relationship between God and the human.

Hezekiah King of Judah (720–692 B.C.E.), he purged the Temple of pagan images and altars.

Hiddur Mitzvah The act of enhancing or beautifying a *mitzvah*.

High Holidays Referring to the festivals of Rosh HaShanah and Yom Kippur.

High priest Chief official in the Temple, this office was conferred on Aaron and his descendants, who held it until the reign of Herod. High priests performed the sacrificial rites on behalf of the people.

Hilkiah High priest in the time of King Josiah (7th century), he found a book of law (2 Kings 22:8) during the repairs to the Temple. Hilkiah is also the name of the father of Jeremiah the prophet.

Hillel Sometimes called "the elder," he was a 1st-century B.C.E scholar who founded the school of Bet Hillel.

Hillel Foundations Organization founded in 1923 and supported by B'nai B'rith, offering religious, cultural, and communal services to thousands of Jewish collegians.

Hillel's sandwich Consisting of a piece of *matzah* with bitter herbs, this sandwich is served on the night of Passover just prior to the main meal.

Hirsch, Baron Maurice de (1831–1890) German financier and philanthropist who was the first to plan for the resettlement of the Jews on a large scale.

Hirsch, Samson Raphael (1808–1888) Important spokesperson for Orthodox Judaism in 19th-century Germany. His main views are expressed in his work *Nineteen Letters of Ben Uzziel*, in which he maintained that until the coming of the Messiah the Jews are not a people but a group of believers performing the obligations of the Written and Oral Law.

Hirsch, Samuel (1815–1889) Radical proponent of Reform Judaism, one of the first to advocate supplementary services on Sunday.

Histadrut Israeli labor federation founded in 1920.

Histadrut Ivrit of America American organization of Hebraists, founded in New York in 1916. It organizes Hebrew adult study and sponsors Hebrew cultural activities.

Holy Convocation An assembly called together for worship at the sanctuary on the three pilgrimage festivals of Sukkot, Passover, and Shavuot.

Holy of Holies The most sacred place in the ancient sanctuary, it held the Ark of the Covenant, which contained the Ten Commandments.

Horah Israeli folk dance, in which people dance in a circle.

Horayot (Hebrew, meaning "decisions") Tenth tractate in the Mishnah order *Nezikin*, dealing with decisions related to religious law made in error by the high priest or the Sanhedrin (Leviticus 4:1–21).

Horovitz, Vladimir (1904–1990) Pianist of Russian birth, he began his European tours in 1924. In 1928 he made his debut in the United States, where he subsequently settled.

Hosea (*c.* 784–725 B.C.E.) First of the Minor Prophets, he predicted the doom of Israel as punishment for its idol worship.

Hoshanah Rabbah Name for the sixth day of the festival of Sukkot. On this day seven circuits are made with the Torah scroll while the worshipers follow carrying their *lulav* and *etrog*.

Houdini, Harry (1874–1926) Born Erich Weiss, he specialized in magic and acrobatics and attained a legendary reputation.

House of David Refers to the descendants of King David. The Jewish messianic hope was attached to David's descendants.

House of Israel Biblical term referring to the whole nation of Israel (Isaiah 5:7).

Howe, Irving (1920–   ) Literary critic and writer best known for *World of Our Fathers*.

"Hymies" Anti-Semitic slur referring to Jews and used by Jesse Jackson during his 1988 presidential campaign.

I

I am that I am The answer Moses receives from God when he asks God to tell him His name in the area of the burning bush (Exodus 3:13–14). This name of God is often understood as "God will be as He will be."

Idolatry The biblical practice of worshiping idols as gods. Judaism was the only religion in the ancient world to oppose idol worship.

Imber, Naphtali Herz (1856–1909) Hebrew poet who lived in the United States and won lasting fame as the composer of *"HaTikvah,"* the national anthem of Israel.

Interfaith Refers to the relationship between people or communities of different religions, particularly Jews and non-Jews.

Intermarriage Refers to the marriage of a Jew to a non-Jew.

Intifada Refers to an Arab uprising; literally, "shaking off."

Isaac Second of the three patriarchs. His parents were Abraham and Sarah.

Isaiah Prophet in Jerusalem (740–701 B.C.E.). In the Book of Isaiah, the prophet protests strongly against moral laxity. One of his important visions described a time when "nation shall not lift up sword against nation, neither shall men learn war anymore" (Isaiah 2:4).

Ishmael Eldest son of Abraham and Sarah's Egyptian handmaid Hagar. He is traditionally believed to be the ancestor of the Arab nation.

Ishmael's Principles of Logic Thirteen principles of logic created by the 2nd-century *tanna* Ishmael ben Elisha. These principles were used by talmudic sages to help explain verses in the Bible.

Israel New name given to the patriarch Jacob after his night of wrestling at Penuel. Israel also refers to the nation that traces its ancestry back to the twelve sons of Jacob (Genesis 34:7).

Israel Bond Chief source of investment capital for Israel's economic infrastructure. Founded in 1951, the Israel Bond Organization has raised billions of dollars to help build roads and communication networks in Israel.

Israel Defense Forces (I.D.F.) Israel's modern army, established in 1948.

Isru Chag Literally, "bind the festival offering," this term applies to the semifestive day following the holidays of Passover, Sukkot, and Shavuot.

Issachar Fifth son of Jacob and Leah, and ancestor of the tribe that settled on Jordan's west bank.

Iyar Second month of the Jewish religious calendar and the eighth month of the civil calendar. Observances in this month include Yom HaShoah, Israel Independence Day, and Lag B'Omer.

J

J School According to the Documentary Hypothesis, the first school of writers to gather the oral traditions and experiences of the Israelites. The J School is named after the name of the Deity, JHVH, that appears in the writings of this first school. The school finished its work in the year 850 B.C.E.

J.A.P. A derogatory term referring to "Jewish American Princess" and stereotyping the Jewish girl as a wealthy, spoiled child with few good values.

Jacob Third of the patriarchs and the younger of the twin sons of Isaac and Rebekah. Jacob cheated his twin brother Esau out of their father Isaac's blessing by impersonating him.

Jacob's ladder A ladder Jacob saw in a dream, with angels descending and ascending upon it. In this vision God promised to bless Jacob and bring his people into the Land of Israel.

Jacobs, Louis (1920–   ) British rabbi and writer of theology. He asserts a human element in the compilation of the Bible.

Jaffa Israel's oldest seaport, located near Tel Aviv along the Mediterranean Sea. The Jaffa orange is internationally famous and an important Israeli export.

Jastrow, Marcus (1829–1903) Zionist leader and rabbi at Rodelph Shalom in Philadelphia. He was an editor of the Talmud department of the *Jewish Encyclopedia*.

Jehovah Traditional but inaccurate Christian reading of the Hebrew tetragrammaton (the four Hebrew consonants "YHVH" that spell God's name). It resulted from overlooking the fact that the vowels with which the letters of God's name YHVH were provided by the Masoretes are those of Adonai.

Jeremiah (7th–6th century B.C.E.) Prophet belonging to a priestly family of Anatoth near Jerusalem. Witnessing the destruction of the First Temple, he prophesied the doom of the Israelites as punishment for their sins. Jeremiah is the second of the Major Prophets.

Jericho City in the south Jordan valley, one of the oldest in the history of civilization. Destroyed by Joshua in biblical times, subsequently it has been destroyed and rebuilt many times. Today modern Jericho is inhabited mostly by Arabs.

Jerusalem City that King David established as Israel's capital in 1000 B.C.E. Situated in the Judean hills, it is today a holy city for Jews, Christians, and Moslems. Among its famous attractions are the Western Wall, the Knesset, and Hebrew University.

Jerusalem Post Israeli English newspaper, founded as the *Palestine Post* in 1932. Its overseas weekly edition is read around the world.

Jerusalem Talmud Compilation of the laws and discussion of the amoraim in Israel, mainly in the academy of Tiberias. The Jerusalem Talmud is much smaller and considered less authoritative than the Babylonian Talmud.

Jeshurun Poetic name for the people of Israel (Deuteronomy 32:15).

Jethro Midianite priest and father of Zipporah, wife of Moses. Jethro advised Moses on legal administration (Exodus 18).

Jewish Agency Prior to Israel's statehood, the World Zionist Organization was designated as the Jewish Agency for advising the administration of Palestine in matters concerning the establishment of Israel as a state. Today the Jewish Agency maintains headquarters in both Jerusalem and New York. Its activities include settling new immigrants, encouraging capital investment by foreigners, and providing Zionist educational materials.

Jewish Chronicle, The English newspaper established in 1841, the oldest Jewish periodical in existence.

Jewish Community Center America Jewish communal institution (originally known as the YM/YWHA) whose aim is to perpetuate Judaism through a program of recreation and education in Jewish culture.

Jewish Encyclopedia, The Twelve-volume encyclopedia, chiefly edited by Isidore Singer.

Jewish Federation Also called Welfare Fund, it is a local overseeing agency and fund-raising arm of a community, having representation through synagogues and other Jewish organizations within the community.

Jewish National Fund (J.N.F.) Institution of the World Zionist Organization for the development and afforestation of land in Palestine. The Jewish National Fund has planted millions of trees in forests since its inception.

Jewish Publication Society (JPS) Nonprofit membership organization founded in 1888 to promote the dissemination of Jewish literature. It is currently located in Philadelphia.

Jewish Quarter Refers to the existence of separate streets or sections of a city for Jews, usually determined by law.

Jewish Telegraphic Agency (JTA) Worldwide Jewish news service established in 1914.

Jewish Theological Seminary of America Rabbinical institution founded in New York in 1886. It has campuses in New York, Los Angeles, South America, and Jerusalem and is the academic arm of Conservative Judaism.

Jewish Welfare Board (JWB) Central organization and coordinating body of Jewish Community Centers.

Jews College Founded in 1855, this rabbinical seminary is located in London.

JHVH An ancient name for God, probably pronounced "Yaweh," which the Christians pronounced Jehovah.

Job Third book in the biblical section called Writings. The theme of this book is the problem of suffering of the righteous. The book's conclusion is that people can never truly understand the mystery of the Lord's ways.

Joel Second book in the order of the Minor Prophets, the Book of Joel calls upon the people of Judea to repent because the Day of Judgment is at hand.

Joint Distribution Committee, The American Jewish Created in 1914, its goals include the dispensing of aid to war victims, caring for orphan children, and the restoration of educational and cultural centers.

Jolson, Al (1886–1950) Entertainer and singer, Jolson starred in the first talking picture, *The Jazz Singer,* in 1927.

Jonathan Eldest son of Saul and devoted friend of King. His bravery in the wars with the Philistines won him great popularity.

Jordan, Kingdom of Formerly known as Transjordan, it was established as a principality of the British in 1923. In 1946 it became independent and adopted its current name of Jordan.

Jordan River Chief river of ancient Israel, running from Mount Hermon to the Dead Sea. Moses was not permitted by God to cross the Jordan River into the Promised Land. The river today is revered by Christians because it was said that Jesus was baptized in its waters.

Joseph Son of Rachel and Jacob, he was their favorite son and was given a "coat of many colors." Joseph's dreams aroused the jealousy of his brothers, who sold him into slavery.

Josephus, Flavius (*c.* 38–*c.* 100) Historian and chronicler, best known for his works the *Jewish Wars* and *Jewish Antiquities*.

Joshua Son of Nun and successor of Moses, he led the Israelites across the Jordan River and defeated the Canaanites. The Book of Joshua is the sixth in the Bible, following the Book of Deuteronomy.

Josiah King of Judah (637–608 B.C.E.), he began a program of religious reform including the repair and purification of the Temple.

Jubilee Year The Bible ordains a rest from agricultural work in ancient Israel once in every 7 years (Leviticus 25:3). The crops in this year are to lie fallow, allowing the land time to replenish itself. The year following these 7 fallow years of rest is known as the Jubilee or 50th year, when cultivation is again prohibited and slaves are set free.

Judah Fourth son of Jacob's first wife, Leah. He was involved in the event that led Joseph to become a slave in Egypt.

Judah the Prince Important scholar whose life work consisted of the editing of the Mishnah.

Judaism as a Civilization Important work of Mordecai Kaplan, in which he articulates the philosophy of Reconstructionist Judaism. Basically it says that Judaism is more than a religion. It is a civilization that includes language, religion, history, a social organization, and spiritual and ethical ideals.

Judea The southernmost of the two kingdoms into which ancient Israel was divided in 933 B.C.E. after the death of King Solomon. Most of the Jewish prophets carried out their activities in Judea.

Judenrat Written by Theodor Herzl in 1896 to advocate the need for the creation of a Jewish state.

Judges (12th and 11th centuries B.C.E.) The Book of Judges spans the period from the death of Joshua to the time of King Saul. Called to leadership by the people, their battles eventually extended Israelite mastery of the land. There were sixteen judges in all. Two of them, Deborah and Samuel, were also prophets.

Jung, Leo (1892–1987) Leading spokesperson of neo-Orthodoxy, he was a professor at Yeshiva University and Columbia University.

K

Kabbalah Referring to the mystical tradition in Judaism.

Kaddish Literally, "consecration," it refers to one of five prayers recited during synagogue services that praise God's Holy Name.

Kal Vahomer A principle of rabbinic explanation. This rule of logical argumentation always compares a lenient to a more stringent case. It asserts that if the law is stringent in a case where we are usually lenient, then it will surely be stringent in a more serious case.

Kalam Arabic scholastic theology that influenced many Jewish philosophers of the Middle Ages.

Kaplan, Mordecai (1881–1983) American rabbi and philosopher, founder of Reconstructionist Judaism. His most famous work is *Judaism as a Civilization*.

Karet A divine punishment (of a short life) for a serious sin.

Karpas Referring to the green vegetable that is served during the Passover meal. It symbolizes rebirth and spring.

Kashrut Regulations determining the Jewish dietary laws.

Kavanah One's devotion and proper intention during prayer services or the performance of any *mitzvah*.

Kedushah Literally, "sanctification," it is the name given to the third of the eighteen blessings of the *Amidah*. The key line in the prayer is, "Holy, holy, holy is the Lord of Hosts, the whole world is filled with His glory."

Kehillah An organized Jewish community or congregation. The Kehilla Movement began in New York in 1909, seeking to direct community affairs in the fields of education, sociology, and religion.

Kelim (Hebrew, meaning "utensils") First tractate in the Mishnah order *Tohorot*, discussing the ritual uncleanliness of vessels (Leviticus 11:32).

Kelippot According to the Kabbalah, *kelippot*, or shells, are the forces of evil that dominate the original light of creation.

Keren Ami Literally, "horn of my people," today it refers to a charity fund whose monies are collected and often sent to assist Israel.

Keriah Act of tearing of one's garment as a sign of mourning. Today a mourner will often cut or tear a black ribbon that is attached to his clothing.

Keritot (Hebrew, meaning "excisions") Seventh tractate in the Mishnah order *Kodashim*, dealing with the punishment of *karet*.

Keter Torah Crownlike ornament placed on the wooden handles at the top of the Torah scroll.

Ketubah Jewish marriage contract, which stipulates the obligations husband and wife have to each other.

Ketubot (Hebrew, meaning "marriage contracts") Second tractate in the Mishnah order *Nashim*, which deals with money to be received by a wife in the case of divorce or widowhood.

Khazars Sovereign Turkish tribe in Eastern Europe whose leaders adopted Judaism.

Kibbutz Israeli collective village, established by the early pioneers. The members of each settlement, known as "kibbutzniks," own its property in common.

Kibud Av Va'em Honoring one's father and one's mother, one of the Ten Commandments.

Kiddush Literally, "sanctification," today it refers to the ceremonial blessing over the wine that ushers in the Sabbath and holidays. The *Kiddush* also refers to the collation following Sabbath and holiday morning services.

Kiddush HaShem Literally, "sanctification of the divine name," it generally refers to martyrdom.

Kiddushin (Hebrew, meaning "betrothals") Seventh and last tractate in the Mishnah order *Nashim* dealing with matters of marriage.

Kilayim (Hebrew, meaning "diverse kinds") Fourth tractate in the Mishnah order *Zeraim*, which deals with prohibitions of mingling different kinds of plants, animals, and clothing (Leviticus 19:19).

King James Bible Alternately called the "Authorized Version." It was King James I of Great Britain who organized a project that resulted in a new translation of the Bible. Fifty translators completed this new Bible in 1611.

King David Hotel Luxury hotel located in Jerusalem. During World War II it was used as administrative headquarters by the British troops.

Kings, Book of In the Bible, the 1st and 2nd Kings cover the history of the kingdoms of Israel and Judah, from King Solomon, 970 B.C.E.., to the destruction of Judah by Babylon in 586 B.C.E..

Kinnim (Hebrew, meaning "bird nests") Eleventh and last tractate in the Mishnah order *Kodashim*, it deals with regulations for bringing a sacrificial offering after childbirth (Leviticus 12:8).

Kippah Skullcap worn by men in synagogue as a sign of reverence for God. In Yiddish it is called a *yarmulke*.

Kishinev Capital of Soviet Moldavia, where many Jews were killed as a result of two massacres (pogroms).

Kislev Ninth month of the Jewish religious calendar and third of the civil calendar. The festival of Chanukah always falls on the 25th of this month.

Kittel White robe sometimes worn by officiants at the Passover Seder. It is also worn by rabbis during the High Holidays and by bridegrooms in traditional marriage ceremonies.

Klal Yisrael Term referring to the entire Jewish people.

Klezmer Eastern Europe instrumental music often including a violin and clarinet.

Knesset Israel's parliament, created in 1949. Its building is located in Jerusalem.

Kodashim (Hebrew, meaning "holy things") Fifth order of the Mishnah, consisting of eleven tractates dealing with the laws of ritual slaughter, sacrifice, and other Temple-related objects.

Kol B'Seder Hebrew for "everything is okay."

Kol Chamirah Formula used to make null and void the *chametz* not found in one's house after the search. It proclaims that any leaven in a person's house that may not have been removed shall be as if it did not exist.

Kol HaNe'arim Refers to the final *aliyah* on the festival of Simchat Torah when all the children are invited to the Torah.

Kol Nidre Formula for the annulment of vows that is recited three times on the eve of Yom Kippur.

Kol Yisrael (Hebrew, meaning "voice of Israel") Israel's official radio station, broadcasting the news of the day hourly.

Kol Yisrael arevim ze lazeh (Hebrew, meaning "all Israelites are responsible for each other") It suggests the responsibility that all Jewish people have for each other's welfare.

Kook, Abraham Isaac (1865–1935) First chief rabbi of Palestine.

Korach A levite related to Moses who rebelled against Moses and Aaron (Numbers 16) in an attempt to seize their leadership. However, the earth opened up and swallowed him (Numbers 26:11).

Kosher Literally, "fit to eat," it refers to food that is permissible to be eaten by Jews according to the Jewish dietary laws. Animals that are kosher must chew their cuds and have split hooves, and kosher fish must have fins and scales.

Koved Honor or respect, alternatively called *kavod*.

Kozu bemuchsaz kozu Secret Hebrew code on the back of every *mezuzah* parchment. The words stand for *Adonai Eloheinu Adonai*, meaning "Adonai is our God."

Kreplach A pastry shell filled with meat, often served in soup.

Kristallnacht Literally, "the night of broken glass." Refers to the Nazi attack on the Jewish community on November 9th and 10th of 1938.

Kugel Noodle pudding.

Kushner, Harold Late-20th-century Conservative rabbi, author of a best-selling book *When Bad Things Happen to Good People.*

Kuzari, The Philosophic work by Judah Halevi that is concerned with the problem of the Jewish fate and exile. This treatise is a polemic against Christianity and Islam and today is regarded as one of the classics of Judaism.

L

Laban Brother of Rebekah and father of Leah and Rachel. He gave his sister Rebekah in marriage to Isaac. Years later, he consented to the marriage of his daughter Rachel to Jacob but substituted her sister Leah at the wedding. Subsequently he also gave Jacob Rachel in exchange for an additional 7 years of service.

Labor Party Political party formed in 1968 by the union of three earlier parties: Mapai, Achdut HaAvodah-Poalei Zion, and Rafi-Israel Labor List.

Ladino Name given to the Judeo-Spanish dialect spoken by the Sephardim of the Mediterranean and written in Hebrew characters.

Lag B'Omer The thirty-third day of the *Omer* period. According to legend, an outbreak of a plague among the students of Rabbi Akiva in the 2nd century ended on this date.

Lamed vavnick A righteous person. *Lamed* and *vav* are two Hebrew letters whose combined numerical value is thirty-six. According to a tradition, in every generation there will be thirty-six righteous persons upon whom the world can depend.

Lamentations Third of the five scrolls in the Hagiographa section of the Bible. It contains five chapters of elegies and mourning over the destruction of Jerusalem. According to rabbinic tradition, the author was the Prophet Jeremiah. Lamentations is read in the synagogue during the summer on the fast of Tisha B'Av.

Land of Milk and Honey A biblical poetic name for the Promised Land (i.e., the Land of Israel). The spies sent by Moses to scout out the land called it "the land of milk and honey" (Numbers 13:27).

Landsman Refers to those who come from the same country.

Landsmanshaft Hebrew Benevolent Society, whose members looked after the needs of their fellow immigrants.

Lashon HaKodesh The holy tongue, referring to the Hebrew language.

Latkes Potato pancakes, called *levivot* in Hebrew, traditionally served during the celebration of Chanukah.

Latter Prophets The Latter Prophets consist of fifteen books that present the teachings of the Israelite prophets. These begin with the three Major Prophets—Isaiah, Jeremiah, and Ezekiel—and conclude with the twelve books of the Minor Prophets. The Minor Prophets include Hosea, Joel, Amos, Obadiah, Jonah, Micah, Nahum, Habakkuk, Zephaniah, Haggai, Zechariah, and Malachi.

Law The Torah (Five Books of Moses) is sometimes referred to as the Book of Law. "Tables of the Law" usually refers to the Ten Commandments.

Lazarus, Emma (1849–1887) American poetess whose words, "Give me your tired, give me your poor . . ." are now inscribed on a plaque embedded in the Statue of Liberty.

L'chayyim Literally, "to life," it is often used as a toast at Jewish ceremonies.

Leah Daughter of Laban and wife of Jacob, who bore him six sons—Reuben, Simeon, Levi, Judah, Issachar, and Zebulun—and a daughter Dinah.

Lebanon Middle Eastern Republic whose capital is Beirut. It is made up of both Arab Moslems and Arab Christians.

Lechah Dodi Mystical prayer of greeting for the Sabbath written in Safed in the 16th century. It is customary for the congregation to turn toward the synagogue entrance while reciting the last verse.

Leeser, Isaac (1806–1868) American religious leader, he became rabbi of Congregation Mikveh Israel in Philadelphia, where he introduced the English sermon into synagogue services. His Bible translation of 1853 served American Jewry as the accepted English version for more than 50 years.

Leprosy A dreaded biblical disease (Leviticus 13:1). According to the Bible, leprosy was acquired as a result of divine punishment.

Leshanah tovah tikatevu Literally, "may you be inscribed for a good year," it is a traditional Rosh HaShanah greeting.

Levenson, Sam (1914–1980) Comedian and educator, known for his stories about the Lower East Side of New York.

Levi 1. Third Son of Jacob and Leah. 2. Social class distinction and biblical tribe, used to designate assistant priests with special responsibilities in the Temple. Today persons who are known to be descended from the Levitical tribe are given the second *aliyah* to the Torah at synagogue services.

Levi Yitzchak of Berdichev Chasid who was well known for standing up to God in the midst of the community.

Leviathan Legendary sea creature described in the Bible in a variety of places (see Job 40:25).

Levirate Marriage Marriage with a brother's childless widow (Deuteronomy 25:5).

Leviticus Third of the Five Books of Moses, it contains a manual for Levites, the priestly ritual of sacrifices, marriage laws, and other laws related to various aspects of life.

Levy, Moses (1665–1728) Prominent merchant in colonial America, he initiated the building of North America's first synagogue.

Levy, Uriah P. (1792–1862) American naval officer, he led the crusade to abolish flogging as a form of discipline in the United States Navy. In 1943 the navy honored his memory by naming a destroyer after him.

Liberal Judaism Generally used as a synonym for Reform Judaism, it denotes the Reform movement in Great Britain.

Lieberman, Saul (1898–1983) Talmudic scholar who served as rector of the Jewish Theological Seminary of America.

Liebman, Joshua (1907–1948) Reform rabbi who gained national attention after publishing his best-selling *Peace of Mind*, a pastoral volume offering comfort to Americans who had suffered during World War II.

Likud Party Major political party in Israel's *Knesset*, it is made up of the Cherut Freedom Party, the Israel Liberal Party, and several smaller parties.

Lishma Meaning "for its own sake," as in study.

Litvak Person who comes from Lithuania.

Lochame Cherut Yisrael Known as Lechi or by its opponents as the Stern Gang, this revolutionary Jewish organization split in 1940 from the Irgun.

Lod (Lydda) Israeli town southeast of Tel Aviv. Today Israel's largest airport, Ben-Gurion, is located near the town.

Lookstein, Joseph (1902–1979) Rabbi who founded the Ramaz School in New York City and was its principal for more than 30 years.

Lot Son of Abraham's brother Haran. The Bible relates Lot's escape from Sodom and the misfortune of his wife, who turned into a pillar of salt.

Lotan One of two *kibbutzim* established in Israel by the Reform movement (the other is Yahel).

Lovers of Zion (Hebrew *Chovevei Zion*) An East European 19th-century organization for the settlement of Jews in Palestine.

Lower East Side Section on the lower part of Eastern Manhattan where thousands of Jewish immigrants lived upon arrival in the United States.

Lox Cured fillet of salmon, often served on a bagel with cream cheese.

Luach Hebrew for Jewish calendar.

Lulav The palm branch used during the festival of Sukkot.

Luria, Isaac ben Solomon (1534–1572) Well-known kabbalist who believed that people could "connect" with the divine spirit through intense concentration and meditation.

M

Maaser Sheni (Hebrew, meaning "Second Tithe") Eighth tractate in the Mishnah order *Zeraim*, dealing with the laws of the second tithe and how it is brought to Jerusalem and redeemed.

Maariv 1. Refers to the daily evening worship service. Tradition ascribes its invention to the patriarch Jacob 2. Israeli mass-circulation paper founded in 1948.

Maccabees Name of the priestly family of the Hasmoneans from the town of Modin in Palestine. In 165 B.C.E. they purified the Temple and the festival of Chanukah was declared.

Maccabiah International Jewish sports festival under the auspices of the Maccabi World Union.

Machpelah Cave near Hebron, which Abraham purchased for his wife Sarah's burial.

Machzor A holiday prayer book.

Maftir Person who reads the *Haftarah*. It also refers to the last Torah reading on a Sabbath or Jewish holiday.

Magid Wandering preacher and storyteller, especially active in 18th-century Poland.

Magnes, Judah L. (1877–1948) Rabbi, community leader, and educator, he headed the New York Kehillah and later became the first president of Hebrew University.

Mah Nishtanah Literally, "why is it different," it refers to the four questions in the Passover *Haggadah*. Tradition allows for the youngest members of the *Seder* to recite these questions.

Maharil (1525–1609) Known as Judah Low ben Bezalel, he was chief rabbi of Moravia, where he wrote many books of rabbinic commentary.

Mailer, Norman (1923–   ) American novelist whose books speak in violent psychological terms.

Maimonides, Moses (1135–1204) Moses ben Maimon, also called the Rambam, known for many works, including the *Guide for the Perplexed*, which attempted to bring philosophy into harmony with religion. This book influenced not only Jewish thinkers but Christian theologians and philosophers as well.

Majdenek Concentration camp on the outskirts of Lublin, Poland. Here 125,000 Jews were exterminated in 1942–1943.

Major Prophets Refers to the biblical prophets Isaiah, Jeremiah, and Ezekiel.

Makhshirin (Hebrew, meaning "predisposings") Eighth tractate in the Mishnah order *Tohorot*, dealing with the laws of ritual impurity in connection with foods that are susceptible to impurity when wet (Leviticus 11:24, 38).

Makkot (Hebrew, meaning "stripes") Fifth tractate in the Mishnah order *Nezikin* dealing with lashings ordered by court decree (Deuteronomy 25:1–3), false witnesses, and cities of refuge (Numbers 35:9–28).

Malachi Last of the biblical prophets (*c.* 460–450 B.C.E.).

Malamud, Bernard (1914–1986) American writer, well known for his novels *The Fixer* and *The Natural.*

Malkhut Literally, "kingdom," referring to the tenth level of the *sefirot* in Kabbalah.

Malkhuyot Refers to the section of the *Amidah* in the additional *Musaf* service during the High Holy Days and acknowledges God's sovereignty.

Mame-loshen Literally, "mother tongue," in Eastern Europe it was used synonymously with Yiddish.

Mamon Material goods or money.

Mamzer (Hebrew, meaning "bastard") Refers to any child of a forbidden sexual relationship.

Manasseh First son of Joseph and Asenath (Genesis 41:50–51). Manasseh was also the name of the King of Judah (692–638 B.C.E.). He was one of the worst biblical kings and was known for his introduction of pagan practices.

Mannah Food eaten by the Israelites in the desert (Exodus 16:4–35). It was found on the ground every morning except for on the Sabbath.

Maot Chittim Literally, "wheat money," it refers to collections made before Passover to assure a supply of flour for *matzah* for the poor.

Maoz Tzur Literally, "fortress rock," a song sung after the lighting of the candles on Chanukah.

Maror Bitter herbs eaten during the Passover *Seder*.

Marrano Literally, "swine," it is a term for Spanish and Portuguese Jews and their descendants who were forced to accept Christianity but continued to practice Judaism in secret.

Marshall, Louis (1856–1929) American lawyer and defender of civil liberties, he became president of the American Jewish Committee in 1912.

Marx, Alexander (1878–1954) Historian and bibliographer, he was a professor at the Jewish Theological Seminary. He collaborated with Max Margolis on a one-volume *History of the Jewish People*.

Masada Stronghold located west of the Dead Sea on a high rock. Herod built a refuge there in 40 B.C.E. Masada became a Zealot fortress until 70 C.E. when the Jews atop Masada committed suicide to avoid being captured by the Romans.

Mashgiach One who supervises the observance of the laws of *kashrut* in the preparation of food.

Maskilim Refers to those who accepted the enlightenment, the *Haskalah*, and worked to refine and further develop it.

Masoretes Jewish scribes from 500–1000 C.E. who carefully copied the Scriptures in an attempt to preserve them. Their work produced the Masoretic Text of the Bible (i.e., the current Hebrew text).

Masoreti Movement Name for the movement of Conservative Judaism in Israel.

Matriarchs The founding mothers of the Israelites, including Sarah, Rebekah, Rachel, and Leah.

Mattathias Priest and father of the Hasmonean brothers, he waged war on the Syrians. After he died, he was succeeded by his son Judah the Maccabee.

Matzah Unleavened bread eaten during Passover.

Maven Yiddish for one who has special knowledge, sometimes in a variety of disciplines.

May Laws Temporary rules issued in 1882 by the Russian minister of the interior that curtailed Jewish residences in villages and reversed the more liberal policy toward the Jews of the previous era.

Mayer, Louis B. (1885–1957) American motion-picture producer and head of Metro-Goldwyn-Mayer (MGM) film productions.

Mazel Literally, "constellation," today it means luck. *Mazel tov* means "good luck."

Mechitzah Divider used in traditional synagogues to separate men from women.

Me'il The mantle or covering of a Torah scroll.

Me'ilah (Hebrew, meaning "trespass," i.e., in regard to holy things) Eighth tractate in the Mishnah order *Kodashim,* it deals with laws concerning profane use of things meant for holy purposes (Leviticus 5:15–16).

Me'sheh'bay'rakh Prayer used to honor or pray for the welfare of a person, often read following the reading of the Torah during synagogue worship services.

Mea Shearim Stronghold of Jewish Orthodoxy, Mea Shearim was established in 1875 in Jerusalem. Today it is home to many *yeshivot* and synagogues.

Megiddo Ancient Palestinian city in the Valley of Jezreel. Excavations here have revealed twenty-one different civilizations. Megiddo's museum is a popular tourist attraction and was the inspiration for writer James Michener's book *The Source*.

Megillah (Hebrew, meaning "scroll") Tenth tractate in the Mishnah order *Moed*, it deals with laws related to reading the Scroll of Esther and regulations for the care of holy objects.

Megillot (Hebrew, meaning "scrolls") In the Hebrew Bible, the Song of Songs, Ruth, Lamentations, Ecclesiastes, and Esther were designated as the Five *Megillot*.

Meir, Golda (1898–1978) Labor Zionist leader and former prime minister of Israel.

Meir, Rabbi Second-century Palestinian *tanna* and student of Rabbi Akiva. His Mishnah formed the basis of the accepted Mishnah of Judah the Prince.

Mekhilta Name applied to certain midrashic works (e.g., The oldest midrashic commentary to the Book of Exodus is called the *Mekhilta*). 2. Also used as a synonym for *masekhet* (i.e., tractate of the Mishnah or Talmud).

Mekhirat Chametz: Legal fiction in which one sells all the *chametz* to a non-Jew.

Melaveh Malkah Literally, "accompanying the Sabbath Queen," it is the concluding Sabbath banquet following the *Havdalah* ceremony.

Men of the Great Assembly One hundred twenty scholarly men whose decisions constituted the supreme authority in matters of religion and law during Second Temple times.

Menachot (Hebrew, meaning "meal offerings") Second tractate in the Mishnah order *Kodashim*, it deals with preparation of the meal offering (Leviticus 2:1–14).

Mendelssohn, Moses (1729–1786) Philosopher par excellence of the German Enlightenment. In his famous work *Jerusalem*, he outlined his ideals of religious and political toleration, separation of church and state, and equality of all citizens.

Menorah Golden seven-branched candelabrum that was one of the prominent features of the Tabernacle and Temple.

Mentsh Literally, "person," today *mentsh* often refers to a person of extraordinary integrity.

Mercaz Movement to reaffirm Conservative Judaism. A member of the World Zionist Organization, Mercaz is the Zionist action organization of the Conservative movement.

Meshuge Yiddish for one who is crazy.

Messianic Age Described in the Bible as a time when peace and serenity will fill the world, the wolf will dwell with the lamb, and the leopard shall lie down with the kid (Isaiah 11:6).

Methuselah Biblical figure, son of Enoch and Lamech. He died at the age of 969, the oldest person recorded in biblical history.

Mezuzah Literally "doorpost," it refers to the parchment scroll placed in a container and affixed to the doorposts of Jewish homes.

Micah (8th century B.C.E.) Prophet in Judah, he speaks for the people against the oppression of the ruling classes. His book is one of the twelve books of the Minor Prophets.

Middot (Hebrew, meaning "measures") Tenth tractate in the Mishnah order *Kodashim* dealing with laws related to the Second Temple architecture.

Midian Bedouin tribe related to Abraham. Its members traveled with caravans of incense from Gilead to Egypt. Jethro, Moses' father, was a Medianite priest.

Midrash Refers to the nonlegal sections of the Talmud and the rabbinic books containing biblical interpretations in the spirit of the *aggadah* (i.e., legend).

Midrash Rabbah Collection of aggadic *midrashim* to the Five Books of Moses and the Five *Megillot*.

Mikra'ot Gedolot Edition of the Bible published in Venice (1524–1525) by Daniel Bomberg. It became the accepted version of the Bible, known as the Masoretic Text, upon which everyone has since relied.

Mikvaot (Hebrew, meaning "ritual baths") Sixth tractate in the Mishnah order *Tohorot*, it deals with the rituals related to ritual bathing (Leviticus 14:8).

Mikveh Ritual bath used by both Jewish men and women. Persons converting to Judaism traditionally immerse in a *mikveh* as well.

Milchig Refers to a meal of dairy or milk products. Jews who keep kosher do not mix dairy meals, *milchig*, with meat meals, called *fleishig*.

Milk and honey Said to flow in the Land of Israel, it refers to the natural beauty of the land.

Miller, Arthur (1915–   ) American playwright whose most famous work, *Death of a Salesman*, won a Pulitzer prize.

Minchah Afternoon worship service, said to have been originally introduced by the patriarch Isaac.

Minhag A custom or observance handed down from generation to generation.

Minhag America American Reform prayer book compiled by Isaac Mayer Wise.

Minor (Hebrew *katan*) A child who has not reached maturity.

Minor Prophets Twelve prophetical books (Hosea, Joel, Amos, Obadiah, Jonah, Micah, Nahum, Habakkuk, Zephaniah, Haggai, Zechariah, and Malachi) placed in the Hebrew Bible after the Book of Ezekiel. Their dates range between the 8th and 5th centuries B.C.E.

Minor Tractate Extracanonical talmudic tractate included in the editions of the Babylonian Talmud in the form of an addenda.

Minyan A group of ten adults (restricted to men in Orthodox Judaism) required for communal prayer.

Miriam Elder sister of Moses, she watched her infant brother when he was placed in a basket on the Nile River. After the Israelites successfully crossed the Red Sea, Miriam led the Israelite women in a song and dance of triumph.

Mishnah Collection of Jewish law complied and edited by Judah the Prince in the early 3rd century. It contains sixty-three tractates and has six divisions: *Zeraim* (agriculture), *Moed* (Festivals), *Nashim* (Marriage), *Nezikin* (Damages), *Kodashim* (Sacrifices), and *Tohorot* (Purity).

Mitnaged Opponent of the chasidic movement. Reasons for opposition included the pantheistic tendencies of the *chasidim*, their use of Sephardic liturgy, and their belief in *tzadikim*.

Mitzvah Commandment traditionally acknowledged to have been given by God or decreed by the rabbis.

Mixed Marriage Marriage between two persons of different faiths, usually Jews and non-Jews. This term is often used interchangeably with intermarriage.

Mizrach Literally, "east," it refers to a wall plaque placed on an eastern wall in one's home to indicate, for purposes of prayer, the direction of Jerusalem.

Mizrachi Religious Zionist movement that made its first appearance as a political party in 1902. Mizrachi of America built Bar Ilan University, the first religious institution of higher academic learning in Israel.

Moab Country in south Transjordan. The Moabites were kindred to the Israelites, traditionally descended from Lot.

Modi'in Ancient Israelite town, southeast of Lydda, home of the Hasmoneans. Today in Israel a burning torch is carried from Modi'in to Jerusalem each Chanukah by relay runners.

Moed (Hebrew, meaning "set feast") Second order of the Mishnah, consisting of twelve tractates dealing with laws related to the Sabbath and festivals.

Moed Katan (Hebrew, meaning "minor festival") Eleventh tractate in the Mishnah order *Moed*, dealing with the kind of work permitted during the intermediate days of Passover and the Feast of Tabernacles. It also deals with the laws of mourning on festivals.

Mohel Ritual circumciser who performs at the ritual of a *Brit Milah*.

Monotheism The belief in one God. Jewish monotheism can be best summed up in the biblical formula, "Hear O Israel, the Lord Our God, the Lord is One" (Deuteronomy 6:4).

Montefiore, Sir Moses (1784–1865) British philanthropist and community worker, known for his contribution of funds for economic development and schools in Palestine. In 1837 he was knighted by Queen Victoria.

Morais, Sabato (1823–1897) Rabbi and leading opponent of Reform Judaism, he became president of the Jewish Theological Seminary of America and helped lay the foundation for Conservative Judaism.

Mordecai Benjamite serving as palace official at Shushan in the reign of Ahasuerus. His neice was Esther, who later became queen and helped save the Jews from destruction (see the Book of Esther).

Moriah, Mount Hill in Jerusalem traditionally identified as the place where Abraham prepared to offer his son Isaac as a sacrifice. Later the Jerusalem Temple was erected there, and currently it is the location of the Dome of the Rock.

Morning Journal, The Yiddish daily newspaper, founded in 1901.

Moses Lawgiver and prophet, Moses led the Israelites out of Egypt. Shortly thereafter he received the Ten Commandments.

Moshav An agricultural village, similar to a *kibbutz*, with the exception that land is privately owned by its settlers. Two of Israel's earliest *Moshavs* were Petach Tikvah and Rishon Le-Zion.

Mourner's Kaddish Prayer recited by a Jewish person who has lost a loved one.

Mourners for Zion Jews who deprived themselves of wine, meat, and other luxuries because of the destruction of the Jerusalem Temple. There is no trace of them after the destruction of the Jerusalem community at the close of the 11th century.

Musaf The additional service recited on sabbaths and holidays.

Musar Ethical guidance and advice encouraging strict behavior regarding Jewish law. It developed into a full-fledged movement in the latter part of the 19th century, led by its founder, Israel Salanter.

Museum of the Diaspora One of Israel's newest and finest museums, located on the campus of Tel Aviv University. The museum uses audio visual aids and traces the history of the Jews from their dispersal after the Roman conquest to the present day.

N

Nachal Branch of the Israel Defense Forces training cadres for agricultural settlements.

Naches Yiddish, it refers to the joy that one may derive from one's children.

Nahum Seventh-century prophet, he foretold the fall of Nineveh. His book is one of the twelve Minor Prophets.

Nahum of Gamzo Second-century *tanna* whose comment on every apparent misfortune was the later proverbial "*Gam zeh letovah*" ("also this is for the good").

Naphtali Sixth son of Jacob. The tribe of Naphtali was active in the war against Sisera and Gideon's campaign against the Midianites.

Nashim (Hebrew, meaning "women") Third order of the Mishnah, consisting of seven tractates dealing with marriage, divorce, and vows of Nazirites. The tractates include: *Yevamot* (sister-in-law), *Ketubot* (marriage deeds), *Nedarim* (vows), *Nazir* (Nazirite), *Sotah* (suspected adulterous woman), *Gittin* (Divorce), and *Kiddushin* (Betrothals).

National Association of Temple Educators (NATE) Professional association of Reform Jewish Educators.

National Community Relations Advisory Council (NCRAC) National community defense agency, which promotes intercommunity relations and monitors anti-Jewish feelings.

National Conference of Christians and Jews American organization founded in 1928, comprised of Protestants, Catholics, and Jews, with the objective of furthering better relations among people of all religions, races and nationalities.

National Conference of Jewish Women (NCJW) American organization founded in 1893 by Hannah Solomon, it is dedicated to furthering human welfare in the Jewish and general communities.

National Conference of Synagogue Youth (NCSY) Youth movement affiliated with Orthodox Judaism.

National Federation of Temple Brotherhoods Synagogue brotherhoods affiliated with the Reform movement and the Union of American Hebrew Congregations, founded in 1923.

National Federation of Temple Sisterhoods (NFTS) Synagogue sisterhoods affiliated with the Reform movement and the Union of American Hebrew Congregations, founded in 1913.

National water carrier Completed in 1964, it brings water from the Sea of Galilee through 81 miles of giant pipes.

Naturai Karta Orthodox Jewish zealots who oppose political Zionism and refuse to recognize the State of Israel.

Navon, Itzkhak In 1978, he became the fifth president of the State of Israel.

Nazareth Israeli town in Lower Galilee, 24 miles east of Haifa. Today Nazareth is the largest town in the Arab part of Israel.

Nazir (Hebrew, meaning "Nazirite") Fourth tractate of *Nashim* dealing with laws related to Nazirite vows (Numbers 6:1–21).

Nazirite Religious devotee who vowed not to drink any liquor or to have his hair cut. Parents could dedicate their children as Nazirites before birth (e.g., Samson).

Near East Region in western Asia and northeastern Africa, often considered the same as the Middle East.

Nebuchadnezzar (or Nebuchadrezzar) King of Babylon (605–562 B.C.E.). In 586 he captured Jerusalem and destroyed the Temple.

Nedarim (Hebrew, meaning "vows") Third tractate of the Mishnah order dealing with regulations concerning vows.

Negaim (Hebrew, meaning "plagues of leprosy") Third tractate in the Mishnah order *Tohorot*, dealing with laws related to leprosy.

Negev The southern, dry land of Israel, extending over an expanse of 5,200 square miles. Beersheba is the largest city in the Negev today.

Nehardea Babylonian town, home of the exilarch.

Nehemiah (5th century B.C.E.) Judean governor who devoted himself to social reforms, including the encouragement of Sabbath observance. His memories form the basis of the biblical Book of Nehemiah in the Hagiographa.

Neilah Literally, "closing," it refers to the last of the prayer services on the Day of Atonement.

Ner Israel Rabbinical College Orthodox college founded in 1933 in Baltimore, Maryland.

Ner Tamid The eternal light in a synagogue.

Neusner, Jacob (1932–   ) American scholar and historian who focuses on the rabbinic period in his writings.

New Amsterdam New World settlement on the tip of Manhattan Island in what is now the city of New York.

Nezikin (Hebrew, meaning "damages") Fourth order of the Mishnah, divided into *Bava Kamma, Bava Metzia,* and *Bava Batra*. It deals with money matters and all damages decided by the courts.

Niddah (Hebrew, meaning "menstruous woman") 1. Seventh tractate in the Mishnah order *Tohorot*, dealing with ritual impurity as a result of menstruation and childbirth (Leviticus 12:1–5). 2. State of ritual impurity of a woman, as a result of a discharge of blood, usually caused by her menstrual period.

Nile River River in Egypt that appears numerous times in the Bible. For example, the infant Moses was sent away in a basket down the Nile River.

Nineveh Capital of the new Assyrian Empire (from 1100 B.C.E.). The Prophet Jonah was sent to Nineveh to persuade its citizens to repent.

Nisan First month of the Jewish religious year. In the Bible it is called the month of Aviv, meaning the month of spring. Passover occurs on the 14th of this month.

Noah Biblical figure and hero of the flood story (Genesis 6) who built an ark to save himself, his family, and the animals.

North American Federation of Temple Youth (NFTY) Youth organization of the Reform movement.

Numbers Fourth book of the Bible, it relates the history of the Israelites in the desert from the second to the fortieth year of the Exodus.

Nuremberg Laws Laws passed in 1935 that reduced the German Jews to second-class citizens.

O

Obadiah Fourth of the twelve Minor Prophets, this one-chapter book severely condemns Edom for having refused to assist Jerusalem in her hour of difficulty.

"Occupied Territories" Refers to the territories of Gaza, the Golan Heights, Judea, and Samaria, which Israel captured during the Six Day War.

Ochs, Adolph S. (1858–1935) Publisher of the *New York Times* in 1896. He coined that paper's famous slogan, "all the news that's fit to print."

Og Amorite king, known as the King of Bashan.

Ohalot (Hebrew, meaning "tents") Second tractate in the Mishnah order *Tohorot*, dealing with ritual impurity as a result of contact with a corpse (Numbers 19:13–20).

Olam HaBa (Hebrew, meaning "the world to come") In theological terms, it generally refers to the period following the advent of the Messiah when all the world will be perfected.

Old City of Jerusalem In the 16th century, the Ottoman sultan Suleiman constructed gates and massive walls around the city of Jerusalem. Until about 100 years ago, the enclosed wall section formed the city's total inhabited area. Today the Old City is divided into Moslem, Christian, Jewish, and Armenian sections.

Old Testament Refers to the Hebrew Bible (*Tanakh*) to distinguish it from the New Testament of Christianity.

Olives, Mount of Mountain to the east of Jerusalem. One of its three summits is occupied by Hebrew University. The New Testament describes Jesus weeping over Jerusalem on the Mount of Olives.

Omer First sheaf cut during the barley harvest, which was offered in the Temple as a sacrifice on the second day of Passover. The 7 weeks beginning from this day and culminating in the festival of Shavuot are known as the period of the counting of the *Omer*. The word *omer* is also a dry measure equal to the tenth part of an *ephah*.

Oneg Shabbat Literally "Sabbath enjoyment," today the term has been expanded to mean any celebration during the Sabbath.

Onkelos Palestinian proselyte and student of Rabbi Akiva. His Aramaic translation of the Five Books of Moses was called the *Targum*.

Operation Exodus Refers to the mobilization of funds to be used for the resettlement of Soviet Jews following Soviet *glasnost* in 1989.

Oral Law Discussions of the *tannaim* are known as the Oral Law, as distinguished from the Written Law—that is, the Bible itself. The Talmud is often referred to as the Oral Law.

Oriental Jews Oriental Jewish communities originating from various Moslem- and Arabic-speaking countries. The Yemenites come from Yemen, in southern Saudi Arabia, the Kurds come from Kurdistan in northern Iraq, and the Persians are from Persia, today called Iran. These and other oriental Jews have established communities throughout the State of Israel.

Orlah (Hebrew, meaning "uncircumcised fruit") Tenth tractate in the Mishnah order *Zeraim*, dealing with the law forbidding the use of the fruit of trees or vineyards for the first 3 years after planting (Leviticus 19:23).

Orlinsky, Harry (1908–1992) Biblical scholar and translator, especially known for his translation of the Five Books of Moses in 1962 for the Jewish Publication Society. He was a professor at Hebrew Union College.

Orthodox Judaism A synonym for traditional Judaism, which acknowledges the divine revelation of Torah and the binding authority of Jewish law.

Outreach Term coined by the Reform movement to refer to the process of "reaching out" to non-Jews married to Jews.

Ozick, Cynthia (1928–   ) American novelist whose works are infused with a variety of disciplines, including psychology and philosophy.

P

P School According to the Documentary Hypothesis, this ancient school of writers is so named because the material has a "priestly" point of view. Most of the Book of Leviticus is believed to be the work of this school of editors.

Paganism Belief in false gods.

Pale of Settlement Refers to twenty-five provinces of czarist Russia where Jews were permitted permanent residence.

Palestine Denotes the land of the Philistines. It is quite probable that the name Palestine was imposed by the Romans on the former Judea to minimize the Jewish association with the name of the country. Palestine was originally called "Canaan" in Hebrew.

Palestinian Liberation Organization (P.L.O.) A terrorist organization, currently headed by Yassir Arafat, whose agenda calls for the world to accept Palestinian rights and for the annihilation of the State of Israel.

Palmach The striking arm of the Haganah in 1941. After 1948 it became an integral part of the Israel Defense Forces.

Parah (Hebrew, meaning "heifer") Fourth tractate in the Mishnah order *Tohorot*, dealing with regulations concerning the red heifer.

Parashah Literally, "section," it denotes a passage in the Bible dealing with a single topic. Today it also denotes the weekly Torah reading, sometimes called a *sidrah*.

Pareve Yiddish expression that originated in Eastern Europe, describing a category of food considered neutral in its relation to dairy products or meat. It can therefore be eaten with either meat or dairy products.

Partition Plan Refers to the division of Palestine into autonomous areas that was proposed at various times before the establishment of the State of Israel. The United Nations recommended that Palestine be divided into an Arab and a Jewish state. The plan was never adopted because Arab forces attacked Israel in the hopes of preventing it from gaining statehood.

Paschal lamb Referring to the lamb that the Israelites sacrificed and whose blood was sprinkled on the doorposts of every house. The angel of the Lord passed over these homes, thus sparing the firstborns from death.

Pasul Ritually unfit and not to be used, such as a *pasul* Torah.

Patriarchs The founding fathers of the Israelites, including Abraham, Isaac, and Jacob.

Peah (Hebrew, meaning "corner") Second tractate of the Mishnah order *Zeraim*, dealing with the setting aside of the corners of one's field for the poor. (Leviticus 19:19).

Peres, Shimon (1923–   ) Israeli politician who was appointed minister of transportation and communications in 1970 and served as prime minister from 1984 to 1986.

Pesach Refers to the Paschal offering. Also the springtime festival celebrating the Exodus of the Israelites from Egypt.

Pesachim (Hebrew, meaning "Paschal lambs") Third tractate in the Mishnah order *Moed*, dealing with the regulations related to the holiday of Passover.

Pesukai Dezimra Preliminary prayers of the daily morning service, consisting mostly of psalms of praise to God.

Pharaoh Permanent title of the king of Egypt in ancient times.

Pharisees Jewish religious and political party during the Second Temple period. They were considered the bearers of traditional Judaism.

Philistines A seafaring people from the Mediterranean who dominated Israel's southern coastal plain. The giant Goliath was a Philistine.

Philo Alexandrian philosopher in the early 1st century C.E. His book *Lives of Moses and the Patriarchs* presents an interpretation of Jewish teachings in philosophical terms. It attempts to reconcile the basic ideas of the Bible with Greek thought.

Pidyon HaBen Redemption of the firstborn. In this ceremony, a firstborn son is symbolically relieved of special service by being redeemed through the payment of five silver coins to a priest.

Pioneer Women Women's Labor Zionist Organization founded in 1925.

Pita A Middle Eastern sandwich of a bread pocket stuffed with diced salad, *felafel*, or various kinds of meat.

Pithom One of the two places (along with Ramses) where the Israelites built storage cities for Pharaoh during their slavery in Egypt.

Pittsburgh Platform Guiding principles of Reform Judaism, produced by fifteen rabbis in 1885.

Piyyut Form of liturgical poetry that began in ancient Palestine. Many of these poems appear in the High Holiday *machzor*.

Plagues, The Ten Afflictions suffered by the Egyptians as a result of Pharaoh's refusal to allow the Israelites to leave the country. The plagues included blood, frogs, lice, flies, cattle disease, boils, heavy hail, locusts, darkness, and slaying of the firstborn.

Po Nikbar Literally, "here rests," its Hebrew letter abbreviation, *pay nun*, often appears on the headstone of the deceased.

Pogrom (Russian, meaning "destruction") An organized massacre of Jewish people and property. It applied to Russian outbreaks from 1881 onward.

Polytheism Belief in, or worship of, a plurality of gods.

Popular Front for the Liberation of Palestine An extreme terrorist group that emerged in the late 1960s and often waged war by attacking planes.

Potiphar Chief of Pharaoh's bodyguards. Joseph was sold to him as a slave.

Potok, Chaim (1929–   ) American novelist, best known for *The Chosen*.

Priestly blessing Formula for the blessing of the people by the descendants of Aaron (Numbers 6:24–26). The priests offered this blessing daily in the ancient Temple.

Prisoners of conscience Term that developed during the 1970s. Refers to the Soviet Jews who were kept in Russia, often in prison or in Siberia, and refused the right to emigrate.

Promised Land Denoting Israel, the land God promised He would give to Abraham and his descendants.

Prophet Refers to persons in the Bible who would bring a message from God to the people.

Protekziah Hebrew for "influence" or "pull."

Protocols of the Elders of Zion Early 20th-century anti-Semitic document, which claims that the Jewish community has a plan to take over the world.

Proverbs Biblical book, the second in the Hagiographa. It consists mostly of moral sayings.

Psalms First book in the Hagiographa section of the Bible, consisting of 150 psalms traditionally ascribed to King David.

Pulitzer, Joseph (1847–1911) Editor and publisher who established the school of journalism at Columbia University in 1903. The Pulitzer prizes for outstanding achievement in journalism and music have been awarded since 1917 under the terms of his will.

Pumbedita Babylonian city and seat of a famous academy founded by Judah ben Ezekiel in the 3rd century.

Purim Literally, "lots," this minor festival commemorates the rescue of the Persian Jews from the hands of Haman. The festival is celebrated by reading the *Megillah* of Esther, eating *hamantaschen*, and giving food baskets to the poor.

Pushke A container used to collect money for charity.

Q

Qumran (also Kumran) Site on the northwest shore of the Dead Sea. The Dead Sea Scrolls were discovered in the nearby caves of Qumran.

Quota system Refers to a limit on jobs, admissions, and immigrations determined by religion and country of origin.

R

Rabban Variant form of "rabbis," used as a title of honor to a select group of scholars in talmudic times.

Rabbi (Hebrew, meaning "my master") First-century term used to address authoritative teachers. The title was used primarily in Palestine, whereas Babylonians addressed their teachers as *Rav*. Today it refers to authoritative Judaic religious teachers who often serve as spiritual leaders of synagogues or educational directors of religious schools.

Rabbi Isaac Elchanan Theological Seminary Orthodox rabbinical school affiliated with Yeshiva University.

Rabbinical Assembly of America Professional union of Conservative rabbis, founded in 1901.

Rabbinical Council of America Orthodox professional organization of rabbis, founded in 1923.

Rabin, Itzkhak (1922–   ) Israeli soldier and politician. In 1964 he headed the Israel Defense Forces and in 1968 he was appointed Israeli ambassador to the United States. He served as prime minister from 1974 to 1977 and in 1992 was reelected prime minister.

Rachel Second wife of Jacob and one of the four matriarchs of the Jewish people. Rachel was the mother of Joseph and Benjamin.

Rachel, tomb of Located in Bethlehem, this is the traditional site of Rachel's burial place, where many Jews still come to pray.

Radical amazement Phrase coined by Abraham Joshua Hershel, who argues for an extraordinary sensitivity to the hidden beauty inherent in seemingly ordinary things.

Rahab Jericho woman who housed and shielded the spies sent by Joshua (2 Joshua). As a reward, Rahab and her family were spared.

Rain, prayer for Special petition in the additional service on Shemini Atzeret for rain in the Land of Israel.

Rainbow In Genesis 9:13, God puts a rainbow in the sky as the sign of his covenant with Noah. The rainbow was God's sign that the world would never again be destroyed by a flood.

Ramah, Camp Camping movement of Conservative Judaism, with locations in the United States, Canada, Israel, and the Soviet Union.

Rameses Ancient Egyptian city in the Nile delta area where Jacob and his family settled. Their descendants were forced to build storehouses for Pharaoh.

Rashbam (c. 1080–1158) Nickname for Samuel ben Meir, a French scholar who, like his grandfather Rashi, was a Bible and Talmud commentator.

Rashi (1040–1105) Rabbi Solomon ben Isaac of Troyes, French biblical and talmudic commentator. His style is simple and concise and attempts to present the literal meaning of the biblical text.

Rashi Script Semicursive form of Hebrew characters, principally used for writing and printing rabbinic commentaries, especially those of Rashi.

Rational Commandments According to Saadia Gaon, commandments that have their basis in reason.

Rebekah Wife of Isaac and mother of Esau and Jacob. She is one of the four Jewish matriarchs and especially known for her kindness.

Rebetzin The wife of a rabbi.

Reconstructionist Movement Fourth and smallest of the four movements in Judaism. Reconstructionist Judaism was founded by Mordecai Kaplan and teaches that Judaism is not only a religion but also a dynamic civilization.

Reconstructionist Rabbinical College Rabbinical school established in Philadelphia for training Reconstructionist rabbis.

Red heifer A congregational sacrifice whose ashes, when mixed with water, removed impurity created by contact with the dead.

Red Sea First identified as the "Reed Sea" crossed by the Israelites during their exodus from Egypt, the Red Sea now forms Israel's southern outlet to the Indian Ocean by way of Eilat.

Redemption (Hebrew *geulah*) Religious and philosophical concept that expresses a person's striving for personal and social improvement, emphasizing the difference between reality and the ideal. Modern philosophers argue that redemption is the triumph of good over evil.

Reform Judaism Liberal religious movement that maintains that to meet contemporary needs, modifications must be introduced into traditional Jewish thought and practice.

Refuge, city of Place of asylum in which an accidental killer was to be safe from the vengeance of the murdered person's kinsmen. There were six cities of refuge in the Bible.

Refugees, Palestinian Arabs who left Israel when the state was created, confident that the Arab armies would destroy it. When Israel survived, many of the Arabs who had left were now homeless. These are the Palestinian refugees of today.

Refuseniks Soviet Jews who have been refused exit visas to emigrate.

Rehovot Israeli town founded in 1890 by the Bilu pioneers. Chaim Weizmann, Israel's first president, made his permanent home there. Modern Rehovot is located 13 miles southeast of Tel Aviv.

Responsa Written replies given to questions on aspects of Jewish law by qualified rabbinic authorities from the time of the later *Geonim* to the present day.

Return, Law of Law passed in 1950 by the *Knesset*, which states that any Jew can become a citizen of Israel just by arriving in Israel and stating an intention to stay.

Reuben Eldest son of Jacob and Leah, he opposed his brothers' plot against Joseph (Genesis 37).

Reubeni, David (*c.* 1491–1535) False Messiah who visited Italy and Portugal and created a stir among the Marranos there.

Revelation The act of communion from God to man and the content of such a communication. The revelation of Moses on Mount Sinai provided the Israelites with the Torah.

Reward and punishment Rabbinic concept suggesting that God rewards good acts and punishes evil behavior.

Rimmon Literally, "pomegranate," today it refers to the ornaments that adorn Torah scrolls.

Rishon Le-Zion Israeli town in the Judean coastal plain founded in 1882 by Russian pioneers. Today Rishon Le-Zion is home of the Carmel wine factory and cellars.

Rishonim (Hebrew, meaning "first ones") Term denoting older authorities, including the *Geonim* and their successors, covering the period between the 6th and the 15th centuries.

Ritual murder Charge by anti-Semites that Jews kill young Christian boys to use their blood in making Passover *matzah.*

Rodgers, Richard (1902–1979) Composer of popular music for comedies, motion pictures, and ballets.

Rosenberg, Israel (1875–1956) Orthodox rabbi who was first acting dean of the Rabbi Isaac Elchanan Theological Seminary in New York City.

Rosenzweig, Franz (1886–1929) Philosopher and theologian whose chief work was *The Star of Redemption.* An exponent of existentialism, he rejected the traditional philosophy that the three main elements we encounter in experience—God, man, and the world—all share the same essence.

Rosh Chodesh Refers to the beginning of a new month and is celebrated today as a minor festival. The Torah is read on Rosh Chodesh and half of the *Hallel* psalms of praise are chanted.

Rosh HaShanah Eighth tractate in the Mishnah order *Moed,* it discusses laws related to the sanctification of the new moon and the blowing of the *shofar* on the festival of the Rosh HaShanah.

Roth, Philip (1933–   ) Novelist who often portrays middle-class American Jews in a sarcastic style.

Rothschild family German Jewish financiers who were very committed to and active in Jewish philanthropies. The fortunes of the family were founded by Mayer Rothchild. His five sons established themselves in different European centers.

Ruth Moabite and ancestor of King David. Her story is told in the Book of Ruth, one of the "Five Scrolls" incorporated in the Hagiographa.

S

Saadia Gaon ben Joseph (882–942) Father of medieval Jewish philosophy. In his most important work, *Belief and Opinion*, he aimed to prove that the Jewish religion is based on reason and does not contradict philosophic thought.

Sabbath The day of rest. It is also described in the Bible as "an everlasting sign between God and the children of Israel" (Exodus 31:17).

Sabbath of Sabbaths Refers to the Day of Atonement, because of its extreme solemnity as Judaism's most important fast day.

Sabbatical year Once in 7 years the Bible orders a year of rest from agricultural work (Leviticus 25:3). Any crops in the seventh year are communal property, and slaves are allowed to go free.

Saboraim (Hebrew, meaning "reasoners") Name given to Babylonian scholars from 500–700 C.E.

Sabra Refers to a native of Israel. The term refers metaphorically to an Israeli's similarity to the prickly pear fruit (*sabra*) grown in Israel, which has a tough exterior and soft interior.

Sacrifice An offering to a deity. Sacrifices during biblical times sought to obtain God's favor. The Israelites prepared both animal and meal offerings as sacrifices.

Sadat, Anwar President of Egypt in 1970. In 1977, he made a historic visit to Israel, a first for any Arab leader. In 1981 he was assassinated.

Sadduccees Second Temple sect whose name derives from Zadok, the high priest. They adhered very closely to the Torah and had no belief in a future world or the resurrection of the soul.

Salanter, Israel (1810–1883) Founder of the ethical Musar movement, he was also a great talmudic authority.

Salomon, Haym (1740–1785) American financier and patriot who became famous for his services in the American Revolution.

Salute to Israel parade Annual spring parade in New York City to commemorate Israel's independence.

Samaria Capital of the biblical northern kingdom of Israel. Today it is part of the West Bank, along with Judea.

Samaritans People with their capital at Samaria, descended from the tribes of Ephraim and Manasseh. For the Samaritans, the whole Bible consisted solely of the Five books of Moses.

Samson Israelite judge, he was a Nazirite from birth. Samson was known for his strength (the secret of which was his long hair).

Samuel Prophet and last of the Israelite judges (11th century B.C.E.). He chose Saul as his successor, and he became the first king. The two books of Samuel in the Bible describe the founding of the kingdom of Israel and the lives of King Saul and King David.

Sandek From the Greek, meaning "with a child." The honorary responsibility at a *Brit Milah* ceremony when a person holds the shoulders of the infant while the *mohel* performs the circumcision.

Sanhedrin Fourth tractate in the Mishnah order *Nezikin*, dealing with courts of justice and criminal law. 2. Name of the higher court of law during Second Temple times.

Sarah Wife of Abraham, mother of Isaac, and one of the four Jewish matriarchs.

Sarna, Nahum (1923–   ) Bible professor and scholar who teaches at Brandeis University.

Satan Usually identified with the devil or the prince of the demons. In the Bible, Satan is no evil spirit but belongs to the divine household like any other angelic being. Satan's function in the Book of Job is that of accuser (Job 1:6).

Saul Selected by Samuel to be Israel's first king, he defeated the Ammonites and fought successfully against the Philistines. In his last battle with them, he fell on his sword and killed himself (1 Samuel 8:31).

Scharansky, Anatoly (1948)–   ) Famous Soviet refusenik who now resides in Israel with the new name Natan Scharansky.

Schechter, Solomon (1847–1915) Scholar and president of the Jewish Theological Seminary. The Conservative movement day schools in America are named after him.

Schiff, Jacob (1847–1920) Financier and philantrophist who founded The American Jewish Committee in 1906.

Schneerson, Joseph Isaac (1880–1950) The Lubavitcher rabbi who built the Chabad community in Brooklyn.

Schocken Books Publishers of Judaicia both in New York City and in Israel.

Scholem, Gershom Twentieth-century scholar who was considered the foremost modern authority on Kabbalah. His well-known work is *Major Trends in Jewish Mysticism*.

Scopus, Mount Mountain in the vicinity of Jerusalem, it is the home of Hebrew University.

Scribe A professional copier of manuscripts and official documents. Scribes were responsible for preserving the biblical traditions concerning the spelling, wording, and meaning of texts.

Second Generation, The Generation of children born to survivors of the Holocaust.

Seder Literally, "order," the *Seder* is the ceremony observed in Jewish homes on Passover during which the *Haggadah* is recited.

Sefer Yetzirah Ninth-century Hebrew work of speculative thought whose central theme is the origin of the universe.

Sefirah Term referring to the counting of the *Omer*, which begins on the second night of Passover and continues until the festival of Shavuot.

Sefirot, Ten The ten stages that emanate from the Ein Sof (God) and form God's ten attributes. Each *sefirah* relates to God's work in creation.

Seixas, Gershom Mendes (1746–1816) Rabbi of Congregation Shearith Israel in New York and Mikveh Israel in Philadelphia. He was one of thirteen clergymen to participate in George Washington's first inauguration.

Selichot Penitential prayers that are recited during the reading preceding Rosh HaShanah. There is always a midnight service on the Saturday before Rosh HaShanah, which is called the *Selichot* service.

Senesh, Channah (1921–1944) A gifted poetess, she joined the parachutists from Palestine in 1943, jumping into Nazi-occupied Europe on a rescue mission. Her poem "Blessed is the Match" has been set to music.

Sephardim Descendants of the Spanish Jews, the Sephardim arrived in Palestine in the 15th century. There are thousands of Sephardic Jews in Israel today.

Septuagint Greek word for "seventy" and the name given to the Greek translation of the Bible (250 B.C.E.).

Seraphim Refers to a class of angels. In Isaiah 6:2, they appear as divine chanters who sing the words, "Holy, holy, holy is the Lord of Hosts, the whole earth is filled with His glory."

Serpent Snake in the early Genesis story that provoked Eve to eat of the Tree of Knowledge. It was later cursed and made to permanently crawl on its belly.

Servant of the Lord Term used by the Prophet Isaiah. In Isaiah 52:12–13, the servant is portrayed as suffering. Judaic commentaries have identified the servant as the people of Israel, the Messiah, and the prophet Isaiah himself.

Seudat Mitzvah A meal that accompanies a religious celebration such as a wedding, circumcision, or *Pidyon HaBen*.

Seudat Shelishit Literally, "third meal," it refers to the dinner meal on *Shabbat,* served in the late afternoon on Saturdays.

Shaatnez A mixture of wool and flax, the wearing of which is prohibited in the Bible. (Leviticus 19:19).

Shabbat The Sabbath, observed from sunset on Friday evening until it gets dark on Saturday evening. The day is marked by holiness, rest, and enjoyment.

Shabbat HaChodesh The Sabbath prior to the month of Nissan is called *Shabbat HaChodesh*, the Sabbath of the month. The Torah reading on this day describes the regulations for Pesach.

Shabbat HaGadol Literally, "great Sabbath," it always occurs on the Saturday before Passover. There is a tradition that rabbis give especially lengthy sermons in their synagogues on this special Sabbath.

Shabbat Nachamu The Sabbath of consolation or comfort, it always follows the commemoration of *Tisha B'Av*.

Shabbat Parah Literally, "Sabbath of the cow," this special Sabbath occurs several weeks before Passover. Its special Torah reading relates the ceremony of purification involving the use of the ashes of a red heifer.

Shabbat Shalom A Sabbath greeting that translates "Sabbath Peace." In Yiddish the greeting is *"Gut Shobbes."*

Shabbat Shekalim This special Sabbath occurs several weeks before Purim. The Torah reading on this day recalls the contribution of a *shekel* to the Temple for its maintenance.

Shabbat Shuvah The Sabbath of Repentance, which always falls between Rosh HaShanah and Yom Kippur.

Shabbat Zakhor The Sabbath of Remembrance, which occurs on the Saturday before Purim. The Torah reading on this day recalls the Amalekites, descendants of Haman.

Shabbes clock A mechanical device that enables modern traditional Jews to have light on the Sabbath without having to turn on a switch.

Shabbes goy A non-Jew employed by a Jew on the Sabbath to carry out tasks prohibited to Jews by traditional Jewish practice on that day.

Shacharit The first prayer service of the day, the one in the morning. Tradition ascribes this service to the patriarch Abraham.

Shadchan (Hebrew, meaning "matchmaker" or "marriage broker") Over the years, many rabbinic scholars were professional matchmakers, and the profession still survives to this day.

Shaddai Divine name found frequently in the Bible, usually translated as "the Almighty."

Shaliach tzibbur The emissary for the congregation who leads the congregation in prayer.

Shalom Hebrew for "hello," "good-bye," or "peace."

Shalom Aleikhem Literally, "Peace unto you," it is a traditional Jewish greeting. It also refers to the name of a traditional Jewish song that is sung on Friday evenings. Additionally, it was the pseudonym of the Yiddish novelist Shalom Rabinovitz.

Shalom Bayit Refers to family harmony, an important value in the Jewish religion.

Shalom Zakhar Ceremony that welcomes a baby boy into the world and is held on the Friday evening before his *Brit Milah*.

Shalosh Regalim Refers to the three pilgrimage festivals on which Jews customarily visited the Jerusalem Temple. These festivals are Sukkot, Passover, and Shavuot.

Shamash Literally, "one who serves," it means a synagogue beadle. It also refers to the additional candle on the *chanukiah* (eight-branched candelabra) that is used to light the other candles.

Shamir, Itzkhak (1915–   ) Leader of the Lochame Cherut Yisrael, with Abraham Stern. He was Israel's prime minister from 1983 to 1984 and again from 1986 to 1992.

Shammai First-century rabbi and a contemporary of Hillel. Unlike Hillel, who was usually lenient, Shammai took a more rigorous point of view.

Sharm-el-Sheikh Located on the southern tip of the Sinai peninsula, its strategic position allowed it to control the Straits of Tiran.

Sharon, Arik General of the Israeli army and minister of defense during the war in Lebanon.

Shas Hebrew initials of *shishah sedarim,* the six orders of the Mishnah forming the basis of the Talmud. Today the term is used synonymously with Talmud.

Shavua Tov Literally, "good week," it is usually spoken as a greeting immediately following the *Havdalah* ceremony on Saturday evening.

Shavuot Literally, "weeks," it is a pilgrimage festival observed on the fiftieth day after Passover. It commemorates the revelation of the Torah on Mount Sinai.

Shazar, Zalman Third president of Israel in 1963, and reelected in 1968.

Shekhinah In kabbalistic literature, the tenth *sefirah*, which represents the feminine aspect of the Godhead. In the Bible the Shechinah often refers to the in-dwelling presence of God on earth.

Sheftall, Mordecai (1735–1797) First recorded *Bar Mitzvah* in the United States. He served in the American Revolution as commissary general for South Carolina and Georgia.

Shehecheyanu Blessing usually said to mark a new occasion, which praises God for His gift of life.

Shekalim (Hebrew, meaning "shekels") Fourth tractate in the Mishnah order *Moed*, dealing with the half-*shekel* tax used for the maintenance of the Temple.

Shekel Silver unit of weight and coin in the time of the Maccabees. The Israelites paid a levy of one-half *shekel* for the maintenance of the Sanctuary.

Shema Judaism's confession of faith, proclaiming God as the absolute unity (Deuteronomy 6:4–9).

Shemini Atzeret The final day of the festival of Sukkot. On it a special prayer for rain is added during the additional *Musaf* service.

Sheol According to the Bible, the dwelling place of the dead (Genesis 37:35) situated far beneath the earth.

Sherut Shared taxi service in Israel.

Sheva Berakhot The seven blessings that are recited over a cup of wine at Jewish marriage ceremonies.

Shevarim Three blasts of the *shofar*.

Shevat Eleventh month of the Jewish religious calendar and fifth month of the civil one. The New Year for trees is celebrated on the 15th of this month.

Shevi'it (Hebrew, meaning "seventh year") Fifth tractate in the Mishnah order *Zeraim*, dealing with the laws of the sabbatical year (Exodus 23:11).

Shevuot (Hebrew, meaning "oaths") Sixth tractate in the Mishnah order *Nezikin*, dealing with types of oaths (Leviticus 5:4) and persons who have become spiritually unclean (Leviticus 5:2–3).

Shiksa Term meaning a non-Jewish female.

Shiloh Located north of Jerusalem, Shiloh was the first Israelite cult center after Joshua conquered Canaan. Both the Ark and the Tabernacle were kept there.

Shivah The 7-day mourning period following a burial.

Shivah Asar B'Tammuz The 17th day of the month of Tammuz, a fast day that commemorates the penetration of the walls of the Jerusalem Temple.

Shloshim Thirty-day period of mourning following a burial.

Shneur Zalman of Liadi (1745–1813) Founder of Chabad Chasidism.

Shoah Refers to the Holocaust and the destruction of 6 million European Jews between the years 1938 and 1945.

Shochet A ritual slaughter of animals.

Shofar Ram's horn sounded on Rosh HaShanah and Yom Kippur. It is also sounded during morning services in the month of Elul. In ancient times it was also used on each Rosh Chodesh.

Shofarot Part of the additional *Musaf* Service for Rosh HaShanah, consisting of verses related to blowing the *shofar* and the theme of redemption.

Shomer Mitzvot A person who observes God's commandments.

Shomer Shabbat A person who observes the Sabbath and meticulously follows its laws.

Shtetl Small communities in Eastern Europe with a unique life-style, often emphasizing ideas of piety, learning, and charity.

Shushan Capital of ancient Persia, it was the place of the royal palace mentioned in the Book of Esther.

Shushan Purim The 15th of the month of Adar, ordained by the Jews in Persia's capital and in big cities.

Siddur A Jewish prayer book.

Sidrah A halakhic discourse related to the Bible portion that was delivered weekly (usually on Sabbath afternoons) by various talmudic rabbis.

Sifra Oldest rabbinic commentary on the Book of Leviticus.

Sifri Oldest rabbinic commentary on Numbers and Deuteronomy.

Siman Tov Literally, a "good sign," it is often used along with *mazel tov* to wish a person happiness.

Simchah The ultimate in Jewish joyous occasions. A Jewish wedding or a *Bar* or *Bat Mitzvah* is called a *simchah*.

Simchat Torah Holiday marking the annual completion of the reading of the Torah. It is customary to take out all of the Torah scrolls and carry them around the sanctuary on this day.

Simeon Second son of Jacob. He and his brother Levi slaughtered the male inhabitants of Shechem (Genesis 34).

Sinai Campaign Israeli military operation directed against Egypt in 1956, resulting in the opening of the Gulf of Eilat to Israeli shipping.

Singer, Isaac Bashevis (1904–1991) Yiddish American writer whose early stories were serialized in *The Forward*.

Sivan Ninth month of the Jewish religious year and third of the civil one. The holiday of Shavuot begins on the 6th of Sivan.

Six Day War War between Israel and Egypt, Jordan, and Syria in 1967. Within 6 days Israel destroyed all of the armies on her frontiers and reunited Jerusalem.

Siyyum Conclusion of the study of a tractate of the Talmud. It is a joyous occasion, often observed by the eating of a festive meal.

Skhakh Thatching used for the roof of a *sukkah*.

Smikhah Literally, "placing of the hands," today it refers to rabbinic ordination.

Sodom and Gomorrah Two evil cities of the Jordan plain that God destroyed with fire and brimstone.

Sofer A scribe who has the expertise in writing a Torah, *mezuzah* parchment, *ketubah*, and so forth.

Solomon King of Israel (*c.* 961–920 B.C.E.), son of King David. Solomon is known for his many wives.

Soloveitchik, Joseph B. (1903–1993) Orthodox rabbi and foremost proponent of modern Orthodox Judaism. His works embody a fusion of classic halakhic Judaism and American culture.

Song of Songs First of the Five Scrolls incorporated in the Hagiographa, consisting of a collection of poems about courtship and love. The book has been interpreted as a metaphor for God and His love for the Jewish people.

Sotah (Hebrew, meaning "errant wife") Sixth tractate in the Mishnah order *Nashim*, dealing with laws concerning a woman suspected of adultery (Numbers 5:11–31).

Spanish and Portuguese Synagogue Called Shearith Israel, it is located in New York city and considered the oldest synagogue in the United States.

Spice box Ritual object used to keep *besamim* (spices) for use in the *Havdalah* ceremony.

Spinoza, Baruch (1632–1677) Dutch philosopher whose unorthodox religious views led to his formal excommunication by the Sephardic community. He advanced a polemic point of view against the Bible.

Spirituality Term that generally refers to some sort of relationship between any person and God.

Steinsaltz, Adin (1937–   ) Contemporary Israeli talmudist who has prepared a modern Hebrew commentary on the Talmud.

Stern, Isaac American violinist who has made successful concert appearances in many parts of the world.

Suez Canal Waterway linking the Mediterranean Sea with the Gulf of Suez and the Red Sea. The canal historically has been the scene of lengthy hostilities between the Egyptians and the Israelis.

Sukkah Booth or hut in which Jews dwell or eat during the festival of Sukkot. It commemorates the special protection given to the Israelites during their 40 years of wandering in the desert.

Sukkot One of the three pilgrimage festivals, recalling the boothlike structures in which Jews dwelled during their wandering in the desert.

Sulzberger, Mayer (1843–1923) Judge and communal leader who helped to organize and was the first president of The American Jewish Committee.

Sunday Laws Also called Blue Laws, they restricted or prohibited the opening of retail establishments on Sundays.

Sunday School Refers to supplementary religious classes, usually held on Sunday.

Sura Babylonian city where a rabbinic academy was established in the early 3rd century.

Synagogue Building for Jewish public prayer. In Yiddish it is called a *shul*.

Synagogue Council of America Established in 1926 for the purpose of overall Jewish religious representation.

Szold, Henrietta (1860–1945) Ardent Zionist who organized Hadassah in 1912.

T

Taanit (Hebrew, meaning "fast") Ninth tractate in the Mishnah order *Moed*, dealing with the designation of fast days in time of drought.

Taanit Esther Fast of Esther, observed on the eve of Purim, commemorating Esther's own fast in the scroll of Esther.

Tabernacle Portable sanctuary set up by Moses in the desert (Exodus 26–27).

Tachlis Refers to the bottom line or the essential element.

Tachrichim The shroud in which a corpse is wrapped.

Tageblatt (Jewish Daily News) First Yiddish daily newspaper in the world, launched in 1885. It lasted until 1928, when it merged with the *Morning Journal*.

Taharah Ritual purification of the body before burial, carried out by the Holy Burial Society.

Takkanah Any regulation that supplements the law of the Torah.

Tali schools Network of schools currently being established in Israel for children of the Masoreti (Conservative) movement.

Tallit Prayer shawl traditionally worn by men and by some women in Reform, Conservative, and Reconstructionist Judaism. Its knotted corners are reminders of God's commandments.

Talmud (Hebrew, meaning "teaching") The name applied to the Babylonian and Jerusalem Talmud, in which are collected rabbinic discussions of Jewish law during several centuries after 200 C.E.. The Talmud consists of the Mishnah and the Gemara.

Talmud Torah Community Judaic elementary school.

Tam, Rabbenu (Jacob ben Meir) Twelfth-century French scholar and grandson of Rashi. His commentary often tried to correct textual corruptions in the Talmud.

Tameh Refers to something that is ritually impure.

Tamid (Hebrew, meaning "perpetual offering") Ninth tractate in the Mishnah order *Kodashim*, dealing with laws related to burnt offerings and priestly duties.

Tammuz Tenth month of the Jewish religious year, usually corresponding to June or July. The 17th of this month is a fast day, commemorating the penetration of the walls of the Jerusalem Temple prior to its destruction.

Tanakh Refers to the complete Hebrew Bible. Its source is the initial letters of *Torah, Neviim*, and *Ketuvim* (Five Books of Moses, Prophets, and Hagiographa).

Tannaim Teachers mentioned in the Mishnah or *Baraita* who lived during the first two centuries C.E.

Targum The Aramaic translation of the Bible.

Tashlich Custom observed on the first day of Rosh HaShanah near a body of water. Crumbs of bread, symbolizing one's sins, are cast into the water and carried away.

Tayku (Hebrew, meaning "let it stand") Means that the question raised in the previous passage remains unsolved. The Hebrew acronym stands for the Hebrew words *Tishbi yitaretz kushyot u'she'alot* ("the Messiah will ultimately solve all difficult questions").

Technion Israel Institute of Technology established in Haifa in 1924. It is rated the most outstanding technological institution in the entire Middle East.

Tefillah A prayer. Among Sephardim, it means a prayer book.

Tefillin Phylacteries or prayerboxes strapped to the head and arm, which traditionally have been worn by men during daily morning services, except on the Sabbath and holidays.

Tekiah One solid blast of the *shofar*.

Tel Aviv Israeli City founded in 1909 as a suburb of Jaffa. Today it is Israel's largest city and hub of its commerce.

Tel Chai Settlement founded in 1917 in the Upper Galilee, it was attacked by Arabs revolting against the French mandatory authorities. Today there is a museum at Tel Chai that many tourists come to visit.

Temple Central building for divine worship in Israel until 70 C.E., situated on Mount Moriah in Jerusalem. The First Temple was built by King Solomon and destroyed in 586 B.C.E. The Second Temple was built 70 years later.

Temurah (Hebrew, meaning "exchange") The sixth tractate in the Mishnah order *Kodashim*, it deals with regulations concerning the exchange of an animal consecrated for a sacrifice (Leviticus 27:10, 33).

Ten Commandments Divine laws spoken by God to Moses and written on two tablets of stone (Exodus 20:2–17 and Deuteronomy 5:6–21).

Ten Days of Repentance First 10 days of the month of Tishri, from the beginning of Rosh HaShanah to the close of Yom Kippur. On each of these days, special prayers of penitence are recited.

Terach Father of Abraham. Legend depicts Terach as an idol maker who challenged Abraham's beliefs during his childhood.

Teruah Nine rapid, short, staccato notes of the *shofar*.

Terumot (Hebrew, meaning "Sanctuary offerings") Sixth tractate in the Mishnah order *Zeraim*, dealing with offerings due the priest from both the Israelite and the Levite (Numbers 18:8). The offerings included produce, the priest's dough offering, and the contribution of the half-*shekel*.

Teshuvah Repentance, a major theme of the High Holidays.

Tevet Fourth month of the Jewish religious year, usually around January. The 10th of this month is a fast day commemorating the besieging of Jerusalem by King Nebuchadnezzar.

Tevilah Ritual immersion in a *mikveh* for purposes of ritual purification and conversion.

Tevul Yom (Hebrew, meaning "one who has bathed that day") Tenth tractate in the Mishnah order *Tohorot*, dealing with ritual uncleanliness that remains after sunset after ritual bathing (Leviticus 15:7–18).

Theresienstadt Town in Czechoslovakia that served as a ghetto between 1941 and 1945. It became a model concentration camp.

Thummim and Urim Sacred means of divination used by the early Hebrews. It was attached to the breastplate of the high Priest.

Tiamat Babylonian deity appearing in its creation myth story.

Tiberias City located on the Sea of Galilee, famous for its hot springs. The Sanhedrin was once located in Tiberias. One of the four holy cities Israel, modern Tiberias is the economic center of the Lower Galilee and is also one of Israel's important health resorts.

Tigris River in southwest Asia, it was regarded as one of the four rivers emerging from the Garden of Eden.

Tikkun 1. Literally, "repair," it refers in kabbalistic terms to the repairing of the vessels that were broken by God during creation. 2. A special book that is used to prepare persons for the reading of the Torah.

Tikkun layl Shavuot Refers to an all-night study evening on Shavuot.

Tikkun Olam (Hebrew, meaning "improvement of the world") Rabbinic ordinances that were instituted to prevent difficulties for people and make the world a better place.

Timbrel A kind of tambourine used to accompany singing and dancing.

Tisha B'Av The 9th of the month of Av, commemorating the destruction of the Jerusalem Temples. On this fast day it is customary to read from the Book of Lamentations.

Tishri Seventh month of the Jewish religious year and first month of the Jewish civil one. The 1st of the month of Tishri is Rosh HaShanah.

Tithe A 10th part of the produce set aside as a religious offering.

Tohorot (Hebrew, meaning "purifications") Sixth and last order of the Mishnah. The name is a euphemism for ritual uncleanliness, and all the tractates of the order deal with laws of impurity. Tractates include *Kelim* (Vessel), *Ohalot* (Tents), *Negaim* (Leprosy), *Parah* (Heifer), *Tohorot* (Purifications), *Mikvaot* (Ritual Baths), *Niddah* (Menstruating Women), *Makshirin* (Preparations), *Zavim* (People Suffering from Secretions), *Tevul Yom* (Immersions), *Yadayim* (Hands), and *Uktzin* (Stems).

Torah In its narrow meaning, the Five Books of Moses. It is also known as the "Written Law" and the "Pentateuch."

Torah Umesorah (National Society for Hebrew Day Schools) Founded in 1944, it is the largest body that serves Orthodox day schools in the United States and Canada.

Tosafot (Hebrew, meaning "addenda") Explanatory notes on the Talmud by French and German scholars (known as tosaphists) of the 12th to 14th centuries. They frequently modify Rashi's talmudic commentary.

Tosefta A supplement to the Mishnah, containing six orders with the same names as of those of the Mishnah. Its paragraphs are called *beraitot*.

Touro, Judah (1775–1854) American philanthropist who gave generously to both the Jewish and Christian communities. Newport's 18th-century synagogue was named after him.

Touro Synagogue Oldest synagogue building in the United States. It is located in Newport, Rhode Island.

Tower of Babel Building intended to reach to heaven, which was erected by the descendants of Noah after the flood. God frustrated the work of the builders by confusing their languages (Genesis 1:1–9).

Tractate (Hebrew *masakhet*) A book of the Mishnah or Talmud.

Treblinka One of the main death camps built by the Nazis during World War II.

Tree of Life One of the two trees specified in the Garden of Eden. Whoever ate of it would live forever.

Trefa Banquet Celebratory banquet in 1883, which consisted of nonkosher seafood and was served upon the first ordination of Reform rabbis. The banquet helped pave the way for the founding of Conservative Judaism.

Trefah That which is ritually unfit to be used or eaten.

Triangle Shirt Factory fire In 1911, 146 workers of the Triangle Shirtwaist Company of New York were killed in a fire due to unsafe building conditions. The fire brought public attention to the cause of safety in labor.

Tribes of Israel Twelve clans into which the Israelites were divided in biblical times. They derived from the sons of Jacob and included Reuben, Simeon, Levi, Judah, Issachar, Zebulum, Joseph, Benjamin, Dan, Naphtali, Gad, and Asher.

Trop Yiddish for musical cantillations that direct the reader in chanting from the Torah or chanting a *haftarah*. In Hebrew they are called *ta amei HaMikra*.

Trumpeldor, Yosef (1880–1921) Zionist leader who worked for the establishment of a Jewish unit to fight with the British against the Turks in Palestine. He was killed in the defense of Tel Chai.

Tsfat (Safed) Mystical town in the Upper Galilee, 22 miles from Tiberias. In the 16th century it became an important holy town for kabbalistic mystics.

Tu BeShevat Jewish arbor day, always occurring on the 15th of the Hebrew month of Shevat. On this day it is customary to plant trees in Israel.

Tzadik A righteous person of great religious faith. A *tzadik* also refers to the leader of a chasidic community.

Tzedakah From the Hebrew word *tzedek*, meaning justice, *tzedakah* is synonymous with charity.

Tzitzit Ritual fringes on the corners of the *tallit*, symbolizing God's commandments.

Tzniut Hebrew for modesty, an important Jewish value.

Tzuris Yiddish for trouble or misfortune.

U

Ufruf The practice of calling a bridegroom (and sometimes a bride) to the Torah on the Sabbath preceding his wedding.

Uktzin (Hebrew, meaning "stalks") Twelfth and last tractate of the Mishnah order *Tohorot*, dealing with ritual impurity brought to a harvested plant when it comes into contact with an unclean person or thing.

Ulpan Intensive language study program whose goal is to immerse the student in spoken Hebrew in a short period of time.

Union of American Hebrew Congregations (UAHC) Established in 1873 as the first national body of synagogues, it provided the framework to establish Hebrew Union College. Today it is the American Reform Jewish synagogue body.

Union of Orthodox Jewish Congregations (UOJCA) Founded in 1899, it is the Orthodox Jewish synagogue body.

Union of Orthodox Rabbis Oldest organization of Orthodox rabbis, founded in 1902.

United Jewish Appeal (UJA) American organization founded in 1939 to coordinate fund-raising campaigns.

United Synagogue of Conservative Judaism Founded in 1913, it is the association of Conservative synagogues.

Universal Jewish Encyclopedia Published in 1941, this encyclopedia puts special emphasis on American Jewish life.

Unleavened bread Flat bread eaten by the Israelites during their hurried exodus from Egypt.

Ur Ancient Babylonian city and the home of Abraham before his family's departure for Haran.

Uris, Leon (1924–   ) American author whose best-selling novels include *Exodus* and *Mila 18*.

Ushpizin Meaning "visitors" in Aramaic, it refers to the symbolic invitation of seven guests (Abraham, Isaac, Jacob, Joseph, Moses, Aaron, and David) into one's *sukkah* during the festival of Sukkot.

V

Vashti Persian queen and wife of King Ahasuerus. She was banished from the kingdom for refusing to appear at her husband's banquet.

Versions of the Bible Term referring to different translations of the Bible (e.g., Septuagint, Targum, and so forth).

Via Dolorosa Located in the Old City, it is the route that Jesus walked on the way to his crucifixion. Franciscan monks lead groups in prayer along the Via Dolorosa every Friday afternoon.

Vidui A confessional prayer, often recited on one's deathbed.

Vilna Lithuanian town. Its best-known scholar is Elijah ben Solomon Zalman, known as the Vilna Gaon.

Vocalization Refers to the placing of vowels into the biblical text, usually associated with the work of the Masoretes.

Vulgate Latin translation of the Bible.

W

Wailing Wall (Western Wall) Together with the southwestern wall, the wailing wall (known in Hebrew as the *Kotel*) comprises the only remains of the enclosures of the Second Temple. Today it serves as an open-air synagogue.

War of Independence This war began with Arab attacks on the Jewish community. In 1948 the armies of Egypt, Transjordan, Iraq, Syria, and Lebanon invaded, killing 6,000 Israelis. The fighting was long and bloody, but Israel finally proved victorious.

Warburg, Felix (1871–1937) Banker and philanthropist who chaired the American Jewish Joint Distribution Committee from 1914 until 1932.

Warsaw Ghetto Uprising Led by Mordecai Anilewicz, the underground in the Warsaw ghetto fought back the advancing German forces. It had a powerful moral effect on Jews and non-Jews who had previously thought that all Jews went to their deaths without a fight.

Waves of Immigration Refers to groups of immigrants who came in large numbers at different periods of time.

Waxman, Meyer (1887–1969) Literary critic and historian whose major work was *The History of Jewish Literature*.

Weiss-Halivni, David (1927–   ) Talmudic scholar who employs a source-critical method. He served as professor of Talmud at the Jewish Theological Seminary of America and is currently a professor at Columbia University.

Weizmann, Chaim (1874–1952) Zionist leader and first president of the State of Israel.

West Bank Area west of the Jordan River annexed by Israel during the Six Day War. Israel refers to this area by the biblical names Samaria and Judea.

Whirlwind Term used by some Holocaust survivors for the Holocaust.

White Papers, British British government statement of Palestinian policy, declaring Britain's intention of setting up an independent Palestinian state in which Jews and Arabs would both participate in the government. The document was opposed by the Zionist movement.

Wiesel, Elie (1928–   ) Twentieth-century author whose writings are reflective explorations of a range of responses to the Holocaust.

Wiesenthal, Simon (1908–   ) Twentieth-century Nazi hunter from Vienna.

Wimpel A binder around a Torah scroll, often presented to the synagogue to commemorate a male child's birth and inscribed with his name.

Wine, Sherwin (1928–   ) Reform rabbi who has rejected the existence of God. He founded the Society for Humanistic Judaism.

Wisdom literature Term applied to certain biblical books (Proverbs, Job, Ecclesiastes, and Psalms 37, 49, and 73). Wisdom in these books is based on the fear of God and knowledge of the commandments.

Wise, Isaac Mayer (1819–1900) Considered by many the father of Reform Judaism, he was the first president of the Hebrew Union College.

World of Our Fathers, The Refers to the ancestors of immigrants from Eastern Europe and their lives on the Lower East Side in New York City after they immigrated to the United States. The book by this name was written by Irving Howe.

Wouk, Herman (1915–   ) American author, known for works such as *Majorie Morningstar* (1955), *This is My God* (1959), and *War and Remembrance*, a story of World War II.

Y

Yad Pointer for indicating the place during the reading of the Torah.

Yad Mordechai Named for Mordecai Anilewicz, this Israeli *kibbutz* was founded in 1943 by Polish Jews. In 1948 it was captured by the Egyptians and rebuilt after its liberation. The battle area has been reproduced and Yad Mordechai is a popular tourist attraction where visitors can relive the bloody battle through an audiovisual program.

Yad Vashem Israel official authority for the commemoration of the massacre of Jews during the Holocaust. Its building is located on Memorial Hill adjoining Mount Herzl in Jerusalem.

Yadayim (Hebrew, meaning "hands") Eleventh tractate in the order *Tohorot*, dealing with rabbinic laws related to the ritual impurity of the hands.

Yadin, Yigal (1917–   ) Israeli soldier and scholar, noted today for his important archaeological research, especially the Dead Sea Scrolls.

Yahel One of two *kibbutzim* established in Israel by the Reform movement. The other is Lotan.

Yahrzeit Anniversary of the death of a close relative, observed by the kindling of a 24-hour candle and the recital of the Kaddish.

Yamim Noraim The Days of Awe, also called the High Holidays (Rosh HaShanah and Yom Kippur).

Yamit Israeli town built in the Sinai after Israel conquered the Sinai from the Egyptians. As part of the Camp David Accord, the Israelis were required to leave the town.

Yasher Koach Literally, "may your strength be increased," this term is traditionally spoken as a congratulatory remark to a person who, for example, has completed an *aliyah* to the Torah. The response to *Yasher Koach* is *"Barukh Tihyeh."*

Yavneh City south of Jaffa where Rabbi Yochanan ben Zakkai opened an academy. There he reestablished the Sanhedrin.

Yellow Badge Yellow star that Jews were required to wear during the Nazi period.

Yemenite An oriental Jew from Yemen, a Moslem area in southern Saudi Arabia.

Yeshiva University The first American University under Jewish auspices, located in New York City. The school is committed to Orthodox Judaism.

Yeshivah Jewish traditional school devoted primarily to the study of the Talmud and other rabbinic literature.

Yeshivah bocher Yiddish for a student who attends a *yeshivah*.

Yetzer ra The evil inclination of a person.

Yetzer tov The good inclination in a person.

Yevamot (Hebrew, meaning "levirates") First tractate in the talmudic order *Nashim*, dealing with the status of the widow of a man who has died childless and whose brother must contract levirate marriage.

Yichud Unchaperoned togetherness of a bride and groom immediately following their wedding ceremony. Together they break their fast with a small repast.

Yichus Distinguished descent or family connection, especially from a scholar.

Yid A Jew; the term sometimes has a negative connotation.

Yiddish Language spoken by a majority of Ashkenazic Jews since the Middle Ages.

Yiddishkeit Ethnic Jewish identity, expression, and lifestyle.

Yigdal Liturgical hymn originating in Italy that enumerates Maimonides' *Thirteen Principles of Faith*.

Yinglish Slang term referring to both the infiltration of Yiddish words into everyday English and the patterns of speech of immigrants whose speech included English and Yiddish.

Yishuv A settlement or population group. More specifically, it refers to the Jewish community of Israel.

Yisrael An Israelite, the masses of the people, as opposed to the Kohen and Levite.

Yizkor (Hebrew, meaning "remember") Opening word of the prayer in commemoration of the dead. It is recited on the three pilgrimage festivals as well as on Yom Kippur.

Yochanan ben Zakkai First-century Palestinian *tanna* and student of Hillel.

Yom HaAtzma'ut Israel Independence Day, commemorated on the 5th of Iyar, in honor of Israel's declaration of independence in 1948.

Yom HaShoah Day of commemorating the Holocaust.

Yom HaZikaron Day of remembrance of Israel's fallen soldiers, observed just prior to Yom HaAtzma'ut.

Yom Kippur The Day of Atonement, observed on the 10th of Tishri as an all-day fast.

Yom Kippur War Beginning on Yom Kippur in 1973, this war took Israel by surprise. It has been considered one of Israel's greatest military victories because it was a victory despite the fact that the Egyptians caught the Israelis unprepared.

Yom Tov A Jewish holiday or festival.

Yoma (Aramaic, meaning "day") Fifth tractate in the order *Moed*, describing the Temple service on the Day of Atonement and dealing with laws of fasting and repenting.

Yordim Israelis who leave Israel for another country.

Young Leadership Division of the United Jewish Appeal that consists of younger persons who are being trained for future leadership positions.

Young Men's/Young Women's Hebrew Association (YM/YWHA) American Jewish communal institution aimed at perpetuating Judaism through a program of recreation, health education, and cultural events. The YM/YWHAs are also known as Jewish Community Centers.

Z

Zavim (Hebrew, meaning "suffers from bodily discharge") Ninth chapter in the talmudic order *Tohorot*, dealing with ritual uncleanliness caused by bodily discharge.

Zealots Members of the Jewish resistance party who fought against the Romans in the 1st century C.E.

Zebulun Sixth son of Jacob and Leah. His ancestors received the territory in the valley of Jezreel.

Zechariah Minor Prophet whose prophecies in his book foretell the ingathering of the exiles and the expansion of Jerusalem.

Zelophehad Israelite of the tribe of Manasseh who died in the desert, leaving five daughters and no sons. His daughters claimed the inheritance, setting the stage for new laws that permitted daughters to inherit a father's property.

Zemirot Sabbath table songs.

Zephaniah Seventh-century Minor Prophet who described in his book *The Day of the Lord* when God will punish all of the wicked and everyone will acknowledge Him as King.

Zeraim (Hebrew, meaning "seeds") First order of the Mishnah and Talmud, dealing with laws of prayer and agriculture. Its eleven tractates include *Berakhot* (Blessings), *Peah* (Corner of Field), *Demai* (Doubtfully Tithed), *Kilayim* (Mixtures), *Shevi'it* (Sabbatical Year), *Terumot* (Contributions to the Priests), *Maaserot* (Tithes), *Maaser Sheni* (Second Tithe), *Challah* (Dough), *Orlah* (Uncircumcised Fruit), and *Bikkurim* (Firstfruits).

Zeresh Wife of Haman, chief minister of King Ahasuerus of Persia.

Zevachim (Hebrew, meaning "animal sacrifices") First tractate in the talmudic order *Kodashim*, it deals with laws of animal sacrifices.

Zevi, Shabbatai (1626–1676) Self-appointed Messiah and leader of the movement called Shabbateanism. The movement climaxed in 1666 when Zevi converted to Islam.

Zikhrano Livrakhah Literally, "May his memory serve as a blessing," traditionally spoken when speaking of the deceased.

Zikhronot Remembrance verses read in the additional *Musaf* service on the festival of Rosh HaShanah.

Zion Jebusite stronghold in Jerusalem, captured by King David.

Zionist Congresses Regular conferences of representatives of the Zionist movement, instituted by Theodor Herzl in 1897. The Zionist Congress constitutes the supreme legislative body of the Zionist Organization.

Zionist Organization of America (ZOA) Zionist organization whose goals include fund-raising and public relations. It was founded in 1918.

Zipporah Wife of Moses and daughter of Jethro. She bore Moses two sons, Gershom and Eliezer (Exodus 2:22; 18:3–4).

Zohar Mystical biblical commentary on sections of the Five Books of Moses and parts of the Hagiographa.

Zugot (Hebrew, meaning "pairs") Term applied to five generations of rabbis preceding the *tannaim*. The *zugot* are: 1. Yose ben Joezer and Yose ben Yochanan 2. Joshua ben Perachia and Nittai the Arbelite 3. Judah ben Tabbai and Simeon ben Shetach 4. Shemaiah and Avtalyon 5. Hillel and Shammai.

PART II

THE JEWISH ALMANAC

BIBLE

Translations of the Bible

The Hebrew Bible (called the "Old Testament" by Christians) has been translated into hundreds of different languages over the centuries. Here is a brief summary of some of the most important early translations of the Bible:

Targum Onkelos This translation, used extensively by Babylonian Jewry, dates back to the beginning of the 2nd century. It is believed that its translator, Onkelos, was a convert to Judaism.

Targum of Jonathan This translation bears the name of Jonathan ben Uzziel. It is a more paraphrastic than true translation and deals with the biblical portions related to the prophets. It was widely used in Babylon in the 4th century.

Targum Yerushalmi or **Pseudo Jonathan** This translation was used extensively by the Jews in Jerusalem in the 7th century.

Samaritan Bible or **Hexateuch** This Bible, written in Hebrew, is a pre-Masoretic text. It is unusual in that it contains six books—the Five Books of Moses and the Book of Joshua.

Septuagint This Bible, written in the second language into which the Bible was translated, Greek, was widely used by the Jews of the Byzantine Empire. The word *septuagint* means seventy, and this Bible was named the Septuagint after the seventy translators who worked on its translation. The Septuagint is the accepted version of the Bible of the Greek church.

Syriac Bible Sometimes called the Peshitta, meaning simple, this Bible is a literal translation from the Hebrew, written in the 2nd century C.E.

Latin Bible or **Vulgate** This authoritative Latin translation of the Bible was called the Vulgate, meaning "the language of the people." It was written in 404 C.E. by Jerome, the bishop of Rome.

Wycliffe Bible This was the first translation of the Christian Bible, containing the Hebrew Bible, the Apocrypha, and the New Testament, all of which were translated into English from the Latin. This Bible's translation has been attributed to John Wycliffe (1320–1384).

Tyndale's Bible   William Tyndale translated his Bible into English directly from the Hebrew and the Greek. This translation was the first to be printed.

King James or **Authorized Version of the Bible**   This Bible, commissioned by King James I of Great Britain, was completed in 1611. It is to this day considered the most historic of all of the translations of the Bible.

The 1854 translation of the Bible   This Bible was the work of Isaac Leeser, a well-known Philadelphia rabbi. It remained an important translation for the Jews for 50 years.

The 1917 translation of the Bible   This Bible was produced by a group of Jewish scholars under the auspices of the Jewish Publication Society of America.

New Version of the Holy Scriptures   This Bible, created in the 1960s, is a revised edition of the 1917 Bible, produced under the auspices of the Jewish Publication Society of America.

Rashi Script

One of the greatest Bible commentators ever to have lived was the French rabbinical scholar Rabbi Solomon Yitzchaki, who is known by the name Rashi (1040–1105). A special form of Hebrew writing (known as Rashi script) has become one of the most common forms of Hebrew writing in printed Hebrew texts. Almost all of the commentaries on the Talmud and the Bible are printed in this script. In fact, the ability to read Rashi script is an essential skill for studying this literature. Here are the letters of Rashi script with the corresponding letters of the Hebrew alphabet:

Rashi Script	Hebrew Alphabet	Rashi Script	Hebrew Alphabet	Rashi Script	Hebrew Alphabet
ע	ע	י	י	א	א
פ	פ	כ	כ	ב	ב
ף	ף	ר	ר	ג	ג
צ	צ	ל	ל	ד	ד
ץ	ץ	מ	מ	ה	ה
ק	ק	ס	ם	ו	ו
ר	ר	נ	נ	ז	ז
ש	ש	ן	ן	ח	ח
ת	ת	ס	ס	ט	ט

✡

The Bible's Best Dressed

Although it is not common to think of biblical characters as being clothes conscious, there are numerous examples of the importance of clothing to a variety of biblical personalities. Here is a cross section of some of the Bible's best-dressed people:

Joseph wore a coat of many colors, which was given to him by his father, Jacob. This coat made him the envy of his brothers, who ultimately stripped Joseph of the coat and sold him into slavery (Genesis 37:3–28).

The **high priest** may have been the best-dressed person in the Bible. His main garment, called the *ephod*, was made of a fine linen of gold, blue, and purple. Golden bells decorated the hem of the *ephod*. Over this garment the high priest wore a breastplate that held twelve gems—each with the name of one of the twelve tribes. Around his head he wore a miter with a gold plate bearing the words, "Holiness to the Lord" (Exodus 28:36).

Job wore an earring of gold (Job 42:11).

Jeremiah was often dressed in crimson clothing with golden ornaments (Jeremiah 4:30).

Ezekiel the prophet was described as wearing an outfit that included shoes of badger's skin, bracelets, a necklace, earrings, a jewel on the forehead, and a beautiful crown (Ezekiel 16:10–13).

The **Phoenicians** wore fine Egyptian linen garments and purple or blue robes (Ezekiel 26:16).

In the Book of Judges the **Midianite camels** wore necklaces (Judges 8:24–26).

The **Israelites** had such fine accoutrements that their garments never got old and their shoes never wore out, although they wandered in the wilderness for 40 years. (Deuteronomy 29:5).

Meanings of Names of the Books of the Bible

Book	Hebrew Name	Meaning
Genesis	Bereshit	In the beginning
Exodus	Shemot	Names
Leviticus	Vayikra	And He called
Numbers	Bamidbar	In the wilderness
Deuteronomy	Devarim	Words
Joshua	Yehoshua	God saves
Samuel	Shmuel	Heard by God
Kings	Malakhim	Kings

Book	Hebrew Name	Meaning
Isaiah	Yeshayahu	God saves
Jeremiah	Yirmiyahu	God lifts us
Ezekiel	Yehezkel	God makes strong
Hosea	Hoshea	Salvation
Joel	Yoel	Jehovah is God
Amos	Amos	Burden
Obadiah	Ovadiah	Worshiper of God
Jonah	Yonah	Dove
Micah	Mikhah	Who is like God
Nahum	Nachum	Comforter
Habakkuk	Chabbakuk	Beloved one
Zephaniah	Tzephaniah	God hides
Haggai	Chaggai	Festive One
Zechariah	Zechariah	God is remembered
Malachi	Malakhi	My messenger
Proverbs	Mishle	Proverbs
Ruth	Rute	Female friend
Lamentations	Eichah	How
Ecclesiastes	Kohelet	Provider
Daniel	Daniel	God is judge
Ezra	Ezra	Help
Nehemiah	Nechemiah	God is consolation
Chronicles	Divrei HaYamin	Words of the days

Torah Portion Summaries

The first of the Five Books of Moses begins with the creation of the world out of the void. It ends with the last days of Moses. Each week a different *sidrah* (Torah portion) is read on Saturday morning in traditional synagogues. Here is a list of the Torah portions for the entire year and a brief summary of each of their contents.

I. Genesis

Contents

The creation of the world. The patriarchs—Abraham, Isaac, and Jacob. Jacob and his sons go down to Egypt. Jacob blesses his sons before his death.

Weekly Portions

Bereshit (1:1–6:8) The world is created in six days.

Noach (6:9–11:32) A flood destroys the world. God's rainbow promises that the world will never again be destroyed in its entirety.

Lekh Lekha (12:1–17:27) Abraham leaves Mesopotamia for the Promised Land.

Vayera (18:1–22:24) Abraham welcomes three angels into his tent and learns that his wife Sarah will give birth to a son.

Chayyei Sarah (23:1–25:18) Eliezer finds a suitable wife, Rebecca, for Abraham's son Isaac.

Toledot (25:19–28: 9) The birth of Esau and Jacob. Isaac blesses Jacob.

Vayetze (28:10–32:3) God appears to Jacob in a dream. Jacob works 14 years and marries Leah and Rachel.

Vayishlach (32:4–36:43) Jacob and Esau reunite after 20 years. Rachel dies and is buried in Bethlehem.

Vayeshev (37:1–40:23) Joseph's brothers strip him of his coat of many colors and throw him into a pit.

Miketz (41:1–44:17) Joseph successfully interprets Pharaoh's dreams. Joseph is appointed viceroy.

Vayigash (44:18–47:27) Joseph reveals himself to his brothers, who are dumbfounded.

Vayechi (47:28–50:26) Jacob blesses his sons. Joseph dies at end of book at age 110.

II. Exodus

Contents

The Israelites are enslaved in Egypt. Moses receives the Ten Commandments. The Israelites build a tabernacle.

Weekly Portions

Shemot (1:1–6:1) Moses is saved by Pharaoh's daughter. God appears to Moses at the burning bush.

Va'era (6:2–9:35) God brings plagues upon the Egyptians. Pharaoh's heart hardens and he refuses to let the Israelites go.

Bo (10:1–13:16) Egyptian firstborn children are slain by God. The Israelites hastily leave Egypt and bake *matzah* from unleavened dough.

Beshallach (13:17–17:16) The waters of the Red Sea divide to make a path for the Israelites.

Yitro (18:1–20:23) Jethro, Moses' father-in-law, advises him to appoint judges so as to ease his burden. Moses receives the Ten Commandments on Mount Sinai.

Mishpatim (21:1–24:18) Moses instructs the Israelites in the Law.

Terumah (25:1–27:19) The tabernacle is constructed.

Tetzaveh (27:20–30:10) Aaron and his sons are put in charge of the *menorah*. The priestly garments are described in great detail.

Ki Tissa (30:11–34:35) The Israelites build a golden calf; when Moses sees it he shatters the tablets containing the Ten Commandments.

Vayakhel (35:1–38:20) The people bring an array of gifts for the tabernacle until they are told to stop.

Pekudei (38:21–40:38) The cloud of glory covers the completed tabernacle as the Israelites stand in the distance.

III. Leviticus

Contents

The priestly code; the rules pertaining to sacrifices, diet, and morality; and the Land of Israel and festivals are discussed.

Weekly Portions

Vayikra (1:1–5:26) God reveals the sacrificial laws.

Tzav (6:1–8:36) Moses anoints Aaron and his sons as priests.

Shemini (9:1–11:47) Laws describing kosher and nonkosher animals are enumerated.

Tazria (12:1–13:59) Cleanliness and uncleanliness are defined in relation to childbirth and leprosy.

Metzora (14:1–15:33) The laws for the purification of the leper after he has healed are discussed.

Acharei Mot (16:1–18:30) Aaron's sons die. Aaron chooses by lot a goat and a scapegoat.

Kedoshim (19:1–20:27) More laws are set forth, including, "Love your neighbor as yourself."

Emor (21:1–24:23) Festival seasons are described in detail.

Behar (25:1–26:2) The sabbatical and jubilee years are discussed.

Bechukkotai (26:3–27:34) The punishment for rejecting God's covenant is discussed.

IV. Numbers

Contents

The Census. More statutes and laws. Adventures of the Hebrews en route to Canaan through the desert.

Weekly Portions

Bamidbar (1:1–4:20) Description of the Israelites' encampments during their journeys through the desert.

Naso (4:21–7:89) Regulations concerning Nazirites and the threefold priestly benediction.

Behaalotekha (8:1–12:16) Kindling of the *menorah*. Seventy elders are delegated to serve under Moses.

Shelach Lekha (13:1–15:41) Twelve spies are dispatched to survey the land of Canaan. Two of the spies return with a positive report.

Korach (16:1–18:32) Korach refuses to accept the leadership of Moses and Aaron. He and his assembly are killed by an earthquake.

Chukkat (19:1–22:1) The laws regarding the red heifer are enumerated. Moses strikes the rock and water gushes forth.

Balak (22:2–25:9) Balak, king of Moab, sends Bilaam to curse the Israelites. Instead, Bilaam gives his blessing to them.

Pinchas (25:10–30:1) The daughters of Zelophechad are given their father's inheritance. Moses chooses Joshua as his successor.

Mattot (30:2–32:42) Moses informs the tribal heads regarding the laws of vowing.

Masei (33:1–36:13) The detailed account of the various way stations on the Israelites' route to the Promised Land. Reference is made to the cities of refuge.

V. Deuteronomy

Contents

A recapitulation of the laws with some additions. Moses addresses the children of Israel and presents them with some warnings.

Weekly Portions

Devarim (1:1–3:22) Moses explains and interprets the law to the people.

Va'et'chanan (3:23–7:11) The Ten Commandments are repeated, with slight variations. The cities of refuge are mentioned. The first section of the *Shema* is begun with, "You shall love the Lord your God."

Ekev (7:12–11:25) The *Shema* continues with the second paragraph, which deals with the theme of reward and punishment.

Re'eh (11:26–16:17) Moses continues his address, telling the people that obedience will bring them blessing, whereas disobedience will bring them curses.

Shoftim (16:18–21:9) Moses warns the people against idolatry. He also reminds the people of the importance of pursuing justice.

Ki Tetze (21:10–25:19) Moses reviews a variety of laws intended to strengthen family life and human decency in Israel. These laws refer to lost property, the educational responsibility of parents to their children, and kindness to animals, among other things.

Ki Tavo (26:1–29:8) The laws of tithing and first fruits are discussed.

Nitzavim (29:9–30:20) Moses continues his farewell speech and God tells the people to choose life.

Vayelekh (31:1–30) Joshua is appointed successor to Moses. Moses completes the writing of the Torah.

Haazinu (32:1–52) Moses' farewell song—a beautiful poem in which he calls upon heaven and earth to witness God's dependability.

Vezot HaBerakhah (33:1–34:12) Moses' final blessing poem and the report of Moses' death on Mount Nebo. Israel now turns to Joshua for leadership.

Parashat Hashavua: Weekly Torah/Haftarah Reading

Name	Torah Text		Prophetic Reading*
Bereshit	Genesis	1:1–6:8	Isaiah 42:5–43:11 (42:5–21)
Noach		6:9–11:32	Isaiah 54:1–55:5 (54:1–10)
Lekh Lekha		12:1–17:27	Isaiah 40:27–41:16
Vayera		18:1–22:24	2 Kings 4:1–37 (4:1–23)
Chayyei Sarah		23:1–25:18	1 Kings 1:1–31
Toledot		25:19–28:9	Malachi 1:1–2:7

Name		Torah Text	Prophetic Reading*
Vayetze		28:10–32:3	Hosea 12:13–14:10 (11:7–12:12)
Vayishlach		32:4–36:43	Hosea 11:17–12:12 (Obadiah 1:1–21)
Vayeshev		37:1–40:23	Amos 2:6–3:8
Miketz		41:1–44:17	1 Kings 3:15–4:1
Vayigash		44:18–47:27	Ezekiel 37:15–25
Vayechi		47:28–50:26	1 Kings 2:1–12
Shemot	Exodus	1:1–6:1	Isaiah 27:6–28:13; 29:22–23 (Jeremiah 1:1–2:3)
Va'era		6:2–9:35	Ezekiel 28:25–29:21
Bo		10:1–13:16	Jeremiah 46:13–28
Beshallach		13:17–17:16	Judges 4:4–5:31 (5:1–31)
Yitro		18:1–20:23	Isaiah 6:1–7:6; 9:5–6 (6:1–13)
Mishpatim		21:1–24:18	Jeremiah 34:8–22; 33:25–26
Terumah		25:1–27:19	1 Kings 5:26–6:13
Tetzaveh		27:20–30:10	Ezekiel 43:10–27
Ki Tissa		30:11–34:35	1 Kings 18:1–39 (18:20–39)
Vayakhel		35:1–38:20	1 Kings 7:40–50 (7:13–26)

Name		Torah Text	Prophetic Reading*
Pekudei		38:21–40:38	1 Kings 7:51–8:21 (7:40–50)
Vayikra	Leviticus	1:1–5:26	Isaiah 43:21–44:23
Tzav		6:1–8:36	Jeremiah 7:21–8:3; 9:22–23
Shemimi		9:1–11:47	2 Samuel 6:1–7:17 (6:1–19)
Tazria		12:1–13:59	2 Kings 4:42–5:19
Metzora		14:1–15:33	2 Kings 7:3–20
Acharei Mot		16:1–18:30	Ezekiel 22:1–19 (22:1–16)
Kedoshim		19:1–20:27	Amos 9:7–15 (Ezekiel 20:2–20)
Emor		21:1–24:23	Ezekiel 44:15–31
Behar		25:1–26:2	Jeremiah 32:6–27
Bechukkotai		26:3–27:34	Jeremiah 16:19–17:14
Bamidbar	Numbers	1:1–4:20	Hosea 2:1–22
Naso		4:21–7:89	Judges 13:2–25
Behaalotekha		8:1–12:16	Zechariah 2:14–4:7
Shelach Lekha		13:1–15:41	Joshua 2:1–24
Korach		16:1–18:32	1 Samuel 11:14–12:22
Chukkat		19:1–22:1	Judges 11:1–33
Balak		22:2–25:9	Micah 5:6–6:8
Pinchas		25:10–30:1	1 Kings 18:46–19:21

Name	Torah Text	Prophetic Reading*
Mattot	30:2–32:42	Jeremiah 1:1–2:3
Masei	33:1–36:13	Jeremiah 2:4–28; 3:4 (2:4–28; 4:1–2)
Devarim	Deuteronomy 1:1–3:22	Isaiah 1:1–27
Va'et'chanan	3:23–7:11	Isaiah 40:1–26
Ekev	7:12–11:25	Isaiah 49:14–51:3
Re'eh	11:26–16:17	Isaiah 54:11–55:5
Shoftim	16:18–21:9	Isaiah 51:12–52:12
Ki Tetze	21:10–25:19	Isaiah 54:1–10
Ki Tavo	26:1–29:8	Isaiah 60:1–22
Nitzavim	29:9–30:20	Isaiah 61:10–63:9
Vayelekh	31:1–30	Isaiah 55:6–56:8
Haazinu	32:1–52	2 Samuel 22:1–51
Vezot HaBerakhah	33:1–34:12	Joshua 1:1–18 (1:1–9)

*Parentheses indicate Sephardic ritual.

Special Readings

Rosh HaShanah	First Day	Genesis 21:1–34; Numbers 29:6	1 Samuel 1:1–2:10

Rosh HaShanah	Second Day	Genesis 22:1–24; Numbers 29:1–6	Jeremiah 31:2–20
Shabbat Shuvah		Weekly portion	Hosea 14:2–10; Micah 7:18–20 or Hosea 14:2–10; Joel 2:15–17 (Hosea 14:2–10; Micah 7:18–20)
Yom Kippur	Morning	Leviticus 16:1–34; Numbers 29:7–11	Isaiah 57:14–58:14
	Afternoon	Leviticus 18:1–30	Jonah 1:1–4:11; Micah 7:18–20
Sukkot	First Day	Leviticus 22:26–23:44; Numbers 29:12–16	Zechariah 14:1–21
	Second Day	Leviticus 22:26–23:44; Numbers 29:12–16	1 Kings 8:2–21
Shabbat Chol HaMoed Sukkot		Exodus 33:12–34:26; Daily portion from Numbers 29	Ezekiel 38:18–39:16
	Eighth Day	Deuteronomy 14:22–16:17; Numbers 29:35–30:1	1 Kings 8:56–66

Simchat Torah		Deuteronomy 33:1–34:12; Genesis 1:1–2:3 Numbers 29:35–30:1	Joshua 1:1–18 (1:1–9)
Chanukah	First Shabbat	Weekly and Chanukah portions	Zechariah 2:14–4:7
Chanukah	Second Shabbat	Weekly and Chanukah portions	1 Kings 7:40–50
Shabbat Shekalim		Weekly portion; Exodus 30:11–16	II Kings 12:1–17 (11:17–12:17)
Shabbat Zakhor		Weekly portion; Deuteronomy 25:17–19	1 Samuel 15:2–34 (15:1–34)
Shabbat Parah		Weekly portion; Numbers 19:1–22	Ezekiel 36:16–38 (36:16–36)
Shabbat HaChodesh		Weekly portion; Exodus 12:1–20	Ezekiel 45:16–46:18 (45:18–46:15)
Shabbat HaGadol		Weekly portion	Malachi 3:4–24
Pesach	First Day	Exodus 12:21–51; Numbers 28:16–25	Joshua 3:5–7; 5:2–6:1; 6:27 (5:2–6:1)
	Second Day	Leviticus 22:26–23:44; Numbers 28:16–25	2 Kings 23:1–9; 21–25
Shabbat Pesach		Exodus 33:12–34:26; Numbers 28:19–25	Ezekiel 36:37–37:14 (37:1–14)

Pesach	Seventh Day	Exodus 13:17–15:26; Numbers 28:19–25	2 Samuel 22:1–51
	Eighth Day	Deuteronomy 15:19–16:17; (on Shabbat 14:22–16:17); Numbers 28:19–25	Isaiah 10:32–12:6
Shavuot	First Day	Exodus 19:11–20:23 Numbers 28:26–31	Ezekiel 1:1–28; 3:12
	Second Day	Deuteronomy 15:19–16:17 (on Shabbat 14:22–6:17) Numbers 28:26–31	Habakkuk (3:1–19) (2:20–3:19)
Tisha B'Av	Morning	Deuteronomy 4:25–40	Jeremiah 8:13–9:23
	Afternoon	Exodus 32:11–14 34:1–10	Isaiah 55:6–56:8
Shabbat Rosh Chodesh		Weekly portion; Numbers 28:9–15	Isaiah 66:1–24
Shabbat immediately preceeding Rosh Chodesh		Weekly portion	1 Samuel 20:18–42

Torah Portions That Can Be Read Together

There are fifty-four portions in the Torah. Because there are certain weeks when a Jewish festival falls on the Sabbath and the regular Torah portion is not read, it is necessary at certain times to combine Torah portions. In this way all of the portions can be read during the course of a year.

Only certain portions can be combined, as determined by the rabbis. They are.

Vayakhel/Pekudei (Exodus 35:1–40:38)
Tazria/Metzora (Leviticus 12:1–15:33)
Acharei Mot/Kedoshim (Leviticus 16:1–20:27)
Behar/Bechukkotai (Leviticus 25:1–27:34)
Chukkat/Balak (Numbers 29:1–25:9)
Mattot/Masei (Numbers 30:1–36:13)
Nitzavim/Vayelekh (Deuteronomy 29:9–31:30)

Occasions When the Torah Is Read

	Number of Aliyot	Haftarah
Shabbat (morning)	7	Yes
Rosh HaShanah (morning)	5	Yes
Yom Kippur (morning)	6	Yes
Yom Kippur (afternoon)	3	Yes
Sukkot (morning)	5	Yes
Passover (morning)	5	Yes
Shavuot (morning)	5	Yes
Intermediate days of festival (morning)	4	No
Shemini Atzeret (morning)	5	Yes
Simchat Torah	As many as needed	Yes
Chanukah (morning)	3	No
Purim (morning)	3	No
Rosh Chodesh (morning)	4	No
Fast Days (morning)	3	No
Fast Days (afternoon)	3	No (except for Yom Kippur and Tisha B'Av)
Mondays and Thursdays (morning)	3	No
Shabbat (afternoon)	3	No

If a festival or the intermediate day of a festival falls on the Sabbath, there are seven aliyot in addition to the maftir.

Torah Portions Named After People

Noach A righteous person who, along with his family, was saved from the flood.

Chayyei Sarah The wife of Abraham and Judaism's first matriarch.

Yitro The father-in-law of Moses.

Korach From the tribe of Levi; he and his followers were consumed by an earthquake.

Balak The king of Moab; he hired Bilaam to curse the Jews.

Pinchas The grandson of Aaron, the high priest.

Tribes of Israel

The nation of Israel was divided into twelve tribes during the time of the judges and the early kings. The tribes were descendants of the twelve sons of Jacob. Each tribe received a portion of land when the Israelites entered Canaan after their exodus from Egypt. The tribes slowly lost their distinct identities when Israel became a more consolidated nation. Here is a summary of the twelve tribes of Israel, their emblems, banners, and jewels:

Name	Emblem	Banner	Jewel
Judah	lion	sky blue	emerald
Issachar	donkey	black; the sun and moon	sapphire
Zebulun	ship	white	diamond
Reuben	mandrake	red	ruby
Simeon	city of Schechem	green	topaz
Gad	encampment	gray	agate
Ephraim	bullock	jet black	onyx
Manasseh	unicorn	jet black	onyx

Name	Emblem	Banner	Jewel
Benjamin	wolf	multicolored	jasper
Dan	serpent	deep blue	emerald
Naphtali	deer	wine color	amethyst
Asher	woman and olive tree	pearl color	beryl
Levi	*urim* and *tummim*	white, red, and black	carbuncle

List of Judges

The period of the judges, or civic leaders, begins with the death of Joshua and ends during the lifetime of the Prophet Samuel. Here is a list of the judges based on P. Wollman-Tsamir, ed. *The Graphic History of the Jewish Heritage* (New York: Shengold Publishers, 1963):

Othniel, son of Kenaz   The first judge to rule during the period of Israelite subjection to Aram.

Ehud, son of Gera   Relieved Israel from vassalage to Eglon, king of Moab.

Shamgar, son of Anath   Relieved Israel from vassalage to the Philistines.

Barak, son of Abinoam and Deborah   Delivered Israel from vassalage to Jabin, king of Canaan, through the defeat of the army of his general, Sisera.

Gideon, son of Joash   Smote the Midianites.

Abimelech, son of Gideon   Killed his seventy brothers.

Tola, son of Puah   A very wise judge, according to the sages.

Jair, the Gileadite   Passed down rule over the cities of Gilead to his sons.

Jephthah, the Gileadite   Keeping his rash vow, he sacrificed his daughter as a victory offering to God.

Ibzan of Bethlehem   Often identified as Boaz, ancestor of David.

Elon, the Zebulunite   No record exists.

Abdon, son of Hillel   Recorded only as having been happy with his children.

Samson, son of Manoah   Nazirite and warrior, with the strength given him through his long hair he delivered Israel from the Philistines.

Eli, the priest   Ruled over Israel in Shiloh.

Samuel, the prophet   The last of the judges and the first of the prophets.

Kings of Israel

After the period of the judges, the kings began to rule in Israel. They were a combination of judge and military leader. Here is a list of the kings of Israel, beginning with the united monarchy. The death of King Solomon spelled the end of the united Israelite kingdom and its division into Judah in the south and Israel in the north.

United Monarchy (1020–928 B.C.E.)

Saul (1020–1004 B.C.E.) was Israel's first king, and helped to unite the tribes of Israel. After a reign of 20 years, he killed himself at the battle of Gilboa.

David (1004–965 B.C.E.) was anointed king by Samuel when he was just a child. He is best known for conquering Jerusalem and making it Israel's capital.

Solomon (965–928 B.C.E.) was famed for his great wisdom and many wives.

Kings of Judah (928–586 B.C.E.)

Rehoboam (928–911 B.C.E.) was the son of Solomon and ruled over Judah. He was accused of idolatry, a sin attributed to the influence of his many foreign wives.

Aviyam (911–908 B.C.E.) attempted to conquer Israel but advanced only a few miles to Bethel.

Asa (908–867 B.C.E.) was a religious reformer who tried to stamp out idolatry.

Jehoshaphat (867–846 B.C.E.) strengthened the army and helped to revive commerce.

Jehoram (846–843 B.C.E.) was accused of idolatry after he married the daughter of Achab and Jezebel of Israel.

Ahaziah (843 B.C.E.) was distinguished by falling through the latticework of an upper room, seriously injuring himself.

Athaliah (842–836 B.C.E.) was the only queen either kingdom ever had. She promoted Baal worship.

Joash (836–798 B.C.E.) was killed by his own officers.

Amaziah (798–769 B.C.E.) was 25 years old when he took a census to conscript an army. In a successful war, he recovered trade routes to the Gulf of Aqaba.

Uzziah (769–758 B.C.E.) took the throne at age 16, making Judah more prosperous than it had been since King Solomon.

Jotham (758–733 B.C.E.) maintained Judah's prosperity and military advantage.

Ahaz (733–727 B.C.E.) was a particularly weak king who indulged in pagan cults.

Hezekiah (727–698 B.C.E.) attempted to restore Israelite worship in Jerusalem and received the backing of the Prophet Isaiah.

Manasseh (698–642 B.C.E.) is noted for the restoration of pagan cults.

Amon (641–640 B.C.E.) continued idolatrous practices and was eventually assassinated by his officers.

Josiah (639–609 B.C.E.) instituted religious reform.

Jehoahaz (609 B.C.E.) tried to be king, but Pharaoh Necho II sent him in chains to Egypt, where he died.

Jehoiakim (608–598 B.C.E.) was appointed puppet ruler of Judah by Pharaoh Necco.

Jehoiachin (597 B.C.E.) was taken captive to Babylon under the reign of Nebuchadnezzar.

Zedekiah (596–586 B.C.E.) rebuilt Jerusalem's defenses and saved the city from the Edomites.

Jeroboam (928–907 B.C.E.) built a new capital at Tirzeh.

Nadav (907–906 B.C.E.) battled with Judah over the location of the border.

Baasha (906–883 B.C.E) unsuccessfully invaded Judah and, in turn, was invaded by Damascus.

Elah (883–882 B.C.E.) was murdered by his officer Zimri while drunk.

Zimri (882 B.C.E.) ruled for only 7 days and died when a burning palace, a fire he had set, collapsed on him.

Omri (882–871 B.C.E.) was a great and wise king who made peace with Judah and won back Moab and other lost territories.

Ahab (871–852 B.C.E.) was a good ruler who continued Omri's peaceable foreign policy and domestic prosperity.

Ahaziah (852–851 B.C.E.) in his first act as king, injured himself by falling from a second story.

Jehoram (851–842 B.C.E.) made abortive attempt to recover Moab.

Jehu (842–814 B.C.E.) stamped out Baal worship.

Jehoahaz (814–800 B.C.E.) lost much territory, and Israel became a dependency of Damascus.

Jehoash (800–784 B.C.E.) punished Jerusalem by breaching the walls and taking treasures and captives.

Jeroboam II (784–748 B.C.E.) was a strong ruler who made peace with Judah and recovered territory until Israel returned to the size it had been during the reign of King David.

Zechariah (748–747 B.C.E.) reigned for 6 months before being assassinated.

Shallum (748–747 B.C.E.) reigned 1 month and was murdered by Menachem.

Menachem (747/746–737/736 B.C.E.) went on a killing spree and suppressed all opposition to his reign.

Pekachiah (737/736–735/734 B.C.E.) collected tribute for Assyria until he was murdered by one of his army officers.

Pekach (735/734–733/732 B.C.E.) attacked Judah and carried off captives.

Hoshea (733/732–724/723 B.C.E.) was a puppet king who collected tribute for Assyria.

Joash (836–798 B.C.E.) was made king when he was 7 years old. Later in his career he repaired the Temple.

The Seven Commandments for All People

In Chapter 9 of the Book of Genesis, there are seven fundamental laws presented that are vital to the existence of human society. In ancient times, an Israelite was expected to carry out all of the commandments of the Torah, whereas obedience only to these seven laws was required of non-Jews living among Israelites.

1. Not to believe in idolatry.
2. Not to curse God.
3. Not to commit murder.
4. To have relations and a normal family life with only one wife.
5. Not to commit thievery.
6. Not to eat a piece of meat that is removed from its source while it is still alive.
7. To establish courts of justice to enforce the observance of the preceding six laws.

Famous Firsts in the Bible

First firemaker	Adam
First farmer	Cain
First world traveler	Cain
First shipbuilder	Noah
First vintager	Noah
First Jew	Abraham
First *matzah* baker	Lot
First matchmaker	Eliezer
First man to be sick	Jacob
First commandment	Be fruitful and multiply
First to have parents	Cain
First real estate transaction	Abraham and Efron
First wrestler	Jacob
First recorded stutterer	Moses
First king of Israel	Saul
First messenger	Raven
First case of disrespectful behavior to parents	Ham
First to receive eviction notice	Adam and Eve
First king of Judah	David
First king of the Ten Tribes	Jeroboam
First women to demand property rights	Daughters of Zelophechad
First woman whose consent for marriage was asked	Rebekah
First skyscraper	Tower of Babel
First man to wear a mask	Moses
First recorded dream	Abimelech
First war	War of the Kings of the North
First pseudonym	Esther, name was used by Hadassah
First person to hold a beauty contest	King Ahasuerus

Biblical Names Used in English

Today, the use of biblical names seems to be increasing in popularity. Here, with their meanings, are some biblical names that are currently used in North America.

Aaron Based on various Hebrew derivatives, the name Aaron may mean, "teaching, singing, to shine, mountain." Aaron was the brother of Moses and head of the priesthood.

Abigail ("joy of my father") A follower of David before he became a king, Abigail was known for both her beauty and her wisdom.

Abraham ("father of a mighty nation") Abraham has always been considered the father of the Jewish people.

Adam ("red" or "earth") The first human being God created.

Benjamin ("son of my right hand") The youngest of Jacob's twelve sons.

Daniel ("God is my judge") A Minor Prophet.

David ("beloved") The second king of Israel.

Deborah ("swarm of bees") An Israelite judge.

Dinah ("judgment") The daughter of Jacob and Leah.

Ezra ("help") A famous scribe who chronicled the Jews return from Babylon.

Isaac ("laughter") Abraham's son and the second Jewish patriarch.

Jacob ("held by the heel") The son of Isaac and Rebekah and the third Jewish patriarch.

Joel ("God is willing") A Minor Prophet.

Joseph ("he will increase") The favorite son of his father, Jacob.

Miriam ("bitter waters") The sister of Moses.

Rebekah   ("to tie or bind") The wife of Isaac.

Sarah   ("princess of God") The wife of Abraham and the mother of Isaac.

The Ten Commandments

The most famous of the 613 commandments are the Ten Commandments, which Moses received on Mount Sinai. In Temple times they used to be read as part of the prayer service. Today, they are read in the portion of Yitro and on the festival of Shavuot:

1. I am the Lord your God who brought you out of the land of Egypt, out of the house of bondage.
2. You shall have no other gods before Me. You shall not make for yourself a graven image.
3. You shall not take the name of the Lord your God in vain.
4. Observe the Sabbath day and keep it holy.
5. Honor your father and your mother.
6. You shall not murder.
7. You shall not commit adultery.
8. You shall not steal.
9. You shall not bear false witness against your neighbor.
10. You shall not be jealous of your neighbor's wife, his house, his field, his man- or maid-servant, his ox, his donkey, or anything that is your neighbor's.

Books of the Apocrypha

The Apocrypha is a series of books, written during the last centuries B.C.E., that were excluded from the Bible. Some of the books were written in Greek, and they were all modeled after the books of the Bible. The following is a summary of the books of the Apocrypha:

Third Book of Ezra   The story of Zerubabel, who received permission from King Darius to visit Judea as the victor's reward in a debate as to what was the strongest thing on earth. (He had said that women were the strongest things on earth.)

1 Maccabees   The story of the Jews from the time of King Antiochus until the death of Simon Maccabee.

2 Maccabees   The history of the Jews from Seleucus IV until the death of Nicanor.

3 Maccabees   The story of God's punishment of Ptolemy IV for polluting the Temple sanctuary.

Book of Tobit   The miraculous story of a man named Tobit and his son Tobias.

Book of Judith   The story of how Judith slew General Holofernes.

Bel and the Dragon   The story of Daniel, who fought the idol Bel and the mythical god Dragon. The story also tells of Daniel's taming of the lions.

Susanna   The story of Susanna, who was falsely accused of adultery by the elders but was eventually vindicated.

Song of the Three Children   The story of Azarias, Chanamia, and Mishoel, who were saved from death in a furnace.

Prayer of Manasseh   The story of Manasseh, king of Judea and the son of Hezekiah.

Book of Baruch   A book of wisdom written by Baruch, a scribe and the secretary of the Prophet Jeremiah.

Epistle of Jeremiah   The story of Jeremiah, who warns the exiles against worshiping idols.

Wisdom of Ben Sira   This book, written by Ben Sira, contains many words of wisdom about religion.

Wisdom of Solomon   A book of philosophy about God, author unknown.

4 Maccabees   A book of stoicism.

Dates of Important Biblical Events and Personalities

(*indicates approximate date)
(All dates are B.C.E.)

Abraham	2000	(*2000–1700) Period of the patri- archs
Isaac		(*1700–1300) Period of the Israelite
Jacob		tribes in Egypt
Joseph	1500	
Moses		(*1300) Exodus of the Israelites from Egypt
		(*1250) Entry into Canaan
		(*1225–1020) Period of the judges
Deborah		
Gideon		
Samson		
Samuel		(1020–1004) King Saul's reign
Saul		
Nathan	1000	(*998–965) King David's reign
David		
Solomon		(*965–926) King Solomon's reign
		(*926) Hebrew kingdom divided; Jeroboam, king of Israel
Elijah		(*882–871) Omri, king of Israel
		(*871–852) Achab, king of Israel
Elisha		
Amos		
Isaiah		
Hosea		
Micah		(721) Assyrian destruction of Israel.
		(621) Book of Deuteronomy Found
Jeremiah		(598) First Babylonian invasion of Judah
		(589) Final Babylonian invasion and start of exile
Ezekiel		
Second Isaiah		(*538) Edict of Cyrus, which per- mitted return of exiles
Ezra	500	(*450) Return of Ezra and Nehemiah

Angels and Demons

In Jewish tradition, God is often conceived of as delegating power to a messenger or angel. These messengers are always bound to perform God's will. Demons are also considered messengers of God, but their role is to bring sorrow and harm to people. Here is a summary of some of the most well known angels and demons in Jewish tradition:

Beelzebub (Lord of the Files) He was the sovereign of the netherworld.

Cherubim Their purpose was to guard the Tree of Life in the Garden of Eden (Genesis 3:24). They are portrayed on the Ark of the Covenant.

Gabriel He is one of the two angels mentioned by name in the Bible (Daniel 8:10). He was the leader of the archangels.

Kategor (Accuser) His function was to call attention to the sins of the people (Zechariah 3:1).

Lilith This female demon reigned in the night (Isaiah 34:14). In Jewish mysticism she is considered the queen of the demons.

Malakh HaMavet (Angel of Death) His purpose was to summon the dying soul from the earth.

Metatron In mystical literature, Metatron is the highest figure in the angelic world, sometimes known as the Angel of the Presence.

Michael He is one of two angels mentioned by name in the Bible (Daniel 10:13).

Ophanim (Wheels) Appearing in the Book of Ezekiel, these angels dress the holy chariot.

Raphael (God heals) One of the seven archangels who brought prayers before God.

Ruziel (Secret of God) He was the angel of magic.

Samael He was the prince of the evil demons.

Sanegor (Defender) His role as an angel was to defend the people in the heavenly court.

Satan (Adversary) One of his primary tasks was to call God's attention to the sins of the people.

Seraphim (Fiery angels) In Isaiah 6:2, these angels declare God's holiness.

Shmodai (Destroyer) He is a destructive angel who was considered the king of all of the demons (Psalm 11).

Uriel Classified as the prince of the Archangels, he is identified by thunder and earthquakes. He warned the people about the end of the world.

Bible Miscellany

There are thirty-nine books in the Jewish Bible, which are divided into three sections: *Torah, Nevi'im* (Prophets), and *Ketuvim* (Writings). The Hebrew acronym for these is *Tanakh*.

Torah Genesis, Exodus, Leviticus, Numbers, Deuteronomy.

Nevi'im Joshua, Judges, 1 Samuel, 2 Samuel, 1 Kings, 2 Kings, Isaiah, Jeremiah, Ezekiel, Hosea, Joel, Amos, Obadiah, Jonah, Micah, Nachum, Habakkuk, Zephaniah, Haggai, Zechariah, Malachi.

Ketuvim Psalms, Proverbs, Job, Song of Songs, Ruth, Lamentations, Ecclesiastes, Esther, Daniel, Ezra, Nehemiah, 1 Chronicles, 2 Chronicles.

The number of verses in the Torah is 5,845. They are divided as follows:

Genesis	1534
Exodus	1209
Leviticus	859
Numbers	1288
Deuteronomy	955

The middle verse of the Torah is Leviticus 8:8: "He put the breastplate on him, and put into the breastplate the Urim and Thummim."

The longest verse in the Tanach is Esther 8:9. It consists of forty-three words.

The shortest chapter in the *Tanakh* is Psalm 117:

Praise God, all nations
Laud Him, all peoples.
His love has overwhelmed us,
His faithfulness lasts forever. Halleluyah.

The longest chapter in the Tanakh is Psalm 119.

The only two books that do not mention the name of God are the Song of Songs and the Book of Esther.

RABBINICS

The Talmud at a Glance

There are six orders to the Babylonian Talmud, each containing a series of tractates (books). Here is a summary of the six orders of the Babylonian Talmud:

I. Order Zeraim (Seeds)

Berakhot (Blessings) Information about benedictions and prayers.

Peah (Corner) Information about corners and gleanings of fields.

Demai (Doubtfully Tithed) Produce suspected of not being tithed.

Kilayim (Mixtures) Prohibited mixtures of animals, plants, and clothes.

Shevi'it (Sabbatical Year) Information about the Sabbatical year.

Terumot (Heave Offerings) Information about heave offerings.

Maaserot (Tithes) Information about tithing.

Maaser Sheni (Second tithes) Information about second tithes.

Challah (Dough) Information about the priestly dough offering.

Orlah (Uncircumcised) Information about fruits of trees during the first four years after planting.

Bikkurim (First Fruits) Information about firstfruits brought to the Temple.

II. Order Moed (Festivals)

Shabbat (Sabbath) Work prohibited on the Sabbath.

Eruvin (Combinations) Extension of Sabbath boundaries.

Pesachim (Passover) Passover laws and the Paschal lamb.

Shekalim (Shekels) Information about the half-shekel tax.

Yoma (The Day) The Day of Atonement.

Sukkah (Tabernacle) Feast of Tabernacles laws.

Betzah (Egg) Work prohibited on festivals.

Rosh HaShanah (New Year) Laws of the New Year.

Taanit (Fast) Laws about public fasts.

Megillah (Scroll) Laws about reading the Book of Esther on Purim.

Moed Katan (Minor Festival) Laws of intermediate days of Sukkot and Passover.

Chagigah (Festival Offering) Private offerings on Passover, Sukkot, and Shavuot.

III. Order Nashim (Women)

Yevamot (Sisters-in-law) Laws about levirate marriage.

Ketubot (Marriage Deeds) Laws about dowries and marriage settlements.

Nedarim (Vows) Laws about vows.

Nazir (Nazarite) Laws about Nazirites.

Sotah (Suspected Adulteress) Laws about a wife suspected of adultery.

Gittin (Divorces) Laws about divorce.

Kiddushin (Betrothals) Laws about marriage.

IV. Order, Nezikin (Damages)

Bava Kamma (First Gate) Laws about injuries and damages.

Bava Metzia (Middle Gate) Laws about found property, trust, buying, selling, lending, hiring, and renting.

Bava Batra (Last Gate) Laws about real estate and commerce.

Sanhedrin (Courts) Laws about courts and capital punishment.

Makkot (Stripes) Laws about false witnesses, cities of refuge, and crimes punishable by stripes.

Shevuot (Oaths) Laws about oaths and promises.

Eduyyot (Testimonies) Laws about testimony.

Avodah Zarah (Idolatry) Laws about idol worship.

Avot (Fathers) Ethics of our ancestors. Maxims and pithy sayings about living life.

Horayot (Decisions) Erroneous decisions and their effects.

The Babylonian Talmud appends to this order these seven tractates of later origin:

Avot de Rabbi Natan (Ethics of the Fathers, by Rabbi Nathan) Extension of the ethics of our fathers.

Soferin (Scribes) Writing of the scrolls of the Five Books of Moses and the Book of Esther.

Avel Rabbati (Mourning) Laws of mourning.

Kallah (Bride) Laws of chastity.

Derekh Eretz Rabbah (Conduct) Laws about prohibited marriages, religious, ethical, and social teachings.

Derekh Eretz Zuta (Conduct) More laws about ethical and social teachings.

Perek Shalom (Chapter on Peace) Laws about making peace.

V. Order Kodashim (Sacred Things)

Zevachim (Sacrifices) Laws about sacrifices.

Menachot (Meal Offerings) Laws about meal and drink offerings.

Chullin (Profane Things) Laws about slaughtering and dietary laws.

Bekhorot (Firstborns) Laws about firstborn men and animals.

Arakhin (Evaluations) Laws about appraisement for redemption.

Temurah (Exchange) Exchange of sanctified things.

Keritot (Excisions) Sins punishable by excision and expiation.

Me'ilah (Trespass) Laws about sacrileges.

Tamid (Daily Sacrifice) Laws about everyday sacrifices.

Middot (Measurements) Laws about measurements and descriptions of the Temple and the courts.

Kinnim (Nests) Sacrifices of fowls and offerings of the poor.

VI. Order Tohorot (Purifications)

Kelim (Vessels) Ritual uncleanliness of clothing and utensils.

Oholot (Tents) Ritual uncleanliness of houses and tents caused by a dead body.

Negaim (Leprosy) Laws about lepers.

Parah (Heifer) Laws about heifers.

Tohorot (Purifications) Lesser degrees of uncleanliness lasting until sunset.

Mikvaot (Ritual Baths) Laws about ritual baths and reservoirs.

Niddah (Menstruant) Laws about menstruation.

Makhshirin (Preparations) Laws about liquids that render seeds and fruit unclean.

Zavim (Sufferers with Gonorrhea) Laws about those suffering from gonorrhea.

Tevul Yom (Immersed at Daytime) Cleanliness acquired at sunset.

Yadayim (Hands) Uncleanliness of hands and their purification.

Uktzin (Fruit Stalks) Laws about fruit stalks and their shells regarding the conveying of uncleanliness.

The 613 Commandments

According to rabbinic tradition there are 613 commandments
(*mitzvot* in Hebrew) in the Torah. There are 365 negative
commandments that tell us what we cannot do, and 248
positive ones that tell us what to do. The list that follows was
set forth by Maimonides in his *Book of Commandments*. The
biblical sources are cited in the margins.

Mandatory Commandments

God

The Jew is required to [1]believe that God exists and to
[2]acknowledge His unity; to [3]love, [4]fear, and [5]serve Him. He is
also commanded to [6]cleave to Him (by associating with and
imitating the wise) and to [7]swear only by His name. One must
[8]imitate God and [9]sanctify His name.

1. Ex. 20:22.	5. Ex. 23:25	6. Deut. 10:20
2. Deut. 6:4	Deut. 11:13	7. Deut. 10:20
3. Deut. 6:5	(Deut. 6:13;	8. Deut. 28:9
4. Deut. 6:13	13:5)	9. Lev. 22:32

Torah

The Jew must [10]recite the *Shema* each morning and evening
and [11]study the Torah and teach it to others. He should bind
tefillin on his [12]head and [13]his arm. He should make [14]*zizit*
for his garments and [15]fix a *mezuzah* on the door. The people
are to be [16] assembled every seventh year to hear the Torah
read and [17]the king must write a special copy of the Torah for
himself. [18]Every Jew should have a Torah scroll. One should
[19]praise God after eating.

10. Deut. 6:7	14. Num. 15:38	17. Deut. 17:18
11. Deut. 6:7	15. Deut. 6:9	18. Deut. 31:19
12. Deut. 6:8	16. Deut. 31:12	19. Deut. 8:10
13. Deut. 6:8		

Temple, and the Priests

The Jews should [20]build a Temple and [21]respect it. It must be
[22]guarded at all times and the [23]Levites should perform their

special duties in it. Before entering the Temple or partici-
pating in its service the priests [24]must wash their hands and
feet; they must also [25]light the candelabrum daily. The priests
are required to [26]bless Israel and to [27]set the shewbread and
frankincense before the Ark. Twice daily they must [28]burn
the incense on the golden altar. Fire shall be kept burning on
the altar[29]continually and the ashes should be [30]removed
daily. Ritually unclean persons must be [31]kept out of the
Temple. Israel [32]should honor its priests, who must be
[33]dressed in special priestly raiment. The priests should
[34]carry the Ark on their shoulders, and the holy anointing oil
[35]must be prepared according to its special formula. The
priestly families should officiate in [36]rotation. In honor of
certain dead close relatives the priests should [37]make themselves ritually unclean. The high priest may marry [38]only a
virgin.

20. Ex. 25:8	27. Ex. 25:30	33. Ex. 28:2
21. Lev. 19:30	28. Ex. 30:7	34. Num. 7:9
22. Num. 18:4	29. Lev. 6:6	35. Ex. 30:31
23. Num. 18:23	30. Lev. 6:3	36. Deut. 18:6–8
24. Ex. 30:19	31. Num. 5:2	37. Lev. 21:2–3
25. Ex. 27:21	32. Lev. 21:8	38. Lev. 21:13
26. Num. 6:23		

Sacrifices

The [39]tamid sacrifice must be offered twice daily and the
[40]high priest must also offer a meal-offering twice daily. An
additional sacrifice (musaf) should be offered [41]every Sabbath, [42]on the first of every month, and [43]on each of the seven
days of Passover. On the second day of Passover [44]a meal
offering of the first barley must also be brought. On Shavuot
a [45]musaf must be offered and [46]two loaves of bread as a
wave offering. The additional sacrifice must also be made
on [47]Rosh HaShanah and [48]on the Day of Atonement when
the [49]Avodah must also be performed. On every day of the
festival of [50]Sukkot a musaf must be brought as well as on the
[51]eight day thereof.

Every male Jew should make [52]pilgrimage to the Temple
three times a year and [53]appear there during the three pilgrim
Festivals. One should [54]rejoice on the Festivals.

On the 14th of Nisan one should [55]slaughter the paschal
lamb and [56]eat of its roasted flesh on the night of the 15th.
Those who were ritually impure in Nisan should slaughter the

paschal lamb on [57]the 14th of Iyyar and eat it with [58]*mazzah* and bitter herbs.

Trumpets should be [59]sounded when the festive sacrifices are brought and also in times of tribulation.

Cattle to be sacrificed must be [60]at least eight days old and [61]without blemish. All offerings must be [62]salted. It is a *mitzvah* to perform the ritual of [63]the burnt offering, [64]the sin offering, [65]the guilt offering, [66]the peace offering and [67]the meal offering.

Should the Sanhedrin err in a decision its members [68]must bring a sin offering which offering must also be brought [69]by a person who has unwittingly transgressed a *karet* prohibition (i.e., one which, if done deliberately, would incur karet). When in doubt as to whether one has transgressed such a prohibition a [70]"suspensive" guilt offering must be brought. For [71]stealing or swearing falsely and for other sins of a like nature, a guilt offering must be brought. In special circumstances the sin offering [72]can be according to one's means.

One must [73]confess one's sins before God and repent for them. A[74]man or [75]a woman who has a seminal issue must bring a sacrifice; a woman must also bring a sacrifice [76]after childbirth. A leper must [77]bring a sacrifice after he has been cleansed.

One must [78]tithe one's cattle. The [79]first born of clean (i.e., permitted) cattle are holy and must be sacrificed. The first-born of man must be [80]redeemed. The firstling of the ass must be [81]redeemed; if not [82]its neck has to be broken.

Animals set aside as offerings [83]must be brought to Jerusalem without delay and [84]may be sacrificed only in the Temple. Offerings from outside the land of Israel [85]may also be brought to the Temple. Sanctified animals [86]which have become blemished must be redeemed. A beast exchanged for an offering [87]is also holy.

The priests should eat [88]the remainder of the meal offering and [89]the flesh of sin and guilt offerings; but consecrated flesh which has become [90]ritually unclean or [91]which was not eaten within its appointed time must be burned.

39. Num. 28:3	45. Num. 28:26–27	51. Num. 29:36
40. Lev. 6:13	46. Lev. 23:17	52. Ex. 23:14
41. Num. 28:9	47. Num. 29:1–2	53. Ex. 34:23
42. Num. 28:11	48. Num. 29:7–8	Deut. 16:16
43. Lev. 23:36	49. Lev. 16	54. Deut. 16:14
44. Lev. 23:10	50. Num. 29:13	55. Ex. 12:6

56. Ex. 12:8	68. Lev. 4:13	80. Ex. 22:28
57. Num. 9:11	69. Lev. 4:27	Num. 18:15
58. Num. 9:11	70. Lev. 5:17–18	81. Ex. 34:20
Ex. 12:8	71. Lev. 5:15,	82. Ex. 13:13
59. Num. 10:10	21–25;	83. Deut. 12:5–5
Num. 10:9	19:20–21	84. Deut. 12:14
60. Lev. 22:27	72. Lev. 5:1–11	85. Deut. 12:26
61. Lev. 22:21	73. Num. 5:6–7	86. Deut. 12:15
62. Lev. 2:13	74. Lev. 15:13–15	87. Lev. 27:33
63. Lev. 1:2	75. Lev. 15:28–29	88. Lev. 6:9
64. Lev. 6:18	76. Lev. 12:6	89. Ex. 29:33
65. Lev. 7:1	77. Lev. 14:10	90. Lev. 7:19
66. Lev. 3:1	78. Lev. 27:32	91. Lev. 7:17
67. Lev. 2:1; 6: 7	79. Ex. 13:2	

Vows

A Nazirite must [92]let his hair grow during the period of his separation. When that period is over he must [93]shave his head and bring his sacrifice.

A man must [94]honor his vows and his oaths which a judge can [95]annul only in accordance with the law.

92. Num. 6:5	94. Deut. 23:24	95. Num. 30:3
93. Num. 6:18		

Ritual Purity

Anyone who touches [96]a carcass or [97]one of the eight species of reptiles becomes ritually unclean; food becomes unclean by [98]coming into contact with a ritually unclean object. Menstruous women [99]and those [100]lying-in after childbirth are ritually impure. A [101]leper, [102]a leprous garment, and [103]a leprous house are all ritually unclean. A man having [104]a running issue is unclean, as is [105]semen. A woman suffering from [106]running issue is also impure.

A [107]human corpse is ritually unclean. The purification water (*mei niddah*) purifies [108]the unclean, but it makes the clean ritually impure. It is a *mitzvah* to become ritually clean [109]by ritual immersion. To become cleansed of leprosy one [110]must follow the specified procedure and also [111]shave off all of one's hair. Until cleansed the leper [112]must be bareheaded with clothing in disarray so as to be easily distinguishable.

The ashes of [113]the red heifer are to be used in the process of ritual purification.

96. Lev. 11:8,
    and 24
97. Lev. 11:29–31
98. Lev. 11:34
99. Lev. 15:19
100. Lev. 12:2
101. Lev. 13:3

102. Lev. 13:51
103. Lev. 14:44
104. Lev. 15:2
105. Lev. 15:16
106. Lev. 15:19
107. Num. 19:14

108. Num. 19:13,21
109. Lev. 15:16
110. Lev. 14:2
111. Lev. 14:9
112. Lev. 13:45
113. Num. 19:2–9

Donations of the Temple

If a person [114]undertakes to give his own value to the Temple he must do so. Should a man declare [115]an unclean beast, [116]a house, or [117]a field as a donation to the Temple, he must give their value in money as fixed by the priest. If one unwittingly derives benefit from Temple property [118]full restitution plus a fifth must be made.

The fruit of [119]the fourth year's growth of trees is holy and may be eaten only in Jerusalem. When you reap your fields you must leave [120]the corners, [121]the gleanings, [122]the forgotten sheaves, [123]the misformed bunches of grapes and [124]the gleanings of the grapes for the poor.

The first fruits must be [125]separated and brought to the Temple and you must also [126]separate the great heave offering (*terumah*) and give it to the priests. You must give [127]one tithe of your produce to the Levites and separate [128]a second tithe which is to be eaten only in Jerusalem. The Levites [129]must give a tenth of their tithe to the priests.

In the third and sixth years of the seven year cycle you should [130]separate a tithe for the poor instead of the second tithe. A declaration [131]must be recited when separating the various tithes and [132]when bringing the first fruits to the Temple.

The first portion of the [133]dough must be given to the priest.

114. Lev. 27:2–8
115. Lev. 27:11–12
116. Lev. 27:14
117. Lev. 27:16,
     22–23
118. Lev. 5:16
119. Lev. 19:24
120. Lev. 19:9

121. Lev. 19:9
122. Deut. 24:19
123. Lev. 19:10
124. Lev. 19:10
125. Ex. 23:19
126. Deut. 18:4
127. Lev. 27:30
     Num. 18:24

128. Deut. 14:22
129. Num. 18:26
130. Deut. 14:28
131. Deut. 26:13
132. Deut. 26:5
133. Num. 15:20

The Sabbatical Year

In the seventh year (*shemittah*) everything that grows is [134]ownerless and available to all; the fields [135]must lie fallow and you may not till the ground. You must [136]sanctify the Jubilee year (50th) and on the Day of Atonement in that year [137]you must sound the *shofar* and set all Hebrew slaves free. In the Jubilee year all land is to be [138]returned to its ancestral owners and, generally, in a walled city [139]the seller has the right to buy back a house within a year of the sale.

Starting from entry into the land of Israel, the years of the Jubilee must be [140]counted and announced yearly and septennially.

In the seventh year [141]all debts are annulled but [142]one may exact a debt owned by a foreigner.

134. Ex. 23:11	137. Lev. 25:9	140. Lev. 25:8
135. Ex. 34:21	138. Lev. 25:24	141. Deut. 15:3
136. Lev. 25:10	139. Lev. 25:29–30	142. Deut. 15:3

Concerning Animals for Consumption

When you slaughter an animal you must [143]give the priest his share as you must also give him [144]the first of the fleece. When a man makes a *herem* (a special vow) you must [145]distinguish between that which belongs to the Temple (i.e., when God's name was mentioned in the vow) and between that which goes to the priests. To be fit for consumption, beast and fowl must be [146]slaughtered according to the law and if they are not of a domesticated species [147]their blood must be covered with earth after slaughter.

Set the parent bird [148]free when taking the nest. Examine [149]beast, [150]fowl, [151]locusts and [152]fish to determine whether they are permitted for consumption.

The Sanhedrin should [153]sanctify the first day of every month and reckon the years and the seasons.

143. Deut. 18:3	147. Lev. 17:13	151. Lev. 11:21
144. Deut. 18:4	148. Deut. 22:7	152. Lev. 11:9
145. Lev. 27:21,28	149. Lev. 11:2	153. Ex. 12:2
146. Deut. 12:21	150. Deut. 14:11	Deut. 16:1

Festivals

You must [154]rest on the Sabbath day and [155]declare it holy at its onset and termination. On the 14th of Nisan [156]remove all leaven from your ownership and on the night of the 15th

[157]relate the story of the exodus from Egypt; on that night [158]you must also eat *mazzah*. On the [159]first and [160]seventh days of Passover you must rest. Starting from the day of the first sheaf (16th of Nisan) you shall [161]count 49 days. You must rest on [162]Shavuot, and on [163]Rosh HaShanah; on the Day of Atonement you must [164]fast and [165]rest. You must also rest on [166]the first and [167]the eighth day of Sukkot during which festival you shall [168]dwell in booths and [169]take the four species. On Rosh HaShanah [170]you are to hear the sound of the *shofar*.

154. Ex. 23:12	160. Ex. 12:16	166. Lev. 23:35
155. Ex. 20:8	161. Lev. 23:35	167. Lev. 23:36
156. Ex. 12:15	162. Lev. 23	168. Lev. 23:42
157. Ex. 13:8	163. Lev. 23:24	169. Lev. 23:40
158. Ex 12:18	164. Lev. 16:29	170. Num. 29:1
159. Ex. 12:16	165. Lev. 16:29,31	

Community

Every male should [171]give half a shekel to the Temple annually.

You must [172]obey a prophet and [173]appoint a king. You must also [174]obey the Sanhedrin; in the case of division, [175]yield to the majority. Judges and officials shall be [176]appointed in every town and they shall judge the people [177]impartially.

Whoever is aware of evidence [178]must come to court to testify. Witnesses shall be [179]examined thoroughly and, if found to be false, [180]shall have done to them what they intended to do to the accused.

When a person is found murdered and the murderer is unknown the ritual of [181]decapitating the heifer must be performed.

Six cities of refuge should be [182]established. The Levites, who have no ancestral share in the land, shall [183]be given cities to live in.

You must [184]build a fence around your roof and remove potential hazards from your home.

171. Ex. 30:12-13	176. Deut. 16:18	181. Deut. 21:4
172. Deut. 18:15	177. Lev. 19:15	182. Deut. 19:3
173. Deut. 17:15	178. Lev. 5:1	183. Num. 35:2
174. Deut. 17:11	179. Deut. 13:15	184. Deut. 22:8
175. Ex. 23:2	180. Deut 19:19	

Idolatry

Idolatry and its appurtenances [185]must be destroyed, and a city which has become perverted must be [186]treated according to the law. You are commanded to [187]destroy the seven Canaanite nations, and [188]to blot out the memory of Amalek, and [189]to remember what they did to Israel.

185. Deut. 12:2;7:5   187. Deut. 20:17   189. Deut. 25:17
186. Deut. 13:17   188. Deut. 25:19

War

The regulations for wars other than those commanded in the Torah [190]are to be observed and a priest should be [191]appointed for special duties in times of war. The military camp must be [192]kept in a sanitary condition. To this end, every soldier must be [193]equipped with the necessary implements.

190. Deut. 20:11–12   192. Deut. 23:14–15   193. Deut. 23:14
191. Deut. 20:2

Social

Stolen property must be [194]restored to its owner. Give [195]charity to the poor. When a Hebrew slave goes free the owner must [196]give him gifts. Lend to [197]the poor without interest; to the foreigner you may [198]lend at interest. Restore [199]a pledge to its owner if he needs it. Pay the worker his wages [200]on time, [201]permit him to eat of the produce with which he is working. You must [202]help unload an animal when necessary, and also [203]help load man or beast. Lost property [204]must be restored to its owner. You are required [205]to reprove the sinner but you must [206]love your fellow as yourself. You are commanded [207]to love the proselyte. Your weights and measures [208]must be accurate.

194. Lev. 5:23   199. Deut. 24:13;   204. Deut. 22:1
195. Deut. 15:8   Ex. 22:25   Ex. 23:4
     Lev. 25:35–36   201. Deut. 23:25–26   205. Lev. 19:17
196. Deut. 15:14   200. Deut. 24:15   206. Lev. 19:18
197. Ex. 22:24   202. Ex. 23:5   207. Deut. 10:19
198. Deut. 23:21   203. Deut. 22:4   208. Lev. 19:36.

Family

Respect the [209]wise, [210]honor and [211]fear your parents. You should [212]perpetuate the human race by marrying [213]according to the law. A bridegroom is to [214]rejoice with his bride for one year. Male children must [215]be circumcised. Should a man die childless his brother must either [216]marry his widow or [217]release her (*halizah*). He who violates a virgin must [218]marry her and may never divorce her. If a man unjustly accuses his wife of premarital promiscuity [219]he shall be flogged, and may never divorce her. The seducer [220]must be punished according to the law. The female captive must be [221]treated in accordance with her special regulations. Divorce can be executed [222]only by means of written document. A woman suspected of adultery [223]has to submit to the required test.

209. Lev. 19:32	215. Gen. 17:10	219. Deut. 22:18–19
210. Ex. 20:12	Lev. 12:3	220. Ex. 22:15–23
211. Lev. 19:3	216. Deut. 25:5	221. Deut. 21:11
212. Gen. 1:28	217. Deut. 25:9	222. Deut. 24:1
213. Deut. 24:1	218. Deut. 22:29	223. Num. 5:15–27
214. Deut. 24:5		

Judicial

When required by the law [224]you must administer the punishment of flogging and you must [225]exile the unwitting homicide. Capital punishment shall be by [226]the sword, [227]strangulation, [228]fire, or [229]stoning, as specified. In some cases the body of the executed [230]shall be hanged, but it [231]must be brought to burial the same day.

224. Deut. 25:2	227. Lev. 21:16	230. Deut. 21:22
225. Num. 35:25	228. Lev. 20:14	231. Deut. 21:23
226. Ex. 21:20	229. Deut. 22:24	

Slaves

Hebrew slaves [232]must be treated according to the special laws for them. The master should [233]marry his Hebrew maidservant or [234]redeem her. The alien slave [235]must be treated according to the regulation applying to him.

232. Ex. 21:2	234. Ex. 21:8	235. Lev. 25:46
233. Ex. 21:8		

Torts

The applicable law must be administered in the case of injury caused by [236]a person, [237]an animal or [238]a pit. Thieves [239]must be punished. You must render judgment in cases of

[240]trespass by cattle, [241]arson, [242]embezzlement by an unpaid guardian and in claims against [243]a paid guardian, a hirer, or [244]a borrower. Judgment must also be rendered in disputes arising out of [245]sales, [248]inheritance and [246]other matters generally. You are required to [247]rescue the persecuted even if it means killing his oppressor.

236. Ex. 21:18	241. Ex. 22:5	245. Lev. 25:14
237. Ex. 21:28	242. Ex. 22:6–8	246. Ex. 22:8
238. Ex. 21:33-34	243. Ex. 22:9–12	247. Deut. 25:12
239. Ex. 21:37–22:3	244. Ex. 22:13	248. Num. 27:8
240. Ex. 22:4		

Prohibitions

Idolatry and Related Practices

It is [1]forbidden to believe in the existence of any but the One God.

You may not make images [2]for yourself or [3]for others to worship or for [4]any other purpose.

You must not worship anything but God either in [5]the manner prescribed for His or [6]in its own manner of worship.

Do not [7]sacrifice children to Molech.

You may not [8]practice necromancy or [9]resort to "familiar spirits" neither should you take idolatry or its mythology [10]seriously. It is forbidden to construct a [11]pillar or [12]dais even for the worship of God or to [13]plant trees in the Temple.

You may not [14]swear by idols or instigate an idolator to do so, nor may you encourage or persuade any [15]non-Jew or [16]Jew to worship idols.

You must not [17]listen to or love anyone who disseminates idolatry nor [18]should you withhold yourself from hating him. Do not [19]pity such a person. If somebody tries to convert you to idolatry [20]do not defend him or [21]conceal the fact.

It is forbidden to [22]derive any benefit from the ornaments of idols. You may not [23]rebuild that which has been destroyed as a punishment for idolatry nor may you [24]have any benefit from its wealth. Do not [25]use anything connected with idols or idolatry.

It is forbidden [26]to prophecy in the name of idols of prophecy [27]falsely in the name of God. Do not [28]listen to the one who prophesies for idols and do not [29]fear the false prophet or hinder his execution.

You must not [30]imitate the ways of idolators or practice their customs, [31]divination, [32]soothsaying, [33]enchanting, [34]sorcery, [35]charming, [36]consulting ghosts or [37]familiar spirits and [38]necromancy are forbidden. Women must not [39]wear male clothing nor men [40]that of women. Do not [41]tattoo yourself in the manner of the idolators.

You may not wear [42]garments made of both wool and linen nor may you shave (with a razor) the sides of [43]your head or [44]your beard. Do not [45]lacerate yourself over your dead.

1. Ex. 20:3	18. Deut. 13:9	33. Deut. 18:10–11
2. Ex. 20:4	19. Deut. 13:9	Deut. 10:26
3. Lev. 19:4	20. Deut. 13:9	34. Deut. 18:10–11
4. Ex. 20:20	21. Deut. 13:9	35. Deut. 18:10–11
5. Ex. 20:5	22. Deut. 7:25	36. Deut. 18:10-11
6. Ex. 20:5	23. Deut. 13:17	37. Deut. 18:10–11
7. Lev. 18:21	24. Deut. 13:18	38. Deut. 18:10–11
8. Lev. 19:31	25. Deut. 7:26	39. Deut. 22:5
9. Lev. 19:31	26. Deut. 18:20	40. Deut. 22:5
10. Lev. 19:4	27. Deut. 18:20	41. Lev. 19:28
11. Deut. 16:22	28. Deut. 13:3,4	42. Deut. 22:11
12. Lev. 20:1	Deut. 13:4	43. Lev. 19:27
13. Deut. 16:21	29. Deut. 18:22	44. Lev. 19:27
14. Ex. 23:13	30. Lev. 20:23	45. Deut. 16:1
15. Ex. 23:13	31. Lev. 19:26	Deut. 14:1
16. Deut. 13:12	Deut. 18:10	also Lev. 19:28
17. Deut. 13:9	32. Deut. 18:10	

Prohibitions Resulting from Historical Events

It is forbidden to return to Egypt to [46]dwell there permanently or to [47]indulge in impure thoughts or sights. You may not [48]make a pact with the seven Canaanite nations or [49]save the life of any member of them. Do not [50]show mercy to idolators, [51]permit them to dwell in the land of Israel or [52]intermarry with them. A Jewess may not [53]marry an Ammonite or Moabite even if he converts to Judaism but should not refuse (for reasons of genealogy alone) [54]a descendant of Esau or [55]an Egyptian who are proselytes. It is prohibited to [56]make peace with the Ammonite or Moabite nations.

The [57]destruction of fruit trees even in times of war is forbidden as is wanton waste at any time. Do not [58]fear the enemy and do not [59]forget the evil done by Amalek.

46. Deut. 17:16	50. Deut. 7:2	55. Deut. 23:8
47. Num. 15:39	51. Ex. 23:33	56. Deut. 23:7
48. Ex. 23:32;	52. Deut. 7:3	57. Deut. 20:19
Deut. 7:2	53. Deut. 23:4	58. Deut. 7:21
49. Deut. 20:16	54. Deut. 23:8	59. Deut. 25:19

Blasphemy

You must not [60]blaspheme the Holy Name, [61]break an oath made by it, [62]take It in vain or, [63]profane It. Do not [64]try the Lord God.

You may not [65]erase God's name from the holy texts or destroy institutions devoted to His worship. Do not [66]allow the body of one hanged to remain so overnight.

60. Lev. 24:16	62. Ex. 20:7	65. Deut. 12:4
rather Ex. 22:27	63. Lev. 22:32	66. Deut. 21:23
61. Lev. 19:12	64. Deut. 6:16	

Temple

Be not [67]lax in guarding the Temple.

The high priest must not enter the Temple [68]indiscriminately; a priest with a physical blemish may not [69]enter there at all or [70]serve in the sanctuary and even if the blemish is of a temporary nature he may not [71]participate in the service there until it has passed.

The Levites and the priests must not [72]interchange in their functions. Intoxicated persons may not [73]enter the sanctuary or teach the Law. It is forbidden for [74]non-priests, [75]unclean priests or [76]priests who have performed the necessary ablution but are still within the time limit of their uncleanness to serve in the Temple. No unclean person may enter [77]the Temple or [78]the Temple Mount.

The altar must not be made of [79]hewn stones nor may the ascent to it be by [80]steps. The fire on it may not be [81]extinguished nor may any other but the specified incense be [82]burned on the golden altar. You may not [83]manufacture oil with the same ingredients and in the same proportions as the annointing oil which itself [84]may not be misused. Neither may you [85]compound incense with the same ingredients and in the same proportions as that burnt on the altar. You must not [86]remove the staves from the Ark, [87]remove the breastplate from the ephod or [88]make any incision in the upper garment of the high priest.

67. Num. 18:5
68. Lev. 16:2
69. Lev. 21:23
70. Lev. 21:17
71. Lev. 21:18
72. Num. 18:3
73. Lev. 10:9-11
74. Num. 18:4

75. Lev. 22:2
76. Lev. 21:6
77. Num. 5:3
78. Deut. 23:11
79. Ex. 20:25
80. Ex. 20:26
81. Lev. 6:6

82. Ex. 30:9
83. Ex. 30:32
84. Ex. 30:32
85. Ex. 30:37
86. Ex. 25:15
87. Ex. 28:28
88. Ex. 28:32

Sacrifices

It is forbidden to [89]offer sacrifices or [90]slaughter consecrated animals outside the Temple. You may not [91]sanctify, [92]slaughter, [93]sprinkle the blood of or [94]burn the inner parts of a blemished animal even if the blemish is [95]of a temporary nature and even if it is [96]offered by Gentiles. It is forbidden to [97]inflict a blemish on an animal consecrated for sacrifice.

Leaven or honey may not [98]be offered on the altar, neither may [99]anything unsalted. An animal received as the hire of a harlot or as the price of a dog [100]may not be offered.

Do not [101]kill an animal and its young on the same day.

It is forbidden to use [102]olive oil or [103]frankincense in the sin offering or [104], [105], in the jealousy offering (sotah). You may not [106]substitute sacrifices even [107]from one category to the other. You may not [108]redeem the firstborn of permitted animals. It is forbidden to [109]sell the tithe of the herd or [110]sell or [111]redeem a field consecrated by the herem vow.

When you slaughter a bird for a sin offering you may not [112]split its head.

It is forbidden to [113]work with or [114]to shear a consecrated animal. You must not slaughter the paschal lamb [115]while there is still leaven about; nor may you leave overnight [116]those parts that are to be offered up or [117]to be eaten. You may not leave any part of the festive offering [118]until the third day or any part of [119]the second paschal lamb or [120]the thanksgiving offering until the morning.

It is forbidden to break a bone of [121]the first or [122]the second paschal lamb or [123]to carry their flesh out of the house where it is being eaten. You must not [124]allow the remains of the meal offering to become leaven. It is also forbidden to eat the paschal lamb [125]raw or sodden or to allow [126]an alien resident, [127]an uncircumcised person or an [128]apostate to eat of it.

A ritually unclean person [129]must not eat of holy things nor may [130]holy things which have become unclean be eaten. Sacrificial meat [131]which is left after the time-limit or [132]which was slaughtered with wrong intentions must not be eaten. The heave offering must not be eaten by [133]a non-priest, [134]a priest's sojourner or hired worker, [135]an uncircumcised person, or[136]an unclean priest. The daughter of a priest who is married to a non-priest may not [137]eat of holy things. The meal offering of the priest [138]must not be eaten, neither may [139]the flesh of the sin offerings sacrificed within the sanctuary or [140]consecrated animals which have become blemished.

You may not eat the second tithe of [141]corn, [142]wine, or [143]oil or [144]unblemished firstlings outside Jerusalem. The priests may not eat the [145]sin-offerings of the trespass-offerings outside the Temple courts or [146]the flesh of the burnt-offering at all. The lighter sacrifices [147]may not be eaten before the blood has been sprinkled. A non-priest may not [148]eat of the holiest sacrifices and a priest [149]may not eat the first-fruits outside the Temple courts.

One may not eat [150]the second tithe while in a state of impurity or [151]in mourning; its redemption money [152]may not be used for anything other than food and drink.

You must not [153]eat untithed produce or [154]change the order of separating the various tithes.

Do not [155]delay payment of offerings—either freewill or obligatory—and do not [156]come to the Temple on the pilgrim festivals without an offering.

Do not [157]break your word.

89. Deut. 12:13
90. Lev. 17:3–4
91. Lev. 22:20
92. Lev. 22:22
93. Lev. 22:24
94. Lev. 22:22
95. Deut. 17:1
96. Lev. 22:25
97. Lev. 22:21
98. Lev. 2:11
99. Lev. 2:13
100. Deut. 23:19
101. Lev. 22:28
102. Lev. 5:11
103. Lev. 5:11
104. Num. 5:15
105 Num. 5:15
106. Lev. 27:10
107. Lev. 27:26
108. Num. 18:17
109. Lev. 27:33
110. Lev. 27:28
111. Lev. 27:28
112. Lev. 5:8
113. Deut. 15:19
114. Deut. 15:19
115. Ex. 34:25
116. Ex. 23:10
117. Ex. 12:10
118. Deut. 16:4
119. Num. 9:13
120. Lev. 22:30
121. Ex. 12:46
122. Num. 9:12
123. Ex. 12:46
124. Lev. 6:10
125. Ex. 12:9
126. Ex. 12:45
127. Ex. 12:48
128. Ex. 12:43
129. Lev. 12:4
130. Lev. 7:19
131. Lev. 19:6–8
132. Lev. 7:18
133. Lev. 22:10
134. Lev. 22:10
135. Lev. 22:10
136. Lev. 22:4

137. Lev. 22:12	144. Deut. 12:17	151. Deut. 26:14
138. Lev. 6:16	145. Deut. 12:17	152. Deut. 26:14
139. Lev. 6:23	146. Deut. 12:17	153. Lev. 22:15
140. Deut. 14:3	147. Deut. 12:17	154. Ex. 22:28
141. Deut. 12:17	148. Deut. 12:17	155. Deut. 23:22
142. Deut. 12:17	149. Ex. 29:33	156. Ex. 23:15
143. Deut. 12:17	150. Deut. 26:14	157. Num. 30:3

Priests

A priest may not marry [158]a harlot, [159]a woman who has been profaned from the priesthood, or [160]a divorcee; the high priest must not [161]marry a widow or [162]take one as a concubine. Priests may not enter the sanctuary with [163]overgrown hair of the head or [164]with torn clothing; they must not [165]leave the courtyard during the Temple service. An ordinary priest may not render himself [166]ritually impure except for those relatives specified, and the high priest should not become impure [167]for anybody in [168]any way.

The tribe of Levi shall have no part in [169]the division of the land of Israel or [170]in the spoils of war.

It is forbidden [171]to make oneself bald as a sign of mourning for one's dead.

158. Lev. 21:7	163. Lev. 10:6	168. Lev. 21:11
159. Lev. 21:7	164. Lev. 10:6	169. Deut. 18:1
160. Lev. 21:7	165. Lev. 10:7	170. Deut. 18:1
161. Lev. 21:14	166. Lev. 21:1	171. Deut. 14:1
162. Lev. 21:15	167. Lev. 21:11	

Dietary Laws

A Jew may not eat [172]unclean cattle, [173]unclean fish, [174]unclean fowl, [175]creeping things that fly, [176]creatures that creep on the ground, [177]reptiles, [178]worms found in fruit or produce or [179]any detestable creature.

An animal that has died naturally [180]is forbidden for consumption as is [181]a torn or mauled animal. One must not eat [182]any limb taken from a living animal. Also prohibited is [183]the sinew of the thigh (*gid ha-nasheh*) as is [184]blood and [185]certain types of fat (*helev*). It is forbidden [186]to cook meat together with milk or [187]eat of such a mixture. It is also forbidden to eat [188]of an ox condemned to stoning (even should it have been properly slaughtered).

One may not eat [189]bread made of new corn or the new corn itself, either [190]roasted or [191]green, before the *omer* offering has been brought on the 16th of Nisan. You may not eat [192]orlah or [193]the growth of mixed planting in the vineyard. Any use of [194]wine libations to idols is prohibited, as is [195]gluttony and drunkenness.One may not eat anything on [196]the Day of Atonement. During Passover it is forbidden to eat [197]leaven (hamez) or [198]anything containing an admixture of such. This is also forbidden [199]after the middle of the 14th of Nisan (the day before Passover). During Passover no leaven may be [200]seen or [201]found in your possession.

172. Deut. 14:7	183. Gen. 32:33	193. Deut. 22:9
173. Lev. 11:11	184. Lev. 7:26	194. Deut. 32:38
174. Lev. 11:13	185. Lev. 7:23	195. Lev. 19:26
175. Deut. 14:19	186. Ex. 23:19	Deut. 21:20
176. Lev. 11:41	187. Ex. 34:26	196. Lev. 23:29
177. Lev. 11:44	188. Ex. 21:28	197. Ex. 13:3
178. Lev. 11:42	189. Lev. 23:14	198. Ex. 13:20
179. Lev. 11:43	190. Lev. 23:14	199. Deut. 16:3
180. Deut. 14:21	191. Lev. 23:14	200. Ex. 13:7
181. Ex. 22:30	192. Lev. 19:23	201. Ex. 12:19
182. Deut. 12:23		

Nazirites

A Nazirite may not drink [202]wine or any beverage made from grapes; he may not eat [203]fresh grapes, [204]dried grapes, [205]grape seeds or [206]grape peel. He may not render himself [207]ritually impure for his dead nor may he [208]enter a tent in which there is a corpse. He must not [209]shave his hair.

202. Num. 6:3	205. Num. 6:4	208. Lev. 21:11
203. Num. 6:3	206. Num. 6:4	209. Num. 6:5
204. Num. 6:3	207. Num. 6:7	

Agriculture

It is forbidden [210]to reap the whole of a field without leaving the corners for the poor, it is also forbidden to [211]gather up the ears of corn that fall during reaping or to harvest [212]the misformed clusters of grapes, or [213]the grapes that fall or to [214]return to take a forgotten sheaf.

You must not [215]sow different species of seed together or [216]corn in a vineyard; it is also forbidden to [217]crossbreed different species of animals or [218]work with two different species yoked together.

You must not [219]muzzle an animal working in a field to prevent it from eating.

It is forbidden to [220]till the earth, [221]to prune trees, [222]to reap (in the usual manner) produce or [223]fruit which has grown without cultivation in the seventh year (*shemittah*). One may also not [224]till the earth or prune trees in the Jubilee year, when it is also forbidden to harvest (in the usual manner)[225]produce or [226]fruit that has grown without cultivation.

One may not[227]sell one's landed inheritance in the land of Israel permanently or [228]change the lands of the Levites or [229]leave the Levites without support.

210. Lev. 23:22	217. Lev. 19:19	224. Lev. 25:11
211. Lev. 19:9	218. Deut. 22:10	225. Lev. 25:11
212. Lev. 19:10	219. Deut. 25:4	226. Lev. 25:11
213. Lev. 19:10	220. Lev. 25:4	227. Lev. 25:23
214. Deut. 24:19	221. Lev. 25:4	228. Lev. 25:33
215. Lev. 19:19	222. Lev. 25:5	229. Deut. 12:19
216. Deut. 22:9	223. Lev. 25:5	

Loans, Business, and the Treatment of Slaves

It is forbidden to [230]demand repayment of a loan after the seventh year, you may not, however, [231]refuse to lend to the poor because that year is approaching. Do not [232]deny charity to the poor or [233]send a Hebrew slave away empty-handed when he finishes his period of service. Do not [234]dun your debtor when you know that he cannot pay. It is forbidden to [235]lend to or [236]borrow from another Jew at interest or [237]participate in an agreement involving interest either as a guarantor, witness, or writer of the contract. Do not [238]delay payment of wages.

You may not [239]take a pledge from a debtor by violence, [240]keep a poor man's pledge when he needs it, [241]take any pledge from a widow or [242]from any debtor if he earns his living with it.

Kidnaping [243]a Jew is forbidden.

Do not [244]steal or [245]rob by violence. Do not [246]remove a landmarker or [247]defraud.

It is forbidden [248]to deny receipt of a loan or a deposit or [249]to swear falsely regarding another man's property.

You must not [250]deceive anybody in business. You may not [251]mislead a man even verbally. It is forbidden to harm the stranger among you [252]verbally or [253]do him injury in trade. You may not [254]return or [255]otherwise take advantage of, a slave who has fled to the land of Israel from his master, even if his master, is a Jew.

Do not [256]afflict the widow or the orphan. You may not [257]misuse or [258]sell a Hebrew slave; do not [259]treat him cruelly or [260]allow a heathen to mistreat him. You must not [261]sell your Hebrew maidservant or, if you marry her, [262]withhold food, clothing, and conjugal rights from her. You must not [263]sell a female captive or [264]treat her as a slave.

Do not [265]covet another man's possessions even if you are willing to pay for them. Even [266]the desire alone is forbidden.

A worker must not [267]cut down standing corn during his work or [268]take more fruit than he can eat.

One must not [269]turn away from a lost article which is to be returned to its owner nor may you [270]refuse to help a man or an animal which is collapsing under its burden.

It is forbidden to [271]defraud with weights and measures or even [272]to possess inaccurate weights.

230. Deut. 15:2	245. Lev. 19:13	259. Lev. 25:43
231. Deut. 15:9	246. Deut. 19:14	260. Lev. 25:53
232. Deut. 15:7	247. Lev. 19:13	261. Ex. 21:8
233. Deut. 15:13	248. Lev. 19:11	262. Ex. 21:10
234. Ex. 22:24	249. Lev. 19:11	263. Deut. 21:14
235. Lev. 25:37	250. Lev. 25:14	264. Deut. 21:14
236. Deut. 23:20	251. Lev. 25:17	265. Ex. 20:17
237. Ex. 22:24	252. Ex. 22:20	266. Deut. 5:18
238. Lev. 19:13	253. Ex. 22:20	267. Deut. 23:26
239. Deut. 24:10	254. Deut. 23:16	268. Deut. 23:25
240. Deut. 24:12	255. Deut. 23:17	269. Deut. 22:3
241. Deut. 24:17	256. Ex. 22:21	270. Ex. 23:5
242. Deut. 24:6	257. Lev. 25:39	271. Lev. 19:35
243. Ex. 20:13	258. Lev. 25:42	272. Deut. 25:13
244. Lev. 19:11		

Justice

A judge must not [273]perpetrate injustice, [274]accept bribes or be [275]partial or [276]afraid. He may [277]not favor the poor or [278]discriminate against the wicked; he should not [279]pity the condemned or [280]pervert the judgment of strangers or orphans.

It is forbidden to [281]hear one litigant without the other being present. A capital case cannot be decided by [282]a majority of one.

A judge should not [283]accept a colleague's opinion unless he is convinced of its correctness; it is forbidden to [284]appoint as a judge someone who is ignorant of the law.

Do not [285]give false testimony or accept [286]testimony from a wicked person or from [287]relatives of a person involved in the case. It is forbidden to pronounce judgment [288]on the basis of the testimony of one witness.

Do not [289]murder.

You must not convict on [290]circumstantial evidence alone.

A witness [291]must not sit as a judge in capital cases.

You must not [292]execute anybody without due proper trial and conviction.

Do not [293]pity or spare the pursuer.

Punishment is not to be inflicted for [294]an act committed under duress.

Do not accept ransom [295]for a murderer or [296]a manslayer.

Do not [297]hesitate to save another person from danger and do not [298]leave a stumbling block in the way or [299]mislead another person by giving wrong advice.

It is forbidden [300]to administer more than the assigned number of lashes to the guilty.

Do not [301]tell tales or [302]bear hatred in your heart. It is forbidden to [303]shame a Jew, [304]to bear a grudge or [305]to take revenge.

Do not [306]take the dam when you take the young birds.

It is forbidden to [307]shave a leprous scall or [308]remove other signs of that affliction. It is forbidden [309]to cultivate a valley in which a slain body was found and in which subsequently the ritual of breaking the heifer's neck (*eglah arufah*) was performed.

Do not [310]suffer a witch to live.

Do not [311]force a bridegroom to perform military service during the first year of his marriage. It is forbidden to [312]rebel against the transmitters of the tradition or to [313]add or [314]detract from the precepts of the law.

Do not curse [315]a judge, [316]a ruler or [317]any Jew.

Do not [318]curse or [319]strike a parent.

It is forbidden to [320]work on the Sabbath or [321]walk further than the permitted limits (*eruv*). You may not [322]inflict punishment on the Sabbath.

It is forbidden to work on [323]the first or [324]the seventh day of Passover, on [325]Shavuot, on [326]Rosh HaShanah, on the [327]first and [328]eighth (*Shemini Azeret*) days of Sukkot and [329]on the Day of Atonement.

273. Lev. 19:15
274. Ex. 23:8
275. Lev. 19:15
276. Deut. 1:17
277. Lev. 19:15,
      rather Ex. 23:3
278. Ex. 23:6
279. Deut. 19:13
280. Deut. 24:17
281. Ex. 23:1
282. Ex. 23:2
283. Ex. 23:2
284. Deut. 1:17
285. Ex. 20:16
286. Ex. 23:1
287. Deut. 24:16
288. Deut. 19:15
289. Ex. 20:13
290. Ex. 23:7
291. Num. 35:30
292. Num. 35:12
293. Deut. 25:12
294. Deut. 22:26
295. Num. 35:31
296. Num. 35:32
297. Lev. 19:16
298. Deut. 22:8
299. Lev. 19:14
300. Deut. 25:23
301. Lev. 19:16
302. Lev. 19:17
303. Lev. 19:17
304. Lev. 19:18
305. Lev. 19:18
306. Deut. 22:6
307. Lev. 13:33
308. Deut. 24:8
309. Deut. 21:4
310. Ex. 22:17
311. Deut. 24:5
312. Deut. 17:11
313. Deut. 13:1
314. Deut. 13:1
315. Ex. 22:27
316. Ex. 22:27
317. Lev. 19:14
318. Ex. 21:17
319. Ex. 21:15
320. Ex. 20:10
321. Ex. 16:29
322. Ex. 35:3
323. Ex. 12:16
324. Ex. 12:16
325. Lev. 23:21
326. Lev. 23:25
327. Lev. 23:35
328. Lev. 23:36
329. Lev. 23:28

Incest and Other Forbidden Relationships

It is forbidden to enter into an incestuous relationship with one's [330]mother, [331]step-mother, [332]sister, [333]half-sister, [334]son's daughter, [335]daughter's daughter, [336]daughter, [337]any woman and her daughter, [338]any woman and her son's daughter, [339]any woman and her daughter's daughter, [340]father's sister, [341]mother's sister, [342]paternal uncle's wife, [343]daughter-in-law, [344]brother's wife and [345]wife's sister.

It is also forbidden to [346]have sexual relations with a menstruous woman.

Do not [347]commit adultery.

It is forbidden for [348]a man or [349]a woman to have sexual intercourse with an animal.

Homosexuality [350]is forbidden, particularly with [351]one's father or [352]uncle.

It is forbidden to have [353]intimate physical contact (even without actual intercourse) with any of the women with whom intercourse is forbidden.

A *mamzer* may not [354]marry a Jewess.

Harlotry [355]is forbidden.

A divorcee may not be [356]remarried to her first husband if, in the meanwhile, she had married another.

A childless widow may not [357]marry anybody other than her late husband's brother.

A man may not [358]divorce a wife whom he married after having raped her or [359]after having slandered her.

An eunuch may not [360]marry a Jewess.

Castration [361]is forbidden.

330. Lev. 18:7	341. Lev. 18:13	352. Lev. 18:14
331. Lev. 18:8	342. Lev. 18:14	353. Lev. 18:6
332. Lev. 18:9	343. Lev. 18:15	354. Deut. 23:3
333. Lev. 18:11	344. Lev. 18:16	355. Deut. 23:18
334. Lev. 18:10	345. Lev. 18:18	356. Deut. 24:4
335. Lev. 18:10	346. Lev. 18:19	357. Deut. 25:5
336. Lev. 18:10	347. Lev. 18:20	358. Deut. 22:29
337. Lev. 18:17	348. Lev. 18:23	359. Deut. 22:19
338. Lev. 18:17	349. Lev. 18:23	360. Deut. 23:2
339. Lev. 18:17	350. Lev. 18:22	361. Lev. 22:24
340. Lev. 18:12	351. Lev. 18:7	

The Monarchy

You may not [362]elect as king anybody who is not of the seed of Israel.

The king must not accumulate an excessive number of [363]horses, [364]wives, or [365]wealth.

362. Deut. 17:15	364. Deut. 17:17	365. Deut. 17:17
363. Deut. 17:16		

Key to Abbreviations: Ex.—Exodus, Deut.—Deuteronomy, Lev.—Leviticus, Num.—Numbers, Gen.—Genesis.

Seven Rabbinic Commandments

In addition to the 613 commandments in the Torah, there are an additional seven commandments that were later added by our rabbis. These innovative commandments were to be accompanied by a special blessing:

1. Saying a blessing before experiencing pleasure in worldly items, for example, before partaking of any food, before smelling fragrant plant, and so forth.
2. Washing hands before partaking of a meal.
3. Lighting Sabbath and festival candles.
4. Saying the *Hallel* psalms of praise.

5. Lighting a *chanukiah* on the festival of Chanukah.
6. Reading the *Megillah* on Purim.
7. Making an *eruv* (a technical term for the rabbinical provision that permits the alleviation of certain Sabbath restrictions).

Famous Sayings from *Ethics of the Fathers*

Ethics of the Fathers is a book of ethical principles set forth by the sages of 450 B.C.E. to 200 C.E. It is one of the most popular books of the Talmud and is included in many editions of the prayer book. Here are several well-known sayings from *Ethics of the Fathers*.

Simeon the Just: The world is based on three principles—Torah, worship, and the performance of good deeds.

Hillel: If I am not for myself, who will be for me? But if I am for myself alone, what am I? And not now, when?

Hillel: Do not separate yourself from the community.

Rabbi Tarfon: The day is short, the task is great, human beings are lazy, the reward is great, and the Master is urgent.

Rabbi Hanina ben Dosa: Anyone who is liked by his fellow men is liked by God; anyone who is not liked by his fellow men is not liked by God.

Rabbi Akiva: Everything is foreseen by God, yet free will is granted to people.

Ben Azzai: Run to perform even a minor *mitzvah*. One good deed brings another good deed.

Some say: There are four characters among people: The person who says: "What is mine is mine, and what is yours is yours" is the average type. The person who says: "What is mine is yours, and what is yours is mine" is ignorant. The person who says: "What is mine is yours, and what is yours is yours" is godly. And the person who says: "What is yours is mine, and what is mine is mine" is wicked.

Rabbi Simon: There are three crowns—the crown of Torah, the crown of priesthood, and the crown of royalty; but the crown of a good name excels them all.

Judah ben Tema: Be bold as a leopard, light as an eagle, swift as a deer, and strong as a lion, to do the will of God in heaven.

Ancient Cures for Diseases

The Talmud, the rabbinic interpretation of the Bible, is filled with many different remedies for diseases. The following are some of the most fascinating remedies for a variety of disorders:

Disorder Asthma
Cure Take three wheat cakes soaked in honey. Eat them and drink undiluted wine. (*Gittin* 69b)

Disorder Bad breath
Cure Eat salt after eating food and after drinking a beverage drink water. (*Berakhot* 40a)

Disorder Coughing
Cure Drink fish oil. (*Divrei Chayyim* II, 52)

Disorder Dog bite
Cure Eat the liver of a mad dog. (*Yoma* 83a)

Disorder Eye infection
Cure Eat fish. (*Nedarim* 54b)

Disorder Fever
Cure Eat radishes. (*Avodah Zarah* 28b)

Disorder Heartburn
Cure Eat black cumin. (*Berakhot* 40a)

Disorder Indigestion
Cure Take 300 grains of long pepper and drink 100 of them each day with wine. (*Gittin* 69b)

Disorder Nosebleed
Cure Take a Kohen whose name is Levi and write his name backwards. (*Gittin* 69a)

Disorder Tapeworms
Cure Eat bread in the morning. (*Bava Metzia* 107b)

Disorder Toothache
Cure Take the top of a garlic with one stalk and grind it with oil and salt. Put it on your tooth and put a piece of dough around it. (*Gittin* 69a)

Occupations of Talmudic Rabbis

Many people believe that the ancient sages were involved only with the study of the Torah. The fact is that many sages had other professions form which they made a living. Here are several famous rabbis and their occupations:

Rabbi Joseph	locksmith
Rav Sheshet	wood carrier
Rabbi Jose	net maker
Rabbi Meir	secretary
Rabbi Yochanan	shoemaker
Rav Papa	brewer
Rav Adah Sabulah	pearl diver
Rabbi Yehudah	baker
Hillel	woodcutter
Shammai	carpenter
Rabbi Chanina	shoemaker
Rabbi Simon ben Lakish	circus performer
Abba Saul	grave digger
Abba ben Abba	silk dealer
Yitzchak Nafcha	blacksmith
Rabbi Meir	scribe
Rabbi Chalafta	leather maker

Rabbinic Quotes about the Diet

It is a religious duty in Judaism for a person to keep healthy.
Throughout the Talmud there are many quotes and sugges-
tions related to keeping healthy by eating the proper foods.
Here are some of the more interesting rabbinic quotes relating
to health and diet:

- Crying chases away the appetite. (*Eichah Rabbah* I).
- Eating until one is satisfied brings sleep (*Yoma* 18).
- Food should be appetizing as well as nourishing
  (*Yoma* 74).
- Talking while eating may cause choking, as may
  eating while lying on one's back or reclining on one's
  right (*Taanit* 5; *Pesachim* 108).
- Cutting one's food and eating it is much better than
  biting off pieces and swallowing them (*Berakhot* 74).
- A meal without soup is not a meal (*Berakhot* 44).
- More people die from overeating than from hunger
  (*Shabbat* 33a).
- One should not eat meat twice a day (*Yoma* 75).
- Bread with salt in the morning and plenty of water
  will banish all sickness (*Bava Kamma* 92b).
- Before the Flood, human beings were vegetarians
  (*Sanhedrin* 159b).
- Raw vegetables that are eaten in the morning cause
  bad breath (*Berakhot* 44b).
- Sweet apples are a cure for almost every sickness
  (*Zohar* III, 74).

Ancient Rabbinic Weather
Forecasting

In an agricultural society, knowing weather patterns was of
great importance. Here is a sampling of some interesting
weather-related rabbinic statements:

Talmud Bava Batra 147a

Abba Saul said: Fine weather during Shavuot is a good sign for the year.

Rabbi Zebid said: If the first day of the New year is warm, all the year will be warm; if cold, the year will be a cold one.

The east wind is always beneficial; the west wind is always harmful; the north wind is beneficial for wheat that has reached the stage of a third of its maturity and harmful for olives that are in blossom. The south wind is injurious for wheat that has reached the stage of a third of its maturity and beneficial for olives in blossom.

Our rabbis taught: If the weather on Shavuot is fine, sow wheat.

Prohibited Activities on the Sabbath

The Torah commands the Israelites to set aside a day of rest, called the Sabbath. But it gives us very few clues as to what refraining from any work on the Sabbath really means. In the talmudic tractate *Shabbat*, the ancient rabbis defined work as all of those activities that were associated with building the portable sanctuary in the desert. Here is a summary of those prohibited categories of work:

I. Growing and preparing food

Ploughing
Sowing
Reaping
Stacking sheaves
Threshing
Winnowing
Selecting out the chaff
Sifting

Grinding
Kneading
Baking

II. Making clothing

Sheepshearing
Bleaching
Combining raw materials
Dyeing
Spinning
Threading a loom
Weaving
Removing a finished article
Separating threads
Tying Knots
Untying Knots
Sewing
Tearing

III. Leatherwork and writing

Trapping an animal
Slaughtering
Flaying skins
Tanning
Scraping
Marking out
Cutting
Writing
Erasing

IV. Providing Shelter

Building
Demolishing

V. Creating fire

Kindling a fire
Extinguishing a fire

VI. Completing work

Putting the final hammer blow on a manufactured object

VII. Transporting goods

Carrying goods in a public place

JEWS IN AMERICA

When Columbus sailed for the New World in 1492, at least five Jews went with him. They were the first of many Jewish men and women who would come to America in search of a different life.

The first Jews to settle in America reached New Amsterdam in 1645. Today, Jews in the United States can look with pride at more than three centuries of accomplishment. Here is a listing of some of those Jewish men and women who played a vital role in the history of America:

Patriotism

Bernard Gratz (1738–1811) One of the key figures in the opening of the West to trade and settlement.

Asser Levy (d. 1681) Member of the first group of Jews to arrive in New Amsterdam in September 1654. He succeeded in having many restrictions on Jews lifted.

Haym Salomon (1740–1785) American financier and patriot who used his own funds to aid patriot leaders such as James Madison and Thomas Jefferson.

Francis Salvador (1747–1776) Revolutionary War hero who served in South Carolina's colonial legislature.

Religion

Cyrus Adler (1863–1940) American communal leader who was a founder and president of the American Jewish Committee and the Jewish Welfare Board.

Isaac Leeser (1806–1868) Rabbi and author who founded the first congregational Hebrew school and the Maimonides rabbis' training college.

Sabato Morais (1832–1897) He was the rabbi of the Sephardic congregation Mikveh Israel in Philadelphia. In 1886 he led in the establishment of the Conservative movement's Jewish Theological Seminary of America.

Solomon Schechter (1847–1925) First president of the Jewish Theological Seminary (1901), he developed its associated organizations such as the United Synagogue of America.

Gershom Mendes Seixas (1745–1816) Headed Congregation Shearith Israel in New York for 50 years. He was one of thirteen clergymen to participate in George Washington's first inauguration.

Isaac Mayer Wise (1819–1900) Father of Reform Judaism, he organized the Central Conference of American Rabbis. He was also the first president of the Hebrew Union College.

Stephen Samuel Wise (1874–1949) Rabbi and Zionist leader, he founded the Jewish Institute of Religion in 1922 to train Reform rabbis.

Abolition

Judah Philip Benjamin (1811–1884) American statesman who became a successful lawyer in Louisiana and was elected to the state legislature in 1842. In 1852 he became a senator.

August Bondi (1833–1907) American abolitionist who participated in the 1848 revolutionary movement. After serving through the Civil War, he held various public offices in Salina, Kansas.

Isidor Bush (1822–1898) Author, editor, and communal leader, he founded the first American Jewish weekly, called "Israel's Herald," in 1849. In the Civil War he served in the rank of captain.

David Einhorn (1809–1879) Reform rabbi who led the extreme Reform wing of American Jewry.

Political Life

Moses Alexander (1853–1932) He became governor of the state of Idaho in 1915, thus becoming the first foreign-born Jew to hold such an office in the United States.

Bernard Baruch (1870–1965) He was a leading figure in the organization of the American economy during World War 1, during which he served on various control commissions. After the war he was an economic adviser for the American Peace Commission.

Herbert Henry Lehman (1878–1963) He was Democratic lieutenant-governor in 1928 and governor of the state of New York in 1932.

Manuel Mordecai Noah (1785–1851) American diplomat and author, he became the sheriff of New York County and the publisher of several newspapers in New York.

Adolphus Simeon Solomons (1826–1910) The American Red Cross was founded in Geneva in 1881 largely as a result of his efforts. He later became the first American vice president of the International Red Cross.

The Military

Uriah P. Levy (1792–1862) American naval officer who became flag officer of the Mediterranean squadron, then the highest post in the navy.

David Marcus (1902–1948) A graduate of West point, he was appointed assistant United States attorney in the southern district of New York. He served with distinction in World War II.

Hyman Rickover (1900–1986) Nuclear energy expert who headed the Naval Reactors Branch of the Atomic Energy Commission. He was responsible for the launching of the World's first atomic submarine.

Edward S. Salomon (1836–1913) He was a brigadier general in the Union Army during the Civil War and governor of Washington territory in 1870. He was also the district attorney of San Francisco County.

Women

Rebecca Gratz (1781–1869) Founder of the Jewish Sunday School movement in Philadelphia.

Emma Lazarus (1849–1887) American poet whose sonnet "The New Colossus" is inscribed on the Statue of Liberty.

Adah Isaac Menken (1835–1868) She was an actress and star of the New York, London, and Paris stage. Her poetry attracted the interest of prominent literary figures.

Henrietta Szold (1860–1945) In 1912, she organized Hadassah, the Women's Zionist Organization in America. She was the first woman to become a member of the Zionist Executive (1927), with responsibility for education and health.

Lillian Wald (1867–1940) American social worker who founded and directed the Henry Street settlement in New York in 1933. She also pioneered the movement to establish playgrounds in America.

The Judicial System

Louis Brandeis (1856–1941) Justice of the United States Supreme Court and Zionist leader. He played a leading role in American Zionism, serving as honorary president of the Zionist Organization of America from 1918 to 1921.

Benjamin Cardozo (1870–1938) In 1914 he was named to the New York Court of Appeals and in 1932 he was elected to the Supreme Court.

Felix Frankfurter (1882–1965) Professor at Harvard Law School (1914–1939) and consultant to several American presidents. In 1939 he was elected to the Supreme Court.

Arthur Goldberg (1908–   ) A labor lawyer in Chicago, he was elected to the Supreme Court by President Kennedy in 1962. In 1977 he was appointed United States envoy to the Belgrade Conference on Human Rights.

Louis Marshall (1856–1929) American jurist and communal leader who defended civil liberties. In 1906 he founded the American Jewish Committee.

Science and Medicine

Simon Baruch (1840–1921) Physician who pioneered in surgery of the appendix. He also was well known for his research on malaria and typhoid fever.

Casimir Funk (1884–1967) A biochemist whose discovery of vitamins led to his appointment as consultant to the United States Vitamin Corporation.

Joseph Goldberger (1874–1929) American pathologist and discoverer of vitamin B_2.

Isaac Hays (1796–1879) Leading ophthalmologist and editor of the *American Journal of the Medical Sciences* who founded the American Medical Association.

Julius Oppenheimer (1904–1967) American physicist who was appointed director of the Institute for Advanced Study. He also served as chairman of the United States Atomic Energy Commission.

Jonas Salk (1914–   ) American scientist whose most well known discovery was the Salk polio vaccine that has saved thousands of lives.

Business

David Lubin (1849–1919) American agriculturalist who headed the international Institute of Agriculture.

David Sarnoff (1891–1971) American industrialist who served as president of the Radio Corporation of America (RCA) and president of the National Broadcasting Company (NBC).

Joseph Seligman (1820–1880) In 1857 he established the J. and W. Seligman banking house. At the outbreak of the Civil War, his clothing business became one of the largest suppliers to the Union Army.

Paul Warburg (1868–1932) A famous banker and philanthropist who founded the Federal Reserve System.

Music

Irving Berlin (1888–1989) Composer who wrote scores of popular American songs (including "God Bless America") and many scores for musical plays and films.

Leonard Bernstein (1918–1990) American composer and conductor, he became permanent conductor of the New York Philharmonic Orchestra in 1957. His compositions include the *Jeremiah* symphony, the ballet *Fancy Free*, and the score for the musical show *West Side Story*.

Aaron Copland (1900–1990) American composer, his compositions include symphonies, ballets, orchestral works, operas, and chamber music.

Leopold Damrosch (1832–1885) Musician and violinist of distinction who founded the Breslau Orchestral Society and the Damrosch Opera Company.

George Gershwin (1898–1937) American composer who introduced the jazz and blues styles into symphonic music.

Beverly Sills (1929–   ) Well-known American opera singer, she has sung in more than seventy operas. She retired in 1980 to become codirector of the New York City Opera.

Writers

Shalom Aleikchem (1859–1916) Great Yiddish writer and humorist whose autobiographical writings include the *Adventures of Mottel* and *The Great Fair.*

Sholem Asch (1880–1957) Yiddish novelist and playwright who arrived in America in 1910. One of his novels, *Three Cities,* describes Jewish experiences in Eastern Europe during the early 20th century.

Dorothy Parker (1893–1967) Poet and short-story writer noted for her ironic wit.

Morris Rosenfeld (1862–1923) Yiddish poet who wrote and published sad lyrics of labor.

Isaac Bashevis Singer (1904–1991) One of the most gifted writers in America, he received numerous literary awards, including the National Book Award for Children's Books (1970) and the National Book Award for Fiction (1974). He was awarded the Nobel Prize for Literature in 1978.

Art

Sir Moses Jacob Ezekiel (1844–1917) Important sculptor whose statues include those of Longfellow, Liszt, Lee, and Stonewall Jackson.

Chaim Gross (1904–   ) Noted for his wood sculptures. Gross was given the Award of Merit for Sculpture from the American Academy of Arts and Letters in 1963.

Myer Myers (1723–1796) Gifted silversmith whose works can be seen in many American museums that maintain colonial silver collections.

Ben Shahn (1898–1969) Artist noted for his outstanding graphic works among which was an illustrated Passover *Haggadah*.

Journalism

Abraham Cahan (1860–1951) Yiddish journalist and editor, he was editor in chief of New York's largest Yiddish daily, *The Forward*.

Ted Koppel (1940–   ) Famous journalist and host of the television show "Nightline."

Adolph S. Ochs (1858–1935) In 1896 he became the publisher of the *New York Times*.

Joseph Pulitzer (1847–1911) Noted newspaper owner, he established Columbia University's School of Journalism in 1903. The Pulitzer prizes for outstanding achievement in journalism, music, and literature have been awarded since 1917 under the terms of his will.

Barbara Walters (1931–   ) Famous journalist who co-hosts "20/20," a news magazine television show.

Theater

David Belasco (1853–1931) Actor, manager, and dramatist, he was a discoverer and trainer of many budding actors who later become stars.

Clifford Odets (1906–1963) Playwright whose reputation was established by the experimental, proletarian plays *Waiting for Lefty* and *Awake and Sing!*

Boris Thomashefsky (1886–1936) Yiddish actor who wrote, adapted, and acted in many successful plays performed in New York City's Yiddish theaters.

Philanthropy

Meyer Guggenheim (1828–1905) Devoted his fortune to philanthropy and to the establishment of foundations that have contributed millions of dollars over the years. The Guggenheim Museum in New York City was donated by his family.

Jacob Henry Schiff (1847–1920) Financier and philanthropist whose charities included the Semitic Museum at Harvard and the Jewish Theological Seminary of America.

Nathan Straus (1848–1931) He and his brother Isidor became heads of the R. H. Macy store in New York in 1896. He made possible the construction by Hadassah of child welfare stations and a health center in Palestine that bore his name.

Judah Touro (1775–1854) Philanthropist responsible for the preservation and maintenance of Newport's 18th-century synagogue.

Felix Warburg (1871–1937) Philanthropist and champion of social causes, he contributed to Hebrew Union College, the Jewish Theological Seminary, and other Jewish and non-Jewish educational institutions.

Sports

Ron Blomberg (1948–   ) The major league baseball's first designated hitter.

Rod Carew (1945–　　) Baseball player who had over 3,000 hits in his career.

Sidney Franklin (1903–1976) A United States matador who became the first non-Latin to win fame in the bullring.

Sid Gillman (1911–　　) A star for the Ohio State football team. He coached many teams during his 40-year career.

Alice Green (1951–　　) A three-time member of the United States Table Tennis Team.

Hank Greenberg (1911–1986) The first Jew elected to the Baseball Hall of Fame.

Abraham Hallandersky He had over 1,300 boxing matches from 1905 to 1918.

Nat Holman (1896–　　) Joined the Original Celtics in 1921 and established himself as one of the greatest players of that time. His nickname was "Mr. Basketball."

Sandy Koufax (1935–　　) Pitched for the Brooklyn Dodgers. In 1961 he refused to pitch on Yom Kippur. In 1972 he became the youngest player ever elected to the Baseball Hall of Fame.

Sid Luckman (1916–　　) An outstanding quarterback for the Chicago Bears who was voted into the Football Hall of Fame.

Barney Sedran (1891–1969) Set an all-time scoring record in 1913. Only 5'4" tall, he was elected to the Basketball Hall of Fame in 1962.

Art Shamsky (1941–　　) Played baseball for Cincinnati and the New York Mets.

Larry Sherry (1935–　　) Baseball player who led the National League with his thirteen relief victories in 1960.

Mark Spitz (1950–　　) Won seven gold medals in swimming at the 1972 Munich Olympics.

ISRAEL

Highlights of Israeli History

Middle Bronze Age (Patriarchs)	2200–1500 B.C.E.
Late Bronze Age (Moses and Joshua)	1550–1200 B.C.E.
Iron Age (Israelite)	1200–587 B.C.E.
Destruction of First Temple	587 B.C.E.
Babylonian and Persian Period	587–322 B.C.E.
Hellenic Period	322–167 B.C.E.
Hasmonean Period	167–63 B.C.E.
Roman Period	63 B.C.E.–324 C.E.
Destruction of Second Temple	70 C.E.
Byzantine Period (Christianity)	324–640 C.E.
Persian Conquest	614–628 C.E.
Arab-Moslem Period	640–1099 C.E.
Crusader Period	1099–1291 C.E.
Mameluke Period (Moslems)	1291–1516 C.E.
First Jewish Colony	1878 C.E.
First Zionist Congress	1897 C.E.
British Mandate	1917–1948 C.E.
State of Israel	May 14, 1948
Sinai Campaign	1956
Six Day War	1967
Yom Kippur War	1973

Israel's Prime Ministers

David Ben-Gurion	1948–1953
Moshe Sharett	1954–1955
David Ben-Gurion	1955–1963
Levi Eshkol	1963–1969
Golda Meir	1969–1974
Yitzchak Rabin	1974–1977
Menachem Begin	1977–1983
Yitzchak Shamir	1983–1984

Shimon Peres	1984–1986
Yitzchak Shamir	1986–1992
Yitzchak Rabin	1992–

Israel's Presidents

Chaim Weizmann	1948–1952
Yitzchak Ben Zvi	1952–1963
Zalman Shazar	1963–1973
Ephraim Katzir	1973–1978
Yitzchak Navon	1978–1983
Chaim Herzog	1983–1993
Ezer Weizman	1993–

Demographic and Geographic
Facts About Israel

Length: 280 miles

Width at widest point: 85 miles

Total area enclosed by boundaries and cease-fire lines: 10,840 square miles

Cities with more than 100,000 inhabitants

Bat Yam 133,000

Beersheba 115,000

B'nai Brak 112,000

Haifa 224,000

Holon 148,000

Jerusalem 504,000

Netanya 120,000

Petach Tikvah 135,000

Ramat Gan 116,000

Rishon LeZion 129,000

Tel Aviv–Jaffa 322,000

Major Mountain Peaks

Mt. Carmel, Haifa 1,792 feet
Mt. Hermon, Golan 9,220 feet
Mt. Meron, Upper Galilee 3,964 feet
Mount of Olives, Jerusalem 2,739 feet
Mt. Tabor, Lower Galilee 1,930 feet

Main inland waters

Dead Sea Lowest point on earth, at 1,300 feet below sea level

Gulf of Eilat one of northern branches of the Red Sea

Jordan River Flows southward from northern Galilee to the Dead Sea—a distance of 127 miles but increased by its meandering to a length of 186 miles

Sea of Galilee 695 feet below sea level, between the Golan Heights and Lower Galilee

People of Israel

Nearly 5 million people from different ethnic, cultural, and religious backgrounds—Jewish, Muslim, Christian.
Jews 81.5 percent of total population
Muslims 14.4 percent of total population
Christians 2.3 percent of total population
Druze and others 1.8 percent of total population

Twelve Important Places in Israel

The Land of Israel is the birthplace and historic homeland of the Jewish people. Here its spiritual, religious, and political identity was shaped. Here it first attained statehood, created cultural values of national and universal significance, and gave the world the Bible.

A pilgrimage to Israel has long been enshrined in the

traditions of the world's major religions. Jews, Christians, and Moslems all come to worship at their own holy shrines.

Here is a map and list of twelve important places in Israel that you may want to visit on your next trip:

1. **Tiberias** (*Teveryah*) A popular holiday resort located in the north on the west shore of the Sea of Galilee. One of the four holy cities of the Jews, Tiberias is rich in historical and religious interest. A main attraction is the synagogue, which was built in the 3rd century.

2. **Safed** (*Tzafat*) Located in the upper Galilean mountains, 22 miles from Tiberias. One of the four holy cities of the Jews and the center of the mystics, today its attractions include several old synagogues and the artists' colony.

3. **Acre** (*Akko*) From ancient times until the 19th century, Acre was the most important seaport of Palestine. Today its attractions include what remains of a Crusader city. It is located 14 miles north of Haifa on the Mediterranean Sea.

4. **Haifa** (*Chaifah*) Haifa is Israel's chief port, lying on the northern slopes of Mount Carmel. Today its attractions include the Baha'i Shrine and Garden, the Haifa Museum, the Maritime Museum, and the Carmelite (Israel's only subway).

5. **Caesarea** (*Keisaria*) This ancient city lies halfway between Tel Aviv and Haifa. Its archaeological ruins include a Roman theater that offers musical concerts in the summer. Its golf course is another popular attraction.

6. **Tel Aviv** Located some 40 miles northwest of Jerusalem on the Mediterranean Sea, Tel Aviv is the hub of Israel's commerce. Among its many places of interest are the Diaspora Museum, the Great Synagogue, the Israeli National Museum, the Carmel Market, and the Tel Aviv Museum.

7. **Ashkelon** Located 35 miles south of Tel Aviv on the Mediterranean Sea, its history goes back to the days of the Canaanites and Philistines. Its archaeological sites are popular tourist attractions, as is its large bathing beach.

8. **Jerusalem** (*Yerushalayim*) The capital of Israel, Jerusalem is undoubtedly Israel's most historic city. Among its many sights are the Bezalel Art School, the Biblical Zoo, Hebrew University, the Israel Museum, the Kennedy Memorial, the Knesset (Israel's Parliament), the Western Wall, the Yad VaShem Holocaust Museum, and Hadassah Hospital with its Chagall windows.

1. Tiberias	7. Ashkelon
2. Safed	8. Jerusalem
3. Acre	9. Dead Sea.
4. Haifa	10. Masada
5. Caesarea	11. Beersheba
6. Tel Aviv	12. Eilat

9. **Dead Sea** (*Yam Hamelach*) This is the lowest place on the earth's surface, 47 miles long and 10 miles wide. At Ein Gedi, located on the west shore, one can float in the Dead Sea and visit the hot springs.

10. **Masada** (*Metzada*) Located on the Dead Sea and rising 1,424 feet above sea level, Masada is most noted as the place where the Zealots managed to hold out against the Romans for 3 years after the fall of Jerusalem. Its sights include the archaeological remains of that stronghold, including the an-

cient synagogue where many American tourists celebrate a
Bar or Bat Mitzvah.

11. **Beersheba** (*Bersheva*) Known as the city of the patriarchs because of its many references in the Five Books of
Moses, today Beersheba has become the "capital" of the
south. Among its many attractions are the Desert Research
Institute and Ben-Gurion University.

12. **Eilat** The southernmost town of Israel, it is situated on
the northern end of the Red Sea. It is a popular tourist
attraction known for its dry, hot climate and excellent coral
beaches.

Twelve Names of Jerusalem

Jerusalem, the capital of Israel, has been known by many
different names in both biblical and postbiblical literature.
Here are some of the better-known ones:

Name	Meaning
Ariel (Isaiah 29:1)	Lion of God
Betulah (Lamentations 1:6)	Virgin
Drushah (Isaiah 62:12)	Sought after
Gilah (Isaiah 65:18)	Joy
Ir HaEmet (Zechariah 8:3)	City of the truth
Kir (Ezekiel 13:14)	City
Kiryat Hannah David (Isaiah 29:1)	City where David camped
Kiriah Ne'emanah (Isaiah 1:25)	Faithful city
Kisei Adonai (Jeremiah 3:17)	Throne of God
Moriah (Genesis 22:2)	Place I will show you
Neveh Tzedek (Jeremiah 31:22)	Righteous dwelling
Shalem (Genesis 14:18)	Peace

Jerusalem Miscellany

Jerusalem, the eternal capital of the Jewish people, has remained throughout the centuries the symbol of hope and

peace. No other place in the world incorporates the mystique and holiness of Jerusalem for the three faiths—Judaism, Christianity, and Islam. Here are some interesting facts about Jerusalem, the city of *shalom*:

- The land of Urusalim was mentioned in correspondence between the Egyptian rulers and their governors of Palestine and Syria over 3,300 years ago.
- Throughout the ages Jerusalem has been called by more than seventy different names.
- King David conquered Jebus and made it the capital in about 1000 B.C.E. (1 Chronicles 10:4–9).
- In about 950 B.C.E., King Solomon built the Temple in Jerusalem.
- Jerusalem is holy to Christians because the final chapter in the life of Jesus took place in Jerusalem.
- Jerusalem is holy to those who follow Islam because they believe that Mohammed prayed there on the sacred rock of the former Temple.
- The Old City of Jerusalem is surrounded by a wall built in 1541 by Suleiman the Magnificent, sultan of the Ottoman Empire. The wall is about 2½ miles long and has eight gates.
- In 1948, the Arabs destroyed the twenty-eight synagogues in the Old City of Jerusalem.
- In 1860, the New City of Jerusalem began to develop, thanks to the generosity of Judah Touro, an American Jew who left 60,000 dollars to Jerusalem charities.
- In 1947, about 2,500 Jews lived in the Old City of Jerusalem and 95,000 in the New City.
- Jerusalem was declared the capital of Israel on January 23, 1950.

How Israel Achieved Statehood (1838–1948)

1838   Moses Montefiore proposes founding a Jewish state.
1854   Jewish hospital established in Jerusalem.
1861   Mishkenot Sha'ananim, the first neighborhood outside Jerusalem City walls, is built.

1863   First Hebrew periodical, *Havazelet*, published.

1878   Petach Tikveh established.

1882   Large-scale immigration from Russia and Yemen begins (Known as First Aliyah).

1897   World Zionist Organization founded.

1904   Second wave of immigration to Israel begins from Poland and Russia.

1909   Deganya, Israeli's first *kibbutz*, is established.

1917   Balfour Declaration pledges British support for Jewish national home in Palestine.

1919   Third wave of immigration begins, mainly from Poland.

1924   Technion, Israel's institute of science, opens in Haifa. Fourth wave of immigration to Israel.

1925   Hebrew University established.

1933   Fifth wave of immigration, from Germany.

1940   Jews from Palestine fight with British army against Nazis.

1945   World War II ends.

1947   United Nations partition plan for Palestine is accepted by Jews but rejected by Arabs.

1948   End of British Mandate. State of Israel is officially proclaimed.

Periods of Foreign Domination of Israel

Due to its location at the junction of three continents, the Land of Israel has always been strategically important. Whoever held it controlled the trade route between East and West. Here is a brief summary of the periods of domination of foreigners of the Land of Israel:

Year (C.E.)	Conqueror
70–313	Romans
313–636	Byzantines

Year (c.e.)	Conqueror
637–1091	Arabs
1091–1098	Seljuks
1099–1291	Crusaders
1291–1516	Mamelukes
1517–1917	Ottoman Turks
1918–1948	British

Israeli Telephone Area Codes

02	Jerusalem, Bethlehem
03	Tel Aviv, Ramat Gan, Givatayim, Ben-Gurion Airport
04	Haifa, Acre, Nahariya
06	Tiberius
08	Ashdod
051	Ashkelon
052	Herziliya
053	Netanya
057	Beersheba
059	Eilat

JEWISH LIFE

False Messiahs

After the Second Temple was destroyed, the Israelites began a period of exile. Living in strange countries, their hopes were often kept alive by a strong belief in the coming of the Messiah. Many individuals, through the centuries, came forth to proclaim themselves the Messiah. Here is a sampling of them:

Abraham ben Samuel Abulafia (1240–1292) This Spaniard was the first of the kabbalistic Messiahs. He even attempted to convert Pope Nicholas III to Judaism!

Abu Isa Isfahani (8th-century Persia) He was the founder of the Issawite sect and claimed to be the last of the five forerunners of the Messiah.

Isaac Luria (1534–1572) This Palestinian mystic was the founder of the modern school of Kabbalah. He felt that he possessed the soul of the Messiah.

Moses Chayim Luzzatto (1707–1747) This Italian believed that the secrets of the Torah had been revealed to him by an angel. Eventually he was excommunicated because of his doctrines.

Solomon Molcho (1500–1532) This Messianist was born in Portugual, and in 1529 he predicted the coming of the Messiah. Eventually he was burned at the stake as a heretic.

Moses of Crete (mid-5th century) He proclaimed himself the Messiah, promising to divide the waters of the Red Sea just as Moses had done. Many of his believers subsequently drowned.

Nissim ben David (13th century) This Spaniard predicted the coming of the Messiah in 1295.

David Reubeni (c. 1491–1535) Many Jews believed he was a forerunner of the Messiah who would lead them back to the Holy Land. He was instrumental in the return to Judaism of many Marranos.

Sabbatai Zevi (1626–1676, Turkey) Claiming to be the Messiah, he attracted hundreds of followers. Eventually, he converted to Islam.

Jacob Frank (1726–1791, Poland) He believed that the soul of the Messiah dwelt within him. Eventually he was excommunicated, and he and thousands of his followers were baptized.

Maimonides' Thirteen Principles of Faith

Maimonides is considered by many the greatest codifier and philosopher in Jewish history. One of the clearest statements of Jewish belief is contained in his *Thirteen Principles of Faith*. Maimonides' principles are found in many prayer books and also form the basis of the well-known synagogue hymn *Yigdal*. Many Jewish people today accept the principles as their personal creed of Judaism.

1. I believe with perfect faith that God is the Creator and Ruler of all things. God alone has made, does make, and will make all things.
2. I believe with perfect faith that God alone is One. There is no unity that is in any way like God's. God alone is our God. God, was, is, and always will be.
3. I believe with perfect faith that God does not have a body. Physical concepts do not apply to God. There is nothing at all that resembles God.
4. I believe with perfect faith that God is the first and God is the last.
5. I believe with perfect faith that it is only proper to pray to God. One may not pray to anyone or anything else.
6. I believe with perfect faith that all the words of the prophets are true.

7. I believe with perfect faith that the prophecy of Moses is absolutely true. He is the chief of all prophets, both before and after him.

8. I believe with perfect faith that the entire Torah that we now have is that which was given to Moses.

9. I believe with perfect faith that this Torah will not be changed, and that there will never be another given by God.

10. I believe with perfect faith that God knows all of a person's deeds and thoughts.

11. I believe with perfect faith that God rewards those who keep God's commandments and punishes those who transgress them.

12. I believe with perfect faith in the coming of the Messiah. Even though the Messiah may tarry, I will await the Messiah's coming every day.

13. I believe with perfect faith that the dead will be brought back to life when God wills it to happen.

Estimated Jewish Population of Some Foreign Cities

Amsterdam	15,000
Antwerp	15,000
Brussels	23,000
Buenos Aires	220,000
Copenhagen	6,700
Glasgow	11,000
Istanbul	22,000
Johannesburg	63,620
Kiev	152,000
Leningrad	165,000
London	225,000
Marseilles	70,000
Melbourne	40,000
Milan	10,000
Montreal	100,000

Moscow	250,000
Nice	25,000
Odessa	120,000
Ottawa	9,000
Paris	350,000
Rio de Janeiro	29,000
Rome	15,000
Stockholm	8,000
Sydney	33,000
Toronto	120,000
Vancouver	18,000
Winnepeg	16,000
Zurich	6,713

Estimated Jewish Population of Cities and Counties in the United States

Alabama
Birmingham	5,100
Montgomery	1,300

Alaska
Anchorage	2,000

Arizona
Phoenix	50,000
Tuscon	20,000

Arkansas
Little Rock	1,300

California
Alameda and Contra Costa Counties	51,500
Fresno	2,000
Long Beach	13,500
Los Angeles Metro Area	501,000
Orange County	80,000
Sacramento	12,500

San Diego	70,000
San Francisco Bay Area	210,000
Santa Monica	8,000
Ventura County	9,000

Colorado

Colorado Springs	1,500
Denver	46,000

Connecticut

Bridgeport	18,000
Hartford	28,000
New Haven	28,000
Norwalk	9,500
Stamford	11,100
Waterbury	2,700

Delaware

Dover	650
Wilmington	9,500

District of Columbia

Greater Washington	165,000

Florida

Boca Raton–Delray	52,000
Fort Lauderdale	140,000
Hollywood	66,000
Jacksonville	7,300
Miami and Dade Counties	226,000
Orlando	18,000
Palm Beach County (except Boca Raton)	55,000
Sarasota	9,500
St. Petersburg	9,500
Tampa	12,500

Georgia

Atlanta Metro Area	67,000
Augusta	1,400
Savannah	2,750

Hawaii

Honolulu (includes all of Oahu)	6,400

Idaho

Boise	220

Illinois

Champaign-Urbana	1,300
Chicago Metro Area	248,000
Rockford	1,000
Springfield	1,000

Indiana

Bloomington	1,000
Ft. Wayne	1,085
Gary	2,200
Indianapolis	10,000
South Bend	1,900

Iowa

Des Moines	2,800
Iowa City	1,200

Kansas

Topeka	500
Wichita	1,000

Kentucky

Lexington	2,000
Louisville	8,700

Louisiana

Baton Rouge	1,200
New Orleans	12,000
Shreveport	960

Maine

Augusta	500
Bangor	1,250
Portland	3,900

Maryland

Annapolis	2,000
Baltimore	94,500
Hartford County	1,000
Howard County	7,200

Massachusetts

Andover	3,000
Boston Metro Region	228,000
Cape Cod	3,000
Fall River	1,780
Greenfield	900

Haverhill	1,500
Lawrence	2,250
Lowell	2,000
Lynn–North Shore Area	25,000
New Bedford	3,000
Pittsfield	3,100
Springfield	11,000
Taunton	1,200
Worcester County	13,700

Michigan
Ann Arbor	5,000
Detroit Metro Area	94,000
Flint	2,000
Grand Rapids	1,725
Kalamazoo	1,000
Lansing	2,100

Minnesota
Duluth	500
Minneapolis	22,000
St. Paul	7,500

Mississippi
Greenville	270
Jackson	700

Missouri
Kansas City Metro Area	19,100
St. Louis	53,500

Montana
Billings	200

Nebraska
Lincoln	1,000
Omaha	6,500

Nevada
Las Vegas	19,000
Reno	1,400

New Hampshire
Manchester	2,500
Portsmouth	950

New Jersey
Atlantic City	15,800

Bergen County	85,000
Camden and Cherry Hill	28,000
Essex County	76,200
Flemington	900
Jersey City	5,500
Middlesex County	58,000
Monmouth County	33,600
Morris–Sussex Counties	33,500
Ocean County	9,500
Passaic County–Clifton	18,700
Princeton	3,000
Somerset County	7,900
Union County	30,000
Vineland	2,200

New Mexico

Albuquerque	4,000
Sante Fe	900

New York

Albany	12,000
Binghamton	3,000
Buffalo	18,125
Ellenville	1,600
Ithaca	1,250
Kingston	4,300
Liberty	2,100
Monticello	2,400
New York Metro Area	1,450,000
Orange County	10,000
Poughkeepsie	6,500
Rochester	22,500
Rockland County	83,100
Schenectady	5,200
Sullivan County	7,425
Syracuse	9,000
Utica	1,900

North Carolina

Asheville	1,350
Chapel Hill-Durham	3,000
Charlotte	4,000
Greensboro	2,700
Raleigh	3,000

North Dakota
Fargo   500

Ohio
Akron   6,000
Butler County   900
Canton   2,400
Cincinnati   23,000
Cleveland   65,000
Columbus   15,600
Dayton   6,000
Toledo   6,300
Youngstown   4,000

Oklahoma
Oklahoma City   2,500
Tulsa   2,750

Oregon
Eugene   2,300
Portland   12,000

Pennsylvania
Allentown   6,000
Chester County   4,000
Easton   1,200
Harrisburg   6,500
Lancaster   2,100
Lower Bucks County   14,500
Philadelphia Area   250,000
Pittsburgh   45,000
Reading   2,800
Scranton   3,150
Wilkes-Barre   3,200
York   1,500

Rhode Island
Providence   14,200
Washington County   1,200

South Carolina
Charleston   4,000
Columbia   2,000
Greenville   800

South Dakota
Sioux Falls   135

Tennessee

Chattanooga	1,350
Knoxville	1,350
Memphis	8,800
Nashville	5,600

Texas

Austin	5,000
Beaumont	800
Corpus Christi	1,400
Dallas	35,000
El Paso	4,900
Ft. Worth	5,000
Houston	42,000
San Antonio	10,000

Utah

Salt Lake City	2,800

Vermont

Burlington	3,000
Newport	550

Virginia

Charlottesville	950
Newport News	2,000
Norfolk–Virginia Beach	18,000
Portsmouth	1,900
Richmond	8,000
Roanoke	1,050

Washington

Seattle	29,300
Spokane	800
Tacoma	1,100

West Virginia

Charleston	1,000

Wisconsin

Madison	4,500
Milwaukee	28,000

Wyoming

Cheyenne	230

United States total	5,798,000

The Hebrew Alphabet

Name	A	B	C	D	E Sound in Ash-kenazi	F Num-erical Value	G Final Forms
Aleph	א	k	ḃ	א	Silent	1	
Bet	ב	ב	3	ב	B	2	
Vet	ב				V		
Gimel	ג	ﻉ	ג	ﻉ	G	3	
Dalet	ד	ך	ר	ך	D	4	
Hay	ה	ה	ס	ה	H	5	
Vav	ו	/	ו	ו	V	6	
Zayin	ז	ﻝ	ﻭ	ז	Z	7	
Het	ח	ת	ם	ח	CH	8	
Tet	ט	ﻉ	צ	ט	T	9	
Yod	י	،	،	ﻭ	Y	10	
Khaf	כ	ﻕﻑ	ﻭ ך	ך ל	K	20	ﻙ SS
Chaf	כ				CH		
Lamed	ל	ﻝ	ﻝ	ל	L	30	
Mem	מ	N ﻕ	ﻕ ﻭ	ﻕﻭ	M	40	ﻭ SS
Nun	נ	ﻝﻝ	ﻭ ﻝ	ﻝﻝ	N	50	ﻝ SS
Samekh	ס	o	ﻕ	ﻕ	S	60	
Ayin	ע	ﻝ	ﻉ	ﻉ	Silent	70	
Pay	פ	ﻑﻝ	ﻝ ﻭ	ﻑ ﻉ	P	80	ﻑ SS
Fay	פ				F		
Tzadi	צ	ﻉ ﻉ	ﻝ ﻭ	ﻉ ﻉ	TZ	90	ﻉ SS
Kof	ק	ﻕ	ﻕ	ק	K	100	

Name	A	B	C	D	E Sound in Ashkenazi	F Numerical Value	G Final Forms
Resh	ר	ר	ר	ר	R	200	* In Modern Hebrew the ת is sounded as T
Shin	שׁ	ℓ	פ	שׁ	Sh	300	
Sin	שׂ				S		
Tav	תּ	ﬨ	ת	ת	T	400	
Sav	ת				S *		

A. Ordinary square form characters: known as *ketav ashurit* (Assyrian), this is the most popular form now used for Hebrew printing.

B. Script or cursive form, used in writing.

C. Rashi script: This script was named after the famous medieval Bible scholar known as Rashi (Rabbi Solomon ben Isaac).

D. Torah script: Used for the Torah as well as *mezuzah* and *tefillin* parchment.

E. These are the sounds in the Ashkenazic dialect.

F. This column contains the number equivalents of each of the Hebrew letters.

G. This column contains the shapes of those Hebrew letters that have a final form.

Jewish Numerology

Numbers have always been important to Jewish culture and are often highly symbolic. For example, the fact that there is one God means that God is unique and unlike any other. Here are some Jewish number clusters for your consideration.

The Number Two in Jewish Life

The two tablets
Two golden cherubim on the top of the Ark of the Covenant
Two boxes for the *tefillin*
Two times a day that traditional Jewish persons recite the *Shema*
Two spies sent by Joshua to spy on Jericho
Two mentionings of the Ten Commandments in the Torah
Two witnesses required to testify in a Jewish court of law

The Number Three in Jewish Life

Three patriarchs—Abraham, Isaac, and Jacob
Three angels came to visit Abraham
Three musical sounds of the *shofar—tekiah*, *shevarim*, *te-ruah*
Three pieces of *matzah* used at the Passover Seder
Three floors of Noah's Ark
Three sections of the Jewish Bible—Five Books of Moses, Prophets, and Writings
Three walls required for building a *sukkah*
Three traditional meals on the Sabbath
Threefold priestly benediction
Three categories of Jews—*Kohanim*, Levites, and Israelites
Three judges required for a Jewish court of law

The Number Four in Jewish Life

Four matriarchs—Sarah, Rebekah, Rachel, and Leah
Four cups of wine at the *Seder*
Four questions asked at the *Seder*
Four types of sons in the *Haggadah*
Four corners of a *tallit*
Four sections of the Torah in the *tefillin* boxes
Four rows of precious stones worn on the breastplate of the high priest
Four couples buried in the Cave of Machpelah

The Number Five in Jewish Life

The Five Books of Moses
The Five *Megillot*
Five double knots in the fringes of a prayer shawl
Five sons of Mattathias

The Number Six in Jewish Life

Six days of creation
Six chapters in the *Ethics of the Fathers*
Six sections to the Mishnah
Six steps leading to the throne of King Solomon

The Number Seven in Jewish Life

Seven benedictions in the Sabbath *Amidah*
Seven Torah processionals on Simchat Torah
Seven marriage blessings
Seven female prophets
Seven days of mourning
Seven lamps on the *menorah*
Seven times *tefillin* are wrapped around the arm

The Number Eight in Jewish Life

Eight days of Chanukah
A male infant is circumcised on the eighth day
Eight different garments worn by a high priest
Eight days of Passover

The Number Ten in Jewish Life

Ten people constitute a *minyan* (quorum)
Ten Commandments
Ten days of repentance
Abraham was tested ten times
Ten plagues
Ten sons of Haman

The Number Twelve in Jewish Life

Twelve tribes of Israel
Twelve Minor Prophets
Twelve constellations
A girl reaches religious maturity at age 12
Twelve loaves of shewbread
Solomon became king at age 12

The Number Forty in Jewish Life

Moses stayed on Mount Sinai for 40 years
It rained for 40 days and nights during the Flood
Spies spent 40 days exploring Israel
Rabbi Akiba was 40 when he began his Jewish studies
Town of Nineveh had 40 days to repent

Names of God

Names have great power. The way in which we think of God will sometimes play an important part in our prayers. Below is a list of some of the names God has been called in various sources in Jewish tradition.

Adonai
Lord
Mighty One of Jacob
God Almighty
Everlasting Rock
YHVH
I am that I am
King of Israel
Rock of Israel
Everlasting God
Shield of Abraham
King of Kings
The Name
The Place
Merciful One
Faithful One
Infinite
Lord of Hosts
Master of the Universe
Eternal One
Peace
God of Abraham
The Good One
Creator
Our Father Our King
Awesome One
My Shepherd
Our Healer
Generous One
Hidden of Hiddens
Mentor
Shaddai
God of Vision

Famous Jews-by-Choice

It is estimated that about 10,000 persons in the United States convert to Judaism annually. This is a list of some famous Jews-by-choice that might surprise you!

Abraham	The first Jew
Ruth	The great-grandmother of King David
Onkelos	A famous Bible translator who translated the Hebrew Bible into Aramaic
King Bulan of Khazaria	Instituted Judaism in his kingdom in the mid-8th century C.E.
Warder Cresson	Born in 1798 into a Quaker family, he was the earliest known American Jew-by-choice
Rod Carew	A now retired ballplayer who was recently inducted into the Baseball Hall of Fame
Elizabeth Taylor	A well-known American actress
Sammy Davis, Jr.	A famous entertainer

Famous Jews Who Changed Their Names

Throughout American history Jewish persons have changed their names, often giving them a more "American" flavor. Here are twenty well-known American Jews who changed their names.

Name	Former Name
Joey Adams	Joseph Abramowitz
Woody Allen	Allen Konigsberg
Rona Barrett	Rona Burstein

Name	Former Name
Jack Benny	Benjamin Kubelsky
Mel Brooks	Melvin Kaminsky
Joyce Brothers	Joyce Bauer
George Burns	Nathan Birnbaum
Howard Cosell	Howard Cohen
Alan King	Irwin Kniberg
Jerry Lewis	Joseph Levitch
Tony Martin	Alvin Morris
Arthur Murray	Arthur Teichman
Tony Randall	Leonard Rosenberg
Joan Rivers	Joan Molinsky
Billy Rose	William Rosenberg
Jill St. John	Jill Oppenheim
Soupy Sales	Milton Hines
Dinah Shore	Francis Rose Shore
Mike Wallace	Mike Wallach
Shelly Winters	Shirley Schrift

Jewish Acronyms

Jewish life has many acronyms—abbreviations that are designed as shortcut devices for long names. Acronyms are not new to Jewish life. Some, like the word *Tanach*, date back to the talmudic period.

Rabbis

Besht	Rabbi Israel Baal Shem Tov
HaGra	Rabbi Elijah ben Solomon Zalman, known as the Vilna Gaon
Ralbag	Rabbi Levi ben Gerson—Gersonides
Ramaz	Rabbi Moses Zacuto
Rambam	Rabbi Moses ben Maimon—Maimonides
Ramban	Rabbi Moses ben Nachman
Rashbam	Rabbi Samuel ben Meir
Rashi	Rabbi Solomon bar Isaac
Rif	Rabbi Isaac bar Jacob haKoen

Jewish Denominations and Their Organizations

Reform

ACC	American Conference of Cantors
CCAR	Central Conference of American Rabbis
HUC/JIR	Hebrew Union College/Jewish Institute of Religion
UAHC	Union of American Hebrew Congregations

Conservative

CA	Cantor's Assembly
JTS	Jewish Theological Seminary
RA	Rabbinical Assembly
UTCJ	Union of Traditional Conservative Judaism
USCJ	United Synagogue of Conservative Judaism

Orthodox

CAA	Cantorial Association of America
RAA	Rabbinical Association of America
RCA	Rabbinical Council of America
UOJCA	Union of Orthodox Jewish Congregations of America
UOR	Union of Orthodox Rabbis
YU	Yeshiva University

Reconstructionist

JRF	Jewish Reconstructionist Foundation
RRA	Reconstructionist Rabbinical Association
RRC	Reconstructionist Rabbinical College

Zionist Organizations

ARZA	Association of Reform Zionists of America
AZF	American Zionist Federation
AZYF	American Zionist Youth Foundation
JNF	Jewish National Fund
LZA	Labor Zionist Organization
MERCAZ	Movement to Reaffirm Conservative Zionism
ZOA	Zionist Organization of America

Youth Organizations

BBYO	B'nai B'rith Youth Organization
NCSY	National Council of Synagogue Youth
NFTY	National Federation of Temple Youth
USY	United Synagogue Youth

Defense Organizations

ADL	Anti-Defamation League of B'nai B'rith
AJC	American Jewish Committee
AJC	American Jewish Congress
JDL	Jewish Defense League

Books

AJYB	*American Jewish Year Book*
EJ	*Encyclopaedia Judaica*
JE	*Jewish Encyclopedia*
TANAKH	*Torah, Nevi'im* (Prophets), and *Ketuvim* (Writings)—better known as the Jewish Bible and also commonly referred to as the Old Testament in Christian circles.

Jewish Charities

AJC	Allied Jewish Charities
CJA	Combined Jewish Appeal
CJF	Council of Jewish Federations
CJP	Council of Jewish Philanthropies
FJC	Federated Jewish Charities
FJP	Federation of Jewish Philanthropies
HIAS	Hebrew Immigrant Aid Society
JFA	Jewish Federated Appeal
UHC	United Hebrew Charities
UJA	United Jewish Appeal

Other Jewish Organizations

AAAPME	American Academic Association for Peace in the Middle East
AIPAC	American Israel Public Affairs Committee

AJCW	Association of Jewish Center Workers
AJHS	American Jewish Historical Society
CAJE	Coalition for the Advancement of Jewish Education
GA	General Assembly (annual meeting of Jewish federations)
JDC	Joint Distribution Committee
JESNA	Jewish Education Service of North America
JTA	Jewish Telegraphic Agency
JWV	Jewish War Veterans
NCJW	National Council of Jewish Women
NCSJ	National Conference on Soviet Jewry
NJCRAC	National Jewish Community Relations Advisory Council
SCA	Synagogue Council of America
SSSJ	Student Struggle for Soviet Jewry
WJC	World Jewish Congress
WUJS	World Union of Jewish Students

Jewish Surnames and Their Meanings

Jewish families that adopted surnames took them from a variety of different sources—occupations, geographical locations, physical characteristics, nicknames, abbreviations, or the first names of their mothers or fathers. Here is a sampling of Jewish surnames and their meanings:

Physical Characteristics

Album	white
Blau	blonde
Bleich	pale
Dick	stout
Fekete	black
Geller	yellow
Gross	large

Jung	young
Klein	small
Kraus	curly
Krumbein	bowlegged
Kurtz	short
Mankuta	left-handed
Roth	red
Rothbart	red-bearded
Schwartz	black
Schwartzbart	black-bearded
Stark	strong
Steinhart	hard stone
Weiss	white
Weisbart	white-bearded

Occupational Names

Abzug	printer
Ackerman	plowman
Ahl	shoemaker
Alembik	distiller
Antman	handyman
Anzieher	shoemaker
Aspis	inn owner
Becker	baker
Berger	shepherd
Bernstein	amber dealer
Braverman	brewer
Breger	brewer
Bronfman	whiskey merchant
Bulka	baker
Burack	beets dealer
Burla	jeweler
Chait	tailor
Chalef	meat slaughterer
Chasin	cantor
Citron	lemon seller
Dauber	pigeon seller
Drucker	printer
Einstein	mason
Emale	enamelware dealer
Feder	scribe

Flaxman	flax merchant
Fleischer	butcher
Fudym	tailor
Futorian	furrier
Galinsky	grain merchant
Geiger	violinist
Giesser	pewterware maker
Gittelmacher	cap maker
Glass	glass trade
Goldschmidt	goldsmith
Graber	grave digger
Handwerker	tradesman
Hirzhman	millet dealer
Imber	ginger seller
Kadar	cooper
Katzoff	butcher
Klinger	junk dealer
Kolatch	baker
Korf	basketmaker
Kotlar	kitchenware maker
Krochmal	starch dealer
Kushner	furrier
Lawentman	weaver
Lederer	tanner
Levandula	cosmetic dealer
Lopata	baker
Mahler	miller
Marmelstein	builder
Mautner	toll collector
Melzner	malt dealer
Messinger	brass dealer
Molotok	carpenter
Muchnik	flour merchant
Netzky	baker
Pechenik	baker
Perlmutter	pearl dealer
Plotkin	fish dealer
Portnoy	tailor
Reifman	wine dealer
Reiter	lumber merchant
Ringle	goldsmith
Salpeter	fertilizer merchant
Scharfstein	knife grinder

Schloss	lock maker
Schulsinger	cantor
Seiler	rope maker
Sholk	silk merchant
Singer	cantor
Spector	tutor
Steuer	tax collector
Tabachnik	manufacturer of snuff
Tendler	dealer in secondhand merchandise
Vigoda	innkeeper
Wapner	lime dealer
Weber	weaver
Weiner	wine seller

Geographical Names

Alkus	Poland
Altfeld	Poland
Anixter	Lithuania
Apter	Galicia
Auerbach	Germany
Bamberg	Bavaria
Barr	Ukraine
Blowitz	Bohemia
Bolotin	Poland
Bragin	White Russia
Bromberg	Poland
Burstein	Poland
Chomsky	White Russia
Dembitz	Galicia
Dissen	Lithuania
Dreebin	Ukraine
Eger	Western Bohemia
Eisenberg	Hungary
Embden	Germany
Erlanger	Bavaria
Floss	Bavaria
Fonseca	Spain
Friedland	Prussia
Fuld	Germany
Ginsburg	Bavaria
Gottinger	Germany

Halperin	Germany
Hammerstein	West Prussia
Jastrow	Prussia
Karletiz	White Russia
Kempler	Galicia
Kissinger	Germany
Kleban	Ukraine
Kolodny	Poland
Kutner	Poland
Lapin	Poland
Lenoff	Poland
Lipsky	Germany
Lubin	Poland
Malin	Ukraine
Melnick	Poland
Mintz	Germany
Nevler	White Russia
Offen	Germany
Pianko	Poland
Pilch	Poland
Prinz	Italy
Ratner	Poland
Ridker	Poland
Samter	Poland
Savitzky	Poland
Silberberg	Poland
Slepin	White Russia
Stendal	Westphalia
Sturm	Poland
Tartakover	Poland
Teplitz	Czechoslovakia
Ticktin	Poland
Turetzky	White Russia
Unna	Germany
Warburg	Germany
Wittenberg	Germany
Yampol	Russia
Zwillenberg	Upper Bavaria

Personal Characteristics

Biederman	honest
Bogatch	rich

Dunkelman	extremely religious
Ehrlich	honest
Fine	nice person
Friedman	free person
Gottlieb	God-loving
Kluger	wise
Lustig	happy
Razumny	clever
Scholem	peaceful
Sharf	brilliant
Sirota	sad
Soroka	talkative
Zaitz	lively person

Tribal Surnames

Cohen

Cohen
Hohen
Kogan
Cogan
Kahane
Cohn
Kahn
Kaplan
Katz

Levites

Levy
Levin
Levine
Levinsky
Levitan
Levitt
Levinthal

Hebrew Names and Their Meanings

Every Hebrew name has a meaning. The following is a cross section of Hebrew names and their meanings.

Masculine

AARON	אהרן	A mountain; tower of strength; teaching
ABEL	אבל	Breath; vanity
ABNER	אבנר	My father is light; paternal
ABRAHAM	אברהם	Father of a multitude; Abram; Abe
ABSALOM	אבשלום	Father of peace; peace-loving
ADAM	אדם	Red earth; man
AKIBA	עקיבא	Held by heel; protect
AMNON	אמנן	Faithful
AMOS	עמוס	Borne (by God); strong; burdened
ARNON	ארנון	Roaring stream
ARYEH	אריה	Lion
ASA	אסא	Healer; physician
ASAPH	אסף	Gatherer
ASHER	אשר	Blessed; happy
AZRIEL	עזריאל	God is my help
BARUCH	ברוך	Blessed
BENJAMIN	בנימין	Son of the right hand; a surety; son of my days
BENONI	בנאני	Son of my sorrow
BEN ZION	בן ציון	Son of Zion; excellent son
BOAZ	בעז	Strength; swiftness
CALEB	כלב	A dog
DANIEL	דניאל	God is my judge; Dan
DAVID	דוד	Darling; beloved
EBENEZER	אבנעזר	Stone of help; Ben; Eben
ELAZAR	אלעזר	God is my help; Eliezer
ELI	עלי	God is the Lord; Elihu, Ellis
ELIAS	אליהו	High; faithful to God
ELIJAH	אליהו	Jehovah is God
ELISHA	אלישע	God is salvation
EMANUEL	עמנואל	God is with us
ENOCH	חנוך	Dedicated; teacher
ENOS	אנוש	Man; mortal being
EPHRAIM	אפרים	Very fruitful
ETHAN	איתן	Firmness; strength; power
EZEKIEL	יחזקאל	God makes strong
EZRA	עזרא	Help: dawn, beginning of joy
GABRIEL	גבריאל	Fighter for God; powerful one

GAMALIEL ——	נמליאל	—Gift of God
GIDEON ———	גדעון	—Deliverer; hewer
HEZEKIAH ——	חזקיה	—God has strengthened
HILIEL ———	הלל	—Praised
HIRAM ———	חירם	—Nobly born; high-souled
HOSEA ———	הושע	—Salvation; God help
IRA ———	שמריה	—Watchful; city watch; descendant
ISAAC ———	יצחק	—Laughter
ISAIAH ———	ישעיה	—Salvation of the Lord
ISRAEL ———	ישראל	—Prince of God; prevailed against God
JACOB ———	יעקב	—Supplanter; held by the heel; Jack
JAMES ———	יעקב	—Supplanter; Jim. Jimmy
JAPHETH ———	יפת	—Enlargement
JARED ———	ירד	—Descent
JEREMIAH ——	ירמיה	—Exalted of the Lord; Jeremy; Jerry, Gerald
JESSE ———	ישי	—Wealthy; gift
JOAB ———	יואב	—God is his father
JOB ———	איוב	—Afflicted; hated
JOEL ———	יואל	—The Lord is God
JOHN ———	יוחנן	—God is gracious; Ivan, Johannes, Hans
JONAH ———	יונה	—A dove
JONATHAN ——	יונתן	—God has given; a gift of God
JORDAN ———	ירדן	—Flowing down; descendent
JOSEPH ———	יוסף	—He shall add; Joe, Jose. Jo
JOSHUA ———	יהושע	—God is deliverance; a Saviour
JOSIAH ———	יאשיהו	—God supports; fire of God
JOTHAM ———	יותם	—God is perfect
JUDAH ———	יהודה	—Praised one; praise the Lord
LABAN ———	לבן	—White
LAZARUS ———	אלעזר	—God has helped
LEMUEL ———	למואל	—Consecrated to God
LEVI ———	לוי	—A bond; joined
LOT ———	לוט	—An envelope; wrap
MALACHI ———	מלאכי	—Messenger
MATTHEW ——	מתתיהו	—Gift of God; reward; Mattathias
MAYER ———	מאיר	—One who brightens; Meyer
MICAH ———	מיכה	—Who is like God; Michael, Mitchell

MOSES	משה	—Drawn out of water; Morris, Morton
NAAMAN	נעמן	—Pleasantness
NAHUM	נחום	—Comforter
NATHAN	נתן	—Given; gift
NATHANIEL	נתנאל	—Gift of God
NEHEMIAH	נחמיה	—Comfort of God
NOAH	נח	—Rest; comfort; consolation
OBADIAH	עבדיה	—Servant of the Lord
PHINEAS	פנחם	—Mouth of brass
RAPHAEL	רפאל	—God hath healed
REUBEN	ראובן	—Behold, a son! Ruben, Rubin
REUEL	רעואל	—God is his friend
SABBATAI	שבתי	—Rest; my Sabbath
SAMSON	שמשון	—Sun's man; brilliant sun
SAMUEL	שמואל	—Named by God; asked of God
SAUL	שאול	—Asked of the Lord
SETH	שת	—Appointed; deep
SIMEON	שמעון	—Hearing; servant of the Lord; Simon
SIMON	שמעון	—Obedient
SOLOMON	שלמה	—Peaceable
THOMAS	תאומא	—Twin; good company
TOBIAH	טוביה	—God is my good; Tobias
URIAH	אוריה	—Flame of god; my light is God
YEHUDI	יהודי	—Jew
ZACHARIAH	זכריה	—God has remembered
ZEBINA	זבינא	—Bought

Feminine

ABIGAIL	אביניל	—My father is joy; source of delight; Gail
ADA	עדה	—An Ornament; happy
ADINA	עדינה	—Delight; adorned
ALMA	עלמה	—Young woman; maiden; a virgin
ANN	חנה	—Grace; gracious; Anne, Annie, Nancy, Nina
ANNABEL	חנה	—Heroine; Anita, Annette
BATHSHEBA	בת שבע	—Daughter of an oath
BEULAH	בעולה	—Married

BESSIE	בתי	—My daughter; Betty, Beth, Betsy
CIVIA	צביה	—Deer
DEBORAH	דבורה	—A bee
DELILAH	דלילה	—Delicate; poor
DINAH	דינה	—Vindicated one; judged
EDNA	עדינה	—Rejuvenation; pleasure
ELIZABETH	אלישבע	—Consecrated to God; Elsie, Eliza, Lisa, Libby
ESTHER	אסתר	—Hadassah; myrtle; star; Estelle, Esta, Essie
EVE	חוה	—Life; Living; Eva
GABRIELLE	גבריאלה	—God is my strength
HANNAH	חנה	—Grace, graciousness
HAZEL	צילה	—Protected by God
HEPZIBAH	חפציבה	—My delight is in her
HULDAH	חלדה	—A weasel
JACOBA	מגנה	—Supplanter
JACQUELINE	מגנה	—Beguiling; supplanter
JANE	מתנה	—Graciousness; God's grace; Janet, Jean
JEMIMA	יונינה	—A dove
JESSICA	חנה	—God's grace; wealthy; Jessie
JOAN	חנה	—Gracious gift of God; Johanna, Joanna
JOSEPHINE	יוסיפה	—Increase
JUDITH	יהודית	—Praised; Judy
LEAH	לאה	—A wild cow; weary one; Lee
MAGDALENE	מגדלה	—Watch tower: high one: Madaline. Maud
MARTHA	מרתה	—Bitter; resigned; lady
MARY	מרים	—Sympathetic: bitter; Maureen, Marlene, Marian, Maria, Marie, May, Molly
MICHELLE	מיכל	—Who is like thee. O Lord!
MIRIAM	מירם	—Bitter; sea of bitterness
NAOMI	נעמי	—Pleasantness; sweet
NANCY	חנה	—Grace; graciousness; Nan, Nanette
POLLY	מרים	—Bitter; nickname for Mary, Miriam
RACHEL	רחל	—Ewe; motherly; Rachelle, Ray
REBECCA	רבקה	—Tied; a snare; Reba

RUTH ————	רות —	Beloved; a friend
SADIE ————	שרה —	Princess; Sally
SALOME ———	שלומית —	Peace
SARAH ————	שרה —	A princess; Sara
SUSAN ————	שושנה —	Lily; Rose; trusting one; Sue, Susie
TABITHA ——	צביה —	Gazelle
TAMARA ——	תמר —	Palm tree; Tamar
TOBEY ———	טובה —	Good; Toba; Tobella
VIDA ————	חיה —	Beloved
ZORA ————	זוהר —	Light; brilliance

Let's Say It in Hebrew

Here are some Hebrew words and phrases that might help you on your next trip to Israel.

Polite Expressions

Please	*Bevakashah*
Hello/good-bye	*Shalom*
See you soon	*Lehitraot*
Excuse me	*Selichah*
Good morning	*Boker tov*
Good evening	*Erev tov*
Good night	*Lailah tov*
How are you?	*Mah shlomkha* [masc]?
	Mah shlomekh [fem]?

People Words

Boy	*yeled*
Girl	*yaldah*
Tourist	*tayar*
Soldier	*chayal*
Police	*shoter*
Taxi driver	*nahag*

Teacher	*moreh* (masc)
	morah (fem)
Man	*ish*
Woman	*ishah*

Food Words

Restaurant	*misadah*
Waiter	*meltzar*
Table	*shulchan*
Food	*okhel*
Menu	*tafrit*
Check	*cheshbon*
Water	*mayim*
Milk	*chalav*
Meat	*basar*
Soup	*marak*
Egg	*beitzah*
Cheese	*gevinah*
Chicken	*of*
Bread	*lechem*
Coffee	*cafeh*
Tea	*tei*
Juice	*mitz*
Ice cream	*gelidah*
Breakfast	*aruchat boker*
Lunch	*aruchat tzaharayim*
Dinner	*aruchat erev*

Places

Apartment	*dirah*
House	*bayit*
Museum	*muzeiyon*
Theater	*teiyatron*
Movie	*kolnoah*
Store	*chanut*
Hotel	*malon*
Room	*cheder*
Post office	*doar*
Synagogue	*Beit Knesset*
Market	*shuk*

Pronouns

I	*ani*
You (sing)	*atah* (masc) *at* (fem)
You (pl)	*atem* (masc), *aten* (fem)
He	*hu*
She	*he*
We	*anachnu*
They	*hem* (masc) *hen* (fem)

Travel

Road	*rechov*
Bus	*autobus*
Car	*mikhonit*
Taxi	*monit*
Bus stop	*tachanah*
Driver	*nahag*
Airport	*sedei te'ufah*
Right	*yeminah*
Left	*smolah*
Straight ahead	*yashar*
Limousine	*sherut*

Clothes

Coat	*me'il*
Hat	*kovah*
Skirt	*chatzit*
Socks	*garbayim*
Raincoat	*me'il geshem*
Bathing suit	*beged yam*
Sunglasses	*mishkefei shemesh*
Boots	*magafayim*
Dress	*simlah*
Shirt	*kutonet*
Belt	*chagorah*
Suit	*chalifah*

Time

What time is it?	*Eizeh shaah?*
The time is . . .	*Hashaah* . . .

Minute	*rega*
Hour	*shaah*
Day	*yom*
Week	*shavuah*
Year	*shanah*
Yesterday	*etmol*
Tomorrow	*machar*

Numbers

One	*achat*
Two	*shtayim*
Three	*shalosh*
Four	*arbah*
Five	*chamesh*
Six	*shesh*
Seven	*shevah*
Eight	*shemoneh*
Nine	*tesha*
Ten	*eser*
Twenty	*esrim*
Fifty	*chamishim*
One hundred	*meiyah*
One thousand	*elef*

Questions

Who?	*Mi?*
Why?	*Lamah?*
What?	*Mah?*
Where is?	*Eifo?*
When?	*Matai?*
How many?	*Kamah?*
How much does it cost?	*Kamah zeh oleh*

Let's Say It in Aramaic

The Gemara, which forms part of the Talmud, was written in the ancient language of Aramaic. The following is a brief summary of some of the most frequently encountered words in the Gemara:

Aramaic Word	Transliteration	Meaning
א	*ah*	on
אוֹרְחָא	*orcha*	path
אוֹרַיְיתָא	*oraita*	Torah
אֲזַל	*azal*	went
אִידִי	*eedee*	this
אִידָךְ	*eedach*	the other
אִיכָּא	*eekah*	there is
אִין	*een*	yes
אֱנָשׁ	*enash*	person
אִית	*eet*	there is
אִיתְּתָא	*eetitah*	woman
אַלְמָא	*alma*	therefore
אַמַּאי	*amai*	why
אֲנָא	*ana*	I
אֲנַן	*anan*	we
אֲתָא	*ata*	he came
אַתְרָא	*atra*	place
בָּבָא	*bava*	gate
בֵּי	*bay*	the house of
בַּר	*bar*	son
בָּתַר	*batar*	after
גַּבֵּי	*gabay*	near
גַּבְרָא	*gavra*	man
גְּמַר	*gemar*	learn
דַּהֲבָא	*dahava*	gold
דּוּכְתָּא	*dukhta*	place
דִּידִי	*deedee*	mine
דָּמֵי	*damei*	similar
הָא	*ha*	this
הֲדָדֵי	*hadadei*	each other
הֲדַר	*hadar*	returned
הֲוָה	*havah*	was
הֵיכִי	*heikhee*	how
הָכָא	*hakha*	here
הָכִי	*hakhee*	thus
הִלְכְתָא	*hilkhita*	law
הַשְׁתָּא	*hashta*	now
זַבֵּין	*zabein*	sold
זוּזָא	*zuza*	money

Aramaic Word	Transliteration	Meaning
זוטָא	zuta	small
חַד	chad	one (masc)
חֲדָא	chada	one (fem)
חֲזָא	chaza	saw
חַמְרָא	chamra	wine
טַבָּחָא	tabacha	butcher
טַעֲמָא	taama	reason
טְפֵי	tefei	more
יוֹמָא	yoma	day
יָתְמָא	yatma	orphan
כּוּלֵי	kulei	all
כִּי	kee	like
לָא	la	not
לִישָׁנָא	leeshana	language
לֵית	leit	there is not
מַאי	mai	what
מַאן	man	who
מַיָּא	maya	water
מִידֵי	meedei	something
מִיהוּ	meehu	in any case
מָנָא	mana	object
מָר	mar	sir
מָתָא	mata	city
נַחֲמָא	nahama	bread
נַמִי	namee	also
נְפַק	nefak	went out
נַפְשֵׁיהּ	nafshei	himself
נַפְשָׁהּ	nafsha	herself
סָבָא	sava	old man
סַגִּי	sagee	enough
סֵיפָא	seifa	end
סָלְקָא דַעְתָּךְ	salka daatakh	you may think
עֲבַד	avad	did
עוּבְדָא	uvda	deed
עָלְמָע	alma	world
פַּלְגָּא	palga	part
פְּלוּגְתָּא	pelugta	dispute
פְּשִׁיטָא	peshita	obvious
צְלוֹתָא	tzlota	prayer
צְרִיכָא	tzreekha	necessary
קָאֵי	kalei	stands
קוּלָא	kula	lenient ruling

Aramaic Word	Transliteration	Meaning
קוּשְׁטָא	*kushta*	truth
קַמָּא	*kama*	first
קְרָא	*kera*	biblical verse
קַשְׁיָא	*kashya*	difficult
רַבָּא	*rabba*	great
רַבָּנָן	*rabbanan*	our Rabbis
רַחֲמָנָא	*rachamana*	All-Merciful God
רֵישָׁא	*reisha*	beginning
שָׁאנֵי	*shanei*	different
שָׁוֵי	*shavei*	treated like
שִׁית	*sheet*	six
שְׁמַיָּא	*shemaya*	sky
שַׁפִּיר	*shapeer*	nice
תָּא	*ta*	come
תְּיוּבְתָּא	*teyuvta*	reply
תְּלָת	*telat*	three
תְּמָנֵי	*temanei*	eight
תְּרֵי	*trei*	two (masc)
תַּרְתֵּי	*tartei*	two (fem)

Some Interesting Facts About the Hebrew Calendar

The Hebrew calendar is based on the phases of the moon; therefore it is a lunar calendar. There are 12 months and 354 days in every Hebrew year. Each month is either 29 or 30 days long. In a Hebrew leap year, which occurs seven times in a 19-year cycle, an extra month is added to the calendar. Every year, twelve groups of stars move across the sky. They are the twelve *mazalot* (constellations). Each Hebrew month has its own constellation.

Here is a summary of the Hebrew months of the Jewish year, including the number of days in each month, important historical events that occurred in that month, and the zodiacal sign of each month.

1. Nisan (30 days)

- On the eve of the 15th of Nisan, the Israelites prepared to leave Egypt.
- Tradition says that Miriam, sister of Moses, died on
  the 10th of Nisan.
- Once every 28 years in the month of Nisan we say a
  blessing for the sun.
- The sign of the zodiac for Nisan is a lamb, reminding
  us of the Paschal lamb.

2. Iyar (29 days)

- Sometimes called Ziv, the month of brightness, be-
  cause during each of its days the sun rises higher in
  the spring sky, making the world lighter and warmer.
- King Solomon began to build the Temple on the 1st of
  Iyar.
- On the 5th of Iyar, in the Hebrew year 5708, the State
  of Israel was established.
- Lag B'Omer, a day of weddings and picnics, is always
  on the 18th of Iyar.
- On the 28th of Iyar, in the year 5727, the city of
  Jerusalem was reunited.
- The sign of the zodiac for Iyar is an ox.

3. Sivan (30 days)

- Third month of the Hebrew calendar.
- On the 6th of Sivan, Moses received the Ten Com-
  mandments atop Mount Sinai.
- King David was born on the 6th of Sivan and died 70
  years later on the same date.
- The sign of the zodiac for Sivan is twins.

4. Tammuz (29 days)

- Tammuz is the fourth month of the year and the first
  month of the summer.
- On the 3rd of Tammuz, the Jews fought a fierce battle
  against the Amorites.

- Moses came down from Mount Sinai on the 17th of Tammuz.
- Noah sent a dove out of the ark on the 17th of Tammuz.
- The sign of the zodiac for Tammuz is a crab.

5. Av (30 days)

- Av is the fifth month of the Hebrew year, and a month of sorrow and mourning.
- Aaron, brother of Moses, died on the 1st of Av.
- Both the First and Second Jerusalem Temples were destroyed on the 9th of Av.
- According to tradition, after 40 years in the desert God forgave the Israelites for the sin of the spies on the 15th of Av.
- The sign of the zodiac for Av is a lion.

6. Elul (29 days)

- Elul is the sixth month of the Hebrew year. It is a popular month for Jewish weddings because Elul's Hebrew initials correspond to the biblical verse *"Ani l'dodi v'dodi li"* (I am my beloved's and my beloved is mine). Every weekday in Elul we blow the *shofar* as a reminder that Rosh HaShanah is around the corner.
- The ten spies died on the 17th of Elul.
- The sign of the zodiac for Elul is a young maiden.

7. Tishri (30 days)

- We count our months from Nisan, when the Jews left Egypt, but our years begin with Tishri, when God created the world. So even though Tishri is the seventh month, it is considered the beginning of the new Hebrew year.
- Tradition has it that Abraham, Isaac, and Jacob were born in Tishri.
- The 1st and 2nd of Tishri are Rosh Hashanah, the beginning of our year.
- Yom Kippur is the 10th of Tishri.
- The festival of Sukkot begins on the 15th of Tishri.

- The sign of the zodiac for Tishri is a pair of scales.
  This is the month in which God "weighs" deeds and
  judges the world.

8. Cheshvan (29 or 30 days)

- Cheshvan, the eighth month, is sometimes called
  Marcheshvan, the bitter month. It was given this
  name because it is the only month with no Jewish
  celebration.
- The flood in the time of Noah began on the 17th of
  Cheshvan.
- Noah came out of the ark on the 28th of Cheshvan.
- Rachel, the matriarch, died on the 14th of Cheshvan.
- The sign of the zodiac for Cheshvan is a scorpion.

9. Kislev (29 or 30 days)

- Kislev is the ninth month of the Hebrew year.
- God blessed Noah in the beginning of Kislev with the
  world's first rainbow.
- On the 25th of Kislev the Jews finished building the
  tabernacle in the desert.
- The festival of Chanukah is celebrated on the 25th of
  Kislev.
- The sign of the zodiac for Kislev is a rainbow.

10. Tevet (29 days)

- Tevet is the tenth month of the year. It begins on the
  6th or 7th day of Chanukah.
- On the 8th of Tevet, King Ptolemy of Egypt forced 72
  Jewish sages to translate the Torah into Greek.
- On the 10th of Tevet (a fast day) the king of Babylon
  began to attack the city of Jerusalem.
- Ezra and Nehemiah died on the 9th of Tevet.
- The sign of the zodiac for Tevet is a goat.

11. Shevat (30 days)

- Shevat is the eleventh month of the Hebrew year.
- On the 1st of Shevat in the 40th year in the desert,

Moses began to review all of the Torah with the Israelites.

- The 15th of Shevat is Jewish Arbor Day, known as Tu BeShevat.
- The sign of the zodiac for Tevet is a vessel filled with water.

12. Adar (29 days)

- When Adar begins, our joy increases. The 14th of Adar commemorates the festival of Purim.
- Moses was born and died on the 7th of Adar.
- In a leap year, a thirteenth month called Adar Sheni (the 2nd Adar), is added to the Hebrew calendar.
- The sign of the zodiac for Adar is a fish, a symbol of blessing and good fortune.

Hebrew Calendar Miscellany

The first day of Passover is always the same day of the week as the 9th of Av.

The second day of Passover is always the same day of the week as Shavuot.

The third day of Passover is always the same day of the week as Rosh Hashanah.

The fourth day of Passover is always the same day of the week as Simchat Torah.

The fifth day of the Passover is always the same day of the week as Yom Kippur.

The sixth day of Passover is always the same day of the week as Purim.

Summary of Jewish Holidays
Shabbat

Date Each week, from sundown on Friday until Saturday night when it gets dark.

Duration One day.

Names of holiday Day of rest (Yom Menuchah).

Source God blessed the seventh day and made it holy. On it God rested from all work (Genesis 2:3).

General Theme The Sabbath, considered the holiest day of the week, celebrates the creation of the world. It is a day of prayer, study, rest, relaxation, spirituality, and enjoyment. The Sabbath is also our weekly reminder that God rested from work as well. Of all of the holidays in the Torah, only the Sabbath is mentioned in the Ten Commandments (Exodus 20:8). We are commanded to observe and remember the Sabbath and to always keep it holy.

Personal theme An opportunity to cease from daily work, proclaiming God as Sovereign of the world and allowing us to rejuvenate ourselves.

Traditional foods Braided loaves of bread (*challot*), gefilte fish, wine, and chicken.

Customs

1. Preparations for the Sabbath include housecleaning, washing ourselves and wearing fresh clothing, and dropping some coins into a *tzedakah* (charity) box before lighting the candles.

2. Two candles are lit just before sunset, and the appropriate blessing is recited.

3. The Friday-evening Sabbath service takes place in synagogue. In most Conservative and Reform communities, family members go to this service after eating the *Shabbat* meal. The traditional greeting on the Sabbath is *Shabbat shalom* (Sabbath peace). Following services is an *Oneg Shabbat*, which is an opportunity to enjoy refreshments with others.

4. It is customary for parents to bless their children before sitting down to the meal. The blessing for boys invokes the shining examples of Jacob's grandchildren Ephraim and Manasseh, who, although raised in Egypt, did not lose their identity as Jews. The blessing for girls refers to the four matriarchs—Sarah, Rebekah, Rachel, and Leah—all of whom were known for their concern and compassion for others.

5. The Friday-evening meal begins with the blessing over the wine. This is followed by the ritual washing of the hands

and the benediction over the two *challot*, which recall the double portion of manna God provided for the Israelites.

6. The *Shabbat* meal should be served and enjoyed at a relaxed pace. Many families sing *Shabbat* songs (*zemirot*) between the courses.

7. The meal concludes with the blessings after the meal (*birkat haMazon*).

8. During services on Saturday morning, a section from the Torah is read, as well as the prophetic portion known as a *haftarah*.

9. *Shabbat* afternoon is a time for a variety of experiences that change the pace of daily life. Taking a nap, reading, studying, and visiting local friends all provide a relaxing shift from weekday pressures.

10. On *Shabbat* afternoon there is a *Minchah* service, which introduces the Torah portion that will be read the following Saturday morning. This is followed by a third *Shabbat* meal—*seudah shelishit*. This meal is usually a simple dairy meal that also customarily includes the singing of *Shabbat* songs.

11. The Saturday-evening service concludes with the reciting of the *Havdalah* (separation) ceremony. The ceremonial objects used in *Havdalah* are a *Kiddush* cup (wine sanctifies reentry into the secular world), a spice box (spices symbolically assure that the memory of the *Shabbat* just gone by will be fragrant and linger), and a braided multiwick candle (fire reminds us that light was what God created right after He completed heaven and earth).

Rosh HaShanah
(Beginning of the Hebrew year)

Date First 2 days of Tishri.

Duration Two days for Conservative, Reconstructionist, and Orthodox Jews and for Jews in Israel. One day for Reform Jews.

Names of holiday Day of Blowing the *Shofar* (Yom Teruah); Day of Remembrance (Yom HaZikaron); Day of Judgment (Yom HaDin); together with Yom Kippur it is known as the Days of Awe (Yamim Noraim).

Source In the seventh month, in the first day of the month, shall be a solemn rest unto you, a memorial proclaimed with the blast of horns, a holy convocation (Leviticus 23:24).

General theme As the new year begins, God judges people for the coming year. In order to judge us fairly, God remembers and weighs all of our acts of the past year before giving a final verdict. Rosh HaShanah also commemorates the birthday of the world.

Personal theme The personal theme of Rosh HaShanah is renewal. In admitting our mistakes, we ask for forgiveness. It is a time for self-examination, new resolutions, and earnest efforts at correcting our faults.

Traditional Foods Round *challah*, suggesting God's crown, and apples dipped in honey, expressing the wish for a sweet and fruitful year.

Customs

1. Festival candles are lit at sunset in the home and the following blessing is recited:

Barukh atah Adonai eloheinu melekh ha'olam asher kidshanu be mitzvotav vetzivanu lehadlik ner shel (shabbat v') yom tov.

Praised are You, Sovereign of the Universe, whose *mitzvot* add holiness to our lives and who gave us the *mitzvah* to kindle light for [Shabbat and for] the Festival.

2. The blessing over the wine (the *Kiddush*) for Rosh HaShanah is recited before eating. This is followed by the reciting of the *shehecheyanu*, the prayer for the gift of life that is used to usher in festivals. The *shehecheyanu* is often said when eating a new fruit for the first time in a season.

3. Apples are dipped in honey, symbolically expressing the hope that sweetness will enter the lives of all Jews in the coming year. The following blessing is recited:

Yehi ratzon milfanekha Adonai eloheinu velohei avoteinu shetechadesh aleinu shanah tovah umetukah.

May it be your desire, God of our ancestors, to renew for us a sweet and good year.

4. The blessing over the bread (*hamotzi*) is recited over a round *challah* in the shape of a king's crown.

Barukh atah Adonai eloheinu melekh ha'olam hamotzi le-chem min haaretz.

Praised are You, Sovereign of the Universe, who brings forth bread from the earth.

5. During synagogue services, the rabbi and the cantor (and congregants who follow this custom) wear white *kittels* (robes). The color white is a symbol of purity and renewal and is reminiscent of the words read on Rosh HaShanah: "Though your sins be as scarlet, they shall become as white as snow" (Isaiah 1:18). It is also Jewish custom to replace the colored ark curtain, Torah mantles, and reader's table cover with white ones.

6. When greeting people, it is customary to use the phrase *Leshanah tovah tikateivu*, meaning, "May you be inscribed for a good year." This phrase also appears on New Year greeting cards, which are often sent to friends and family. Other traditional greetings include *Shanah tovah* ("Have a good year") and *Ketivah vechatimah tovah* ("May you be inscribed and sealed for a good year").

7. The *shofar* (ram's horn) is sounded during services (except on the Sabbath), awakening us to repentance.

8. On the first day of Rosh HaShanah, in the afternoon (or on the second day in the afternoon if the first day is the Sabbath), Jews customarily gather at a nearby stream or river to symbolically cast away their sins. This ceremony is called *Tashlikh* (meaning to cast off), and includes the verse from the Book of Micah (7:19), "And You will cast [*vetashlikh*] all their sins in the depths of the sea."

9. Some people visit the graves of departed family members before Rosh HaShanah, during the month of Elul.

Yom Kippur (Day of Atonement)

Date Tenth of Tishri.

Duration One day for Reform, Conservative, Orthodox, and Reconstructionist Jews.

Names of holiday Together with Rosh HaShanah, it is known as the Days of Awe (Yamim Noraim); Sabbath of Sabbaths (Shabbat Shabbaton).

Source On the tenth day of the seventh month is the day of atonement. You shall have a holy convocation and you shall afflict your souls (Leviticus 23:27).

General Theme We abstain from eating, confess our sins, and ask for forgiveness, hoping that we will be sealed in God's Book of Life. We all feel responsible to one another.

Personal theme Integrity, renewal, and a desire that our fast will lead us to lending a hand to others in distress.

Customs

1. We serve a festive meal at sunset on the eve of Yom Kippur.
2. The holiday is ushered in by lighting two candles and reciting the following blessing:

Praised are You, Sovereign of the Universe, whose *mitzvot* add holiness to our lives and who gave us the *mitzvah* to kindle light for (*Shabbat* and for) Yom Kippur.

This is followed by the recitation of the *shehecheyanu:*

Barukh atah Adonai eloheinu melekh haolam shehecheyanu vikimanu vihigiyanu lazman hazeh.

Praised are You, Sovereign of the Universe, for granting us life, for sustaining us, and for enabling us to reach this day.

3. It is customary to light a *yahrzeit* candle, as a memorial to the deceased members of the family, just before leaving for services.
4. Rabbi, cantor, and congregants who follow the custom, wear white gowns, called *kittels,* as is the custom on Rosh HaShanah.
5. At the evening Yom Kippur service, called *Kol Nidre,* the *tallit* (prayer shawl) is worn, symbolizing the added piety of the occasion.
6. The abstinence on Yom Kippur includes total fasting for adults (except the sick or weak), abstaining from sexual relations, and not wearing leather shoes (out of compassion for animals) or cosmetics.
7. Memorial services for the dead *(Yizkor)* are said on Yom Kippur during services.

8. On Yom Kippur afternoon, at the *Minchah* service, the entire Book of Jonah is chanted, reminding us that God's forgiveness is universal.

9. At the end of the Yom Kippur service, a long blast of the *shofar* is sounded and the words *leshanah habaah biyerushalayim* ("next year in Jerusalem") are proclaimed.

10. The greeting at the end of Yom Kippur is *G'mar chatimah tovah* ("May you be sealed for a good verdict").

Sukkot

Date Begins on the 15th of Tishri.

Duration Eight days for Conservative, Reconstructionist, and Orthodox Jews. Seven days for Reform Jews and Jews in Israel.

Names of holiday Day of Ingathering (Hag HaAsif); The Holiday (HeChag); Day of Rejoicing (Zeman Simchateinu); Harvest Festival (Chag HaKatzir).

Source On the fifteenth day of the seventh month is the feast of tabernacles for seven days. And you shall take on the first day the fruit of the goodly trees, branches of palm trees, and willows of the brook, and you shall rejoice before God seven days. And you shall dwell in booths seven days (Leviticus 23:34, 40, 42).

General theme Sukkot marks the end of the fall harvest season, when the Israelites brought their firstfruits to the Temple as a sign of thanksgiving for God's kindness. We are urged to remember the Israelites' 40 years of wandering in the desert. They built fragile huts to protect them from the elements. We are commanded to do the same today, reminding us of the fragility of life itself.

The Bible also commands us to use the "four species" on Sukkot. These consist of the *etrog* (citron), a *lulav* (palm branch) and, attached to the *lulav*, the two sets of leaves—*hadassim* (myrtles, which are short and round) and *aravot* (willows, which are long and narrow). Various explanations have been given for the four species, including the one in which the etrog represents the heart, the lulav represents the spine, the myrtles symbolize the eyes, and the willows are symbolic of the lips and mouth. The symbols indicate that we should serve God with every fiber of our being.

Personal theme Festival of Thanksgiving that is closely related to the American Thanksgiving festival.

Traditional foods

Stuffed cabbage and *kreplach* (fried pockets of dough) containing fruit or fall harvest vegetables; dishes made with honey, such as *tsimmes* (prunes and other fruit, carrots, and honey) and *taiglakh* (honey pastry) are served in the *sukkah* to symbolize the hope for a sweet year.

Customs

1. The holiday is ushered in with the lighting of two candles and the reciting of this blessing:

Barukh atah Adonai eloheinu melekh ha'olam asher kidshanu beemitzvotav vetzivanu lehadlik ner shel Yom tov.

Praised are You, Sovereign of the Universe, whose *mitzvot* add holiness to our lives and who gave us the *mitzvah* to kindle light for the Festival.

2. The festival blessing over wine (*Kiddush*) is chanted in the *sukkah*, followed by the *shehecheyanu* blessing and the special blessing for dwelling in the *sukkah*. The latter blessing is:

Barukh atah Adonai eloheinu melekh ha'olam asher kidshanu bemitzvotav vetzivanu leisheiv basukkah.

Praised are You, Sovereign of the Universe, whose *mitzvot* add holiness to our lives and who gave us the *mitzvah* to dwell in the *sukkah*.

3. By tradition, the walls of the *sukkah* are hung with tablets bearing the names of seven *ushpizin*, or special guests, whom we invite to be with us in the *sukkah* each day: Abraham, Isaac, Jacob, Joseph, Moses, Aaron, and David.

4. During Sukkot morning services, the *lulav* and *etrog* are waved during certain selections in the Hallel service. The Hallel psalms recall the celebration of festivals in the ancient Temple and express our gratitude for God's protection and deliverence. (Note: The *lulav* and *etrog* are not used when Sukkot falls on the Sabbath.)

5. The *lulav* and *etrog* are carried in a processional during morning services. In these *hakafot* (circuits), *hoshannot* (prayers of redemption) are recited.

6. Meals are customarily served in the *sukkah* throughout the festival.

7. The seventh day of Sukkot is called Hoshannah Rabbah (the great help) because of the special Hoshannah prayers of redemption recited on this day. On Hoshannah Rabbah the cantor dons a white gown (*kittel*). Our sages suggest that on this day God's judgment, sealed on Yom Kippur, receives final confirmation. Seven circuits are made around the sanctuary as the Torah carrier is followed by all persons holding their *lulav* and *etrog*. Toward the end of the service, bunches of willow leaves (called *hoshannot*) are taken by each person and struck against a chair or table. Just as the tree, after losing its leaves, renews its life by rain and warmth, so can people gain fresh strength in life's struggles and cares by renewed faith in God.

8. When one of the intermediate days of Sukkot falls on the Sabbath, the biblical book of Ecclesiastes (*Kohelet*) is read before the reading of the Torah.

9. The greeting during Sukkot is *chag same'ach*. ("Happy holidays") or *Mo'adim lesimchah* ("May your festival be happy").

Shemini Atzeret and Simchat Torah

Date The 22nd and 23rd of Tishri.

Duration Two days for Conservative, Reconstructionist, and Orthodox Jews. One day for Reform Jews and Jews living in Israel.

Source On the eighth day shall be a holy convocation for you . . . it is a day of solemn assembly (Leviticus 23:36).

General theme These 2 days are attached to the end of the festival of Sukkot. Since Sukkot was one of the three pilgrimage festivals, the people extended their festivities and lingered in Jerusalem—thus the added 8th day of Shemini Atzeret. On Simchat Torah (the 9th day), the reading from the Book of Deuteronomy concludes the cycle of Torah readings, which is begun again immediately with the reading of the first verses of Genesis.

Personal theme A new beginning in anticipation of an improved and better new year.

Customs

1. Two candles are lit to usher in both Shemini Atzeret and Simchat Torah, and the festival blessing is chanted. A *yahrzeit* candle to the memory of the departed is lit as well.

2. The festival blessing over the wine (the *Kiddush*) and the blessing over the bread (*hamotzi*) are recited.

3. On Shemini Atzeret the *Yizkor* memorial prayers for the departed are recited. In addition, the solemn prayer for rain in Israel (called *Tefillat Geshem*) is added to the additional *Musaf* service, for at this time of year the rainy season is due to begin in Israel, where the crops depend heavily on the abundance of rainfall. In most synagogues the cantor is attired in a white gown (*kittel*) because of the importance of the prayer for rain.

4. On Simchat Torah there is great merriment in the synagogue. People sing and dance while marching with all of the Torah scrolls. Children often carry banners and flags topped with apples. During the service a very special honor is awarded to two members of the congregation. The one called on to read the concluding paragraph of the Torah is referred to as *Chatan Torah* (the bridegroom of the Torah), and the one who reads the opening paragraphs of Genesis is called *Chatan Bereshit* (the bridegroom of Genesis). There is also a custom to call up adults to the Torah for an aliyah. Often adults are called up collectively to say the Torah blessings, and they stand under a large prayer shawl (*tallit*). Children , too, are also presented with an opportunity to recite the blessings over the Torah, standing under a prayer shawl as well.

Chanukah

Date Begins on the 25th of Kislev.

Duration Eight days.

Names of holiday Chag HaUrim (Festival of Lights).

Source They purified the Temple, removed the stones which defiled it . . . they took unhewed stones, as the law commands, and built a new altar on the model of the old one. They rebuilt the sanctuary and restored its interior and courts. They fixed the sacred vessels and menorah. When they had the shew bread on the table and had hung the curtains, and all their work was complete, then early on the twenty-fifth day of the month of Kislev . . . it was rededicated with hymns of Thanksgiving . . . . Then Judah, his brothers, and the whole congregation of Israel decreed that the rededication of the altar should be observed with joy and gladness at the same time each year (1 Maccabees 4:39–59).

General theme Chanukah marks the first time in recorded history that a war was launched for freedom of religion. About 2,100 years ago, Antiochus, the Syrian tyrant, set out to destroy the Jewish religion and replace it with Greek idol worship. He suffered a stunning defeat by the Maccabees, who not only defeated the enemy but also recaptured the Jerusalem Temple and rededicated it. Through a miracle, the little cruse of pure oil that had been found burned for 8 days. That is why the Jewish people light candles on each of the 8 days of the festival. The special Chanukah candle holder is called a *chanukiah*.

Personal theme Religious freedom and dedication. On Chanukah many Jews have become involved in seeking freedom and opportunities for all people.

Traditional foods Foods fried in oil, especially potato pancakes (called *latkes* or *levivot* in Hebrew). In Israel the custom is to serve jelly doughnuts (*sufganiot*).

Customs

1. Each night of Chanukah the *chanukiah* is lit and the appropriate blessings are recited. The song *"Ma'oz tzur"* is often chanted upon the completion of lighting the *chanukiah*.

2. In the synaogogue the *chanukiah* is also lit during the morning Shaharit service, but the blessings are not recited.

3. During the morning service the Torah is read (Numbers, chap. 7). The reading tells of the identical gifts that were brought by the princes of the tribes of Israel at the dedication of the altar.

4. The *Hallel* psalms of praise are chanted in the synagogue during the morning services. In addition, the special paragraph *al hanissim* is added to the *Amidah* prayer. The *al hanissim* thanks God for the miraculous deliverance of our ancestors in other days as well as in our time.

5. Chanukah games are played throughout the festival. The most popular one is spinning a *dreidel*, which is a spinning top with four sides. On each side is found one of the following letters: *nun, gimel, hay*, or *shin*. These letters stand for the words *Nes gadol hayah sham* (A great miracle occurred there). If the dreidel falls on the *nun*, the player gets nothing; if it falls on the *gimel*, the player takes the whole pot; if it falls on the *hay*, the player takes half; if it falls on the *shin*, the player must add to the pot.

6. Sharing and exchanging gifts, including Chanukah *gelt* (money).

7. Some people affix a new *mezuzah* to a doorpost in the home that has yet to receive one. Since the word *Chanukah* itself means dedication, affixing a *mezuzah* is the spiritual way to dedicate a room.

8. Some people use the festival of Chanukah to affix a *mizrach* to an eastern wall in their home. Years ago when the Temple still existed, Jews outside Jerusalem would face the city when praying. For many of the world's Jews, this meant facing East. The custom then developed of marking the eastern wall of the home in some manner so that one would always be aware of the direction of Jerusalem. Today a *mizrach* usually refers to some sort of decoration that is hung on the east wall of the house or synagogue to indicate the direction of Jerusalem for correct orientation in prayer.

Purim (Festival of Lots)

Date Fourteenth of Adar.

Duration One day.

Source Wherefore they called these days Purim after the name of Pur (Book of Esther 9:26).

General theme Purim commemorates the Jewish people's miraculous escape about 2,400 years ago in Persia. Because the Jews refused to bow down to Haman, the adviser to King Ahasuerus, he drew lots (*purim* in Hebrew) to determine on which day the Jews would be exterminated. Through the intervention of Mordecai and his niece, Queen Esther, the Jewish people were saved.

Personal theme Giving to the poor and sharing food with one's friends.

Traditional Foods *Hamantaschen* (triangular pastries filled with prunes, poppy seeds, cherries, and the like) are served. The shape of these pastries is reminiscent of the three-cornered hat worn by Haman.

Customs

1. Some Jews follow the custom of fasting on the day before Purim. This fast, called the Fast of Esther (*Taanit Ester*) is in honor of Esther, who abstained from food for 3 days before petitioning King Ahasuerus.

2. The Scroll of Esther (*Megillat Ester*) is publicly chanted aloud in both the evening and the morning. At these services, people are encouraged to masquerade in costume and use noisemakers (called *greggars* or *raashanim* in Hebrew) to drown out the name of Haman each time his name is read.

3. Many synagogues and Jewish Community Centers hold Purim carnivals for participants to enjoy eating festive food, costumes, and playing carnival games.

4. A festive Purim meal (called the Purim *seudah*) is customarily served. This meal affords family members, relatives, and friends the opportunity to be together on a joyous occasion.

5. The exchanging of food baskets (called *mishloach manot*) with family and friends is also part of the Purim festival custom. Making charitable donations to various organizations is also very much in the spirit of the festival.

6. A special paragraph called *al hanissim* is added during the *Amidah* prayer. This paragraph offers gratitude to God for the miraculous deliverance of our ancestors in days of old as well as in modern times.

Passover

Date Begins the 14th of Nisan.

Duration Lasts 8 days for Conservative, Reconstructionist, and Orthodox Jews and 7 days for Reform Jews and Jews living in Israel.

Names of holiday Feast of Unleavened Bread (Chag HaMatzot); Holiday of Freedom (Zeman Heruteinu); Festival of Spring (Chag He'Aviv).

Note: The name Passover (Pesach) derives from the fact that the angel of the Lord "passed over" the homes of the Israelites while smiting the firstborn Egyptians (Exodus 12:27).

Source On the fifteenth day of the same month is the feast of unleavened bread for God. Seven days you shall eat unleavened bread (Leviticus 23:5).

General theme This holiday commemorates the exodus of the Israelites from Egypt under the leadership of Moses some 3,300 years ago. During their hasty departure, the Israelites did not have time to fully bake their bread and allow it to rise. The result was the creation of *matzah* cakes (unleavened bread), which Jews today eat on Passover as a reminder of that Egyptian slavery. Passover also has an agricultural theme. It heralds the arrival of spring and the beginning of the spring grain harvest.

Personal theme Religious freedom.

Traditional Foods

1. During the Passover *Seder* meal, the following special foods are placed on the *Seder* plate:

a. *Charoset*: A mixture of chopped nuts, apples, wine, and cinnamon, resembling the mortar used by the Israelite slaves to make bricks for the Egyptian pyramids.

b. Roasted bone (*zeroa*): Represents the Paschal lamb that was sacrificed by our ancestors.

c. Roasted egg (*beitzah*): Symbolizes both the sacrifice made by everyone in the Jerusalem Temple on each holiday and the mourning over the destruction of the Temple.

d. Bitter herbs (*maror*): Pure horseradish, which reminds us of the bitterness of slavery.

e. Parsley (*karpas*): Dipped into salt water, the parsley symbolizes the tears of misery that were shed by our enslaved ancestors. The parsley itself symbolizes spring and hope for the future.

2. Food that is *chametz* (leavened) is forbidden to be eaten on Passover. This would include food made of the grains wheat, rye, barley, oats, and spelt. Thus foods such as biscuits, cakes, cereals, crackers, bread, and liquids made from grain alcohols are expressly forbidden. Foods not *chametz* include meat, fish, fowl, all fruits, vegetables (except

peas and beans), and, from freshly opened packages, spices, coffee, tea, sugar, and salt.

All kinds of packaged and prepared foods are available for Passover. To be acceptable, they should carry both the seal of a rabbinical group and the inscription "kosher for Passover" (*kosher l'Pesach*).

Customs

1. Before the festival begins, the house is scrubbed and special care is taken to remove all bread items. Special Passover pots and dishes are used during the holiday.

2. On the eve of Passover, it is customary to search for any leftover *chametz* in a ceremony called "searching for *chametz*" (*bedikat chametz*). Traditionally the ceremony is conducted using a candle for light, a feather as a broom, and a wooden spoon as a dustpan. The following morning, the *chametz* that was gathered the previous evening is burned.

All *chametz* that is not burned is stored away in one's home. In many communities this *chametz* is sold to a rabbi who in turn sells the community *chametz* to a non-Jew. After Passover, the *chametz* reverts to its original owner.

3. A Passover *Seder* is conducted on the first 2 nights of Passover (one night for Reform Jews). The Passover text used during the meal is the *Haggadah*.

4. Candles are lit and the appropriate blessing recited on the first 2 nights and last 2 nights of Passover.

5. Historically, "wheat money" (*ma'ot chittin*) was given to the poor. Today, one customarily makes a charitable *tzedakah* donation.

6. Beginning on the second night of Passover, Jews begin to count the *omer*. The *omer* (literally "sheaf") refers to an offering from the new barley crop that was brought to the ancient Temple on the eve of the second day of Passover. *Omer* has come to be known as the name of the period between Passover and Shavuot. By counting the days of this period (*sefirat ha'omer*), we recall the events to which these days connect in the Jewish calendar: the liberation from slavery commemorated by Passover, and the revelation of the Torah commemorated by Shavuot. We count the days to heighten our anticipation of celebrating the revelation of the Torah.

7. The first 2 days and last 2 days of Passover are holy days, with work restrictions. In the synagogue, the *Hallel* psalms of praise are chanted. A special prayer for dew (*tefillat*

tal) is recited by the cantor at morning services on the first day of Passover. The Torah is chanted throughout the entire festival of Passover. On the first 2 days the reading is Exodus 12:21–51 and Leviticus 22:26–23, respectively. The readings for the last 2 days are Exodus 13:17–15:26 and Deuteronomy 15:19–16:17.

8. On the evening of the 8th day of Passover, it is customary to light a *yahrzeit* memorial candle in memory of one's departed loved ones. The following morning at services there is a *Yizkor* memorial service in memory of the departed.

9. Some synagogues follow the custom of reading selections from the Song of Songs on the Intermediate Sabbath of Passover. Rabbinic tradition interprets the book as a love song, where the beloved is taken to mean God and the bride to mean the Israelites. This tradition made the book especially appropriate to Passover, because it marked, as it were, the beginning of the courtship of Israel and God before, metaphorically speaking, they finally became wedded at Mount Sinai by Israel's acceptance of the Torah.

Shavuot

Date Begins on the 6th of Sivan.

Duration Two days for Conservative, Reconstructionist, and Orthodox Jews. One day for Reform Jews and Jews living in Israel.

Names of holiday Season of the giving of the Torah (Zeman Matan Torateinu); Holiday of Firstfruits (Chag HaBikkurim); Pentecost.

Source Unto the morrow after the seventh week shall you number fifty days . . . (Leviticus 23:16).

General theme This holiday, which occurs 7 weeks after the 2nd day of Passover, commemorates the receiving of the Torah at Mount Sinai. Shavuot, like Passover and Sukkot, is one of the three pilgrimage festivals. During Temple days the Israelites brought an offering of their firstfruits (*bikkurim*). Thus Shavuot has also come to be known as the spring harvest festival of firstfruits.

Personal theme Accepting religious obligations (*mitzvot*) and reaffirming our covenant with God.

Traditional foods Blintzes, cheesecake, and other dairy foods are eaten on Shavuot. One reason for this custom is that it is derived by our sages from the passage "honey and milk shall be under your tongue" (Song of Songs 4:11), which implies that the words of the Torah may be as pleasant and acceptable to our ears and hearts as milk and honey are to our tongues.

Customs

1. Candles are lit on both evenings of Shavuot to usher in the holiday. This is followed by the festival blessing over the wine for Shavuot and the blessing over the bread.

2. It is customary to spend many hours on Shavuot night in reading and studying various Jewish texts. Called in Hebrew *leil tikkun shavuot*, this special gathering to study is often held in the synagogue as well as in various homes in the Jewish community.

3. Synagogues are usually decorated with greenery and flowers reflecting the agricultural aspect of Shavuot.

4. During the morning services of Shavuot, the special Hallel psalms of praise are recited. In addition, the Torah is read on both days of Shavuot. On the 1st day, the reading includes the Ten Commandments (Exodus 19 and 20). On the 2nd day, the reading is from Deuteronomy 15:19–16:17 and includes a description of the three pilgrimage festivals of Sukkot, Passover, and Shavuot.

5. On the evening of the 2nd night of Shavuot it is customary to light a *yahrzeit* memorial candle in memory of one's deceased loved ones. At services on the morning of the 2nd day of Shavuot, there is a *Yizkor* memorial service.

6. Many synagogues invite their Hebrew high school students to participate in a Confirmation service on Shavuot. These students lead the service, confirm their allegiance to God, and often are presented with Confirmation diplomas.

7. On the 1st day of Shavuot, a special liturgical poem called *Akdamut* is recited at morning services before the Torah reading. The poem suggests the unspeakable majesty of God.

8. On Shavuot day it is customary to read the Book of Ruth. The reasons for its association with the festival are the

story of how Ruth, a Moabite woman, embraced the religion of Israel, and the account it gives of the grain harvest and the treatment of the poor in the harvest season. There is also a tradition that King David was born and died on Shavuot. Because David descended from Ruth, the reading of this book, in which the birth of David is recorded, is appropriate to the occasion.

Other Jewish Commemorations

Tisha B'Av (9th of Av)

Date Ninth of Av.

Duration One day.

Theme Tisha B'Av commemorates the destruction of the First and Second Temples in Jerusalem. The 3 weeks prior to Tisha B'Av are known as the "Three Weeks." This is a corresponding period of lesser mourning. The 9 days starting with the 1st day of Av and ending with Tisha B'Av are known as the "Nine Days," during which we remember with sadness the destruction of the Temple. Many people refrain from eating meat (except on the Sabbath) during these days, because eating meat was considered joyous.

Customs

1. On the night of Tisha B'Av, the lights are dimmed in the synagogue. Congregants often sit on low benches (or on the floor). In this mourning posture they follow the reading from the Book of Lamentations (*Eikhah*). The fast of Tisha B'Av now begins.

2. During morning services the next day, the prayers are spoken rather than chanted. *Tefillin* and *tallit* are not worn. The reading is taken from Deuteronomy 4:25–40 and the *haftarah* from the Book of Jeremiah (8:13–9:23), which opens with the words, "I will utterly consume them, says God."

3. In the afternoon, during the *Minchah* service, the mood begins to change. Both *tallit* and *tefillin* are worn. The Torah

is read (Exodus 32:11–14; 34:1–10) and so is the *haftarah* (Isaiah 55:6–56:8).

4. Bathing and conjugal relations are forbidden during the commemoration of Tisha B'Av.

Tu BeShevat (Jewish Arbor Day)

Date Fifteenth of Shevat.

Duration One day.

Names of holiday New Year for Trees (Rosh HaShanah L'Ilanot).

Source The Mishnah (1:1) of the talmudic tractate of *Rosh HaShanah* mentions the New Year for trees.

Theme Tu BeShevat commemorates the beginning of the spring season in Israel, when the trees begin to blossom. The official organization responsible for planting trees in Israel is called Keren Kayemet L'Yisrael (Jewish National Fund). In Israel, children plant trees on this holiday. In the Diaspora it is customary to purchase Jewish National Fund certificates.

Traditional foods Fruits and vegetables are customarily eaten on Tu BeShevat. These include the Israeli fruits mentioned in the Bible, including grapes, pomegranates, figs, dates, olives, and *bokser* (St. John's bread), the fruit of the carob tree.

Customs

1. Many synagogues and families hold a Tu BeShevat Seder using four cups of wine (one white, symbolizing winter; the second, light red, symbolizing spring; the third, deep red, symbolizing summer; and the fourth, red mixed with white, symbolizing fall). A Tu BeShevat *Haggadah* is commonly used to recite blessings over the various fruits, reminding us of the importance of trees.

2. In Israel, children plant saplings in the Jewish National Fund forests. In Western countries it is customary to purchase tree certificates in honor and memory of friends and relatives.

Yom HaShoah (Holocaust Memorial Day)

Date Twenty-seventh of Nisan.

Duration One day.

Theme A day to recall the 6 million Jews of Europe who were tortured and murdered during the Second World War.

Customs A community memorial service is held, commemorating the martyred dead. Holocaust survivors and their children often speak at the service. A six-branched candelabrum is lit in commemoration of the 6 million.

Yom HaZikaron (Remembrance Day)

Date Fourth of Iyar.

Duration One day.

Theme A memorial day observed for those who fell during active service in the Israel War of Independence, and subsequently. It is observed in solemn, civil, military, and religious ceremonies throughout Israel.

Customs

1. In Israel, memorial candles are lit in army camps, schools, synagogues, and public places, and flags are flown at half-mast.
2. Throughout the day, ex-servicemen and soldiers serve as guards of honor at war memorials in all towns and villages. Families of the fallen participate in memorial ceremonies at military cemeteries.
3. In Israel all places of entertainment are closed on the eve of Yom HaZikaron.
4. During the morning, a siren marks a 2-minute silence, which brings all activity to a standstill.
5. Special prayers for the previous Sabbath and for Yom HaZikaron include the recital of Psalm 9: "For the leader, on the death of the son," and Psalm 144: "Blessed be God, my Rock, who trains my hands for war and my fingers for battle."

Yom HaAtzma'ut (Israel Independence Day)

Date Fifth of Iyar.

Duration One day.

Theme Commemorates the establishment of the State of Israel on May 14, 1948, corresponding to the 5th of Iyar, 5708.

Traditional Foods Israeli foods, such as pita bread, felafel, and hummus.

Customs

1. Many public gatherings and celebrations are observed, including an Israeli Day parade in New York City, usually held on the Sunday closest to the 5th of Iyar.
2. Included in the synagogue prayers of the day are the Hallel psalms of praise and the addition of *al hanissim* in the *Amidah*, thanking God for miraculous deliverance.

Rosh Chodesh (New Month)

Date The first day of each Jewish month is known as Rosh Chodesh.

Duration One or 2 days. When observed for 2 days, the first day always falls on the 30th of the preceding Hebrew month and the 2nd day falls on the 1st day of the new month.

Source On your new moons, you shall present a burnt offering to God (Numbers 28:11).

General theme In biblical times, Rosh Chodesh was observed as a holiday accompanied by special sacrificial offerings.

Personal theme An opportunity for reflection on the month past and the ways we can improve.

Customs

1. A blessing for the new Hebrew month is recited on the Sabbath immediately preceding that month (except for the month of Tishri).
2. *Hallel* psalms of praise are recited during the morning service, and the Torah reading (Numbers 28:1–15) describes the special sacrificial offerings proffered in biblical times for each new month.

Lag B'Omer (thirty-third day of the *omer*)

Date Eighteenth of Iyar.

Duration One day.

Theme The days between Passover and Shavuot are a solemn period of the Jewish year, recalling the suffering the Jews endured under Roman persecution. During this time, joyous celebrations such as weddings are not permitted. Lag B'Omer breaks the series of solemn days. According to Jewish folklore, Bar Kokhba won a great victory over the Romans on the 33rd day of the *omer*. Another story tells of a plague that was raging among Rabbi Akiba's students and suddenly stopped on that day. This is why Lag B'Omer has been called the "scholar's holiday."

Customs

1. Weddings are often held on Lag B'Omer because of the relief it provides from the solemnity of the days that precede and follow it.

2. Picnics, outings, games with bows and arrows, sporting events, and bonfires are popular ways of celebrating the day.

3. Traditional Jews often will give their children their first haircut on Lag B'Omer. Because the days before Lag B'Omer are days of mourning when haircutting is not permitted, Lag B'Omer affords the first new opportunity to cut hair.

Fast Days in the Hebrew Calendar

Yom Kippur (Day of Atonement) is undoubtedly the most well known of all of the Jewish fast days. However, there are several lesser known fast days as well. Here is a summary of them:

Date	Name	Reason	Time of Observance
3 Tishri	Fast of Gedaliah	Assassination of Gedaliah (2 Kings 25:25)	Dawn to dusk

Date	Name	Reason	Time of Observance
10 Tishri	Yom Kippur	Atonement for one's sins (Leviticus 26–32)	Dusk to dawn
10 Tevet	Fast of Asarah B'Tevet	King Nebuchadnezzar captures Jerusalem (2 Kings 25:1)	Dawn to dusk
13 Adar	Fast of Esther	Esther decrees a fast day (Esther 4:16)	Dawn to dusk
14 Nisan	Fast of First-born	Commemorates tenth plague (Exodus 12:29)	Dawn to dusk
17 Tammuz	Fast of Shivah Asar B'Tammuz	Jerusalem walls breached by King Nebuchadnezzar (2 Kings 24:10–7)	Dawn to dusk
9 Av	Fast of Tisha B'Av	Destruction of Temples (2 Kings 25: 8–9)	Dusk to dawn

✡

Summary of Jewish Holidays and Their Dates

Approximate English Date	Hebrew Date		Holiday
September	29 Elul (evening)		*Eve of Rosh HaShanah (New Year)

Approximate English Date	Hebrew Date		Holiday
	1 Tishri	♆	*First day, Rosh HaShanah
	2 Tishri	♆	*Second day, Rosh HaShanah
September–	9 Tishri (evening)	♆	*Kol Nidre, opening prayer of
October	10 Tishri		*Yom Kippur (Day of Atonement)
October	14 Tishri	♆	*Eve of Sukkot
	15 Tishri	♆	*First day, Sukkot (Tabernacles)
	16 Tishri		*Second day, Sukkot
	21 Tishri	♆	*Eve of Hoshanah Rabbah
	22 Tishri	♆	*Shemini Atzeret (Feast of Conclusion, 8th Day of Solemn Assembly)
	23 Tishri		*Simchat Torah (Rejoicing of the Law)
December	24 Kislev (eve)		°First Chanukah light
	to		
	1 Tevet		(8 nights in all)
January	15 Shevat		°Tu BeShevat (New Year of the Trees)
March	13 Adar		°Eve of Purim (*Megillah* reading)
	14 Adar		°Purim
March–April	14 Nisan	♆	*Passover, first *Seder* (evening)
	15 Nisan	♆	*Second *Seder*
	20 Nisan	♆	*Eve of
	21 Nisan	♆	*Concluding days of Passover, 7th day
	22 Nisan		*Eighth day

Approximate English Date	Hebrew Date		Holiday
April–May	16 Nisan to 5 Sivan		Counting the *omer* (49 days, no weddings)
	27 Nisan		°Remembrance Day (Yom HaShoah, memorializing victims of the Holocaust)
April–May	5 Iyyar		°Israel Independence Day (Yom Ha'Atzma'ut)
	18 Iyyar		°Lag b'Omer (33rd day of counting *omer*, weddings allowed)
May–June	5 Sivan (eve)	♆	*Eve of Shavuot, Bikkurim
	6 Sivan	♆	*First day, Shavuot (Feast of Weeks or Firstfruits)
	7 Sivan		*Second day, Shavuot
August	9 Av		°Tisha b'Av (Fast of the 9th of Av, commemorating the destruction of the Temple)

♆ Candles lit   * Festivals, High Holidays   ° Minor holidays

Ten-Year Calendar of Jewish Holidays

	5754 1993	5755 1994	5756 1995	5757 1996	5758 1997	5759 1998
Rosh HaShanah	Sept. 16	Sept. 6	Sept. 25	Sept. 14	Oct. 2	Sept. 21
Yom Kippur	Sept. 25	Sept. 15	Oct. 4	Sept. 23	Oct. 11	Sept. 30
Sukkot	Sept. 30	Sept. 20	Oct. 9	Sept. 28	Oct. 16	Oct. 5
Simchat Torah	Oct. 8	Sept. 28	Oct. 17	Oct. 6	Oct. 24	Oct. 13
Chanukah	Dec. 9	Nov. 28	Dec. 18	Dec. 6	Dec. 24	Dec. 14
	1994	1995	1996	1997	1998	1999
Tu BeShevat	Jan. 27	Jan. 16	Feb. 5	Jan. 23	Feb. 11	Feb. 1
Purim	Feb. 25	Mar. 16	Mar. 5	Mar. 23	Mar. 12	Mar. 2
Passover	Mar. 27	Apr. 15	Apr. 4	Apr. 22	Apr. 11	Apr. 1
Shavuot	May 16	June 4	May 24	June 11	May 31	May 21

	5760 1999	5761 2000	5762 2001	5763 2002	5764 2003
Rosh HaShanah	Sept. 11	Sept. 30	Sept. 18	Sept. 7	Sept. 27
Yom Kippur	Sept. 20	Oct. 9	Sept. 27	Sept. 16	Oct. 6
Sukkot	Sept. 25	Oct. 14	Oct. 2	Sept. 21	Oct. 11
Simchat Torah	Oct. 3	Oct. 22	Oct. 10	Sept. 29	Oct. 19
Chanukah	Dec. 4	Dec. 22	Dec. 10	Nov. 30	Dec. 20
	2000	2001	2002	2003	2004
Tu BeShevat	Jan. 22	Feb. 8	Jan. 28	Jan. 18	Feb. 7
Purim	Mar. 21	Mar. 9	Feb. 26	Feb. 16	Mar. 7
Passover	Apr. 20	Apr. 8	Mar. 27	Apr. 17	Apr. 6
Shavuot	June 9	May 28	May 17	June 6	May 26

Sabbath and Holiday Greetings

Sabbath

Shabbot Shalom: Sabbath Peace
Gut Shabbos: Yiddish for "Good Sabbath"

After *Havdalah*

Shavua tov: Have a good week
A gut voch: Yiddish for "Have a good week"

General Holiday

Gut Yontif: Yiddish for "Happy holiday"
Chag Same'ach: Happy holiday
Mo'adim LeSimcha: Happy holiday

Rosh HaShanah

Shanah tovah: Have a good year
Shanah tovah u'metukah: Have a good and sweet year
Shanah tovah tikateivu: May you be inscribed for a good
   year

During Ten Days of Repentance
(i.e., between Rosh HaShanah and Yom Kippur)

Gemar chatimah tovah: May your inscription in the Book of
   Life be concluded
Tzom kal: Have an easy fast (said prior to Yom Kippur)

Yom Kippur

Shanah tovah tikateivu vechatameinu: May you be inscribed
   and sealed in the Book of Life for a good year

Daily Greetings

Shalom: Hello, good-bye, peace
Boker tov: Good morning
Boker or: Good morning
Erev tov: Good evening
Lailah tov: Good night
Chalomot tovim: Sweet dreams
Lehitra'ot: See you soon

Kadosh, Kadosh, Kadosh: Holy People, Places, and Things

The vocabulary of Judaism is filled with references to sacred people, places, and things. Throughout the Bible, the Israelites are called God's holy people. Here is a brief summary of the use of the Hebrew word *kadosh* (holy) as it is applied to people, places, and things in Judaism.

People

Am kadshekha—People of your holiness (Isaiah 63:18)
Zerah kodesh—Holy seed (Isaiah 6:13)
Goy kadosh—Holy nation (Exodus 19:6)
Anshei kodesh—Holy People (Exodus 22:30)

Places

Admat kodesh—Holy ground (Exodus 3:5)
Makom HaKodesh—Holy place (Joshua 5:15)
Mikdash—Sanctuary (Exodus 25:8)
Har HaKodesh—Holy Mountain (Isaiah 11:19)
Kodesh HaKodashim—Holy of Holies (Exodus 26:33)
Ir HaKodesh—Holy city (Isaiah 48:2)
Bet HaMikdash—House of Holiness (Refers to Jerusalem Temple)

Sacred Things

Kadashim—Holy objects (Exodus 38:38)
Klei kodesh—Holy vessels (Exodus 38:38)
Bigdei kodesh—Holy garments (Exodus 28:2)
Aron HaKodesh—Holy Ark (Exodus 25:10)

Names and Phrases

Kadosh, Kadosh, Kadosh—Holy, Holy, Holy (Isaiah 6:3)
Kedushah—Prayer of Sanctification
Kaddish—Prayer for the Dead
Kedushin—Marriage Ceremony
Ruach HaKodesh—Holy Spirit

Kosher Symbols

In the United States and Canada, Orthodox rabbis generally supervise the *kashrut* of manufactured foods, although in some communities Conservative rabbis have assumed that role. Today, there are more than fifty major kosher certifying organizations in the United States. Here is a sampling of some of the kosher organizations and their symbols.

 Canadian Jewish Congress of Toronto
4600 Bathurst Street
Downsview, Ontario, Canada
M2R 3V2

Chicago Rabbinical Council
3525 West Peterson Avenue
Chicago, IL 60659

Denver Association of Intensive
Torah Education
1560 Winona Court
Denver, CO 80204

Kashruth Alliance (Igud Harabonim)
156 Fifth Avenue
New York, NY 10010

Kashruth Inspection Service of the
    Vaad Hoier of St.Louis
4 Millstone Campus
St. Louis, MO 63146

Kashruth Supervision Service
7111 Park Heights Avenue
Baltimore, MD 21215

Kehila De Los Angeles
186 North Citrus
Los Angeles, CA 90030

KO Kosher Service
5871 Drexel Road
Philadelphia, PA 19131

Kosher Supervision Service
1444 Queen Anne Road
Teaneck, NJ 07666

Montreal Vaad Hair
5491 Victory Avenue
Montreal, Quebec, Canada

Rabbi Harry Cohen
165 West 91st Street
New York, NY 10024

Rabbi Bernard Poupko
5715 Beacon Street
Pittsburgh, PA 15217

Rabbi Joseph Ralbag
225 West 85th Street
New York, NY 10024

Rabbinical Council of California
244-13 Hendrick Avenue
Lomita, CA 90717

Sephardic Rabbinical Council of America
2030 Ocean Parkway
Brooklyn, NY 11223

Union of Orthodox Jewish Congregations
45 West 36th Street
New York, NY 10018

The Vaad Harabbonim of Flatbush
1618 Coney Island Avenue
Brooklyn, NY 11230

Vaad Horabonim of Greater Detroit
17071 West Ten Mile Road
Southfield, MI 48075

Vancouver Kashrus
3476 Oak Street
Vancouver, BC, Canada V6H 2L8

Tombstone Symbols

In the Book of Genesis (35:20) we are told that Jacob set up a
pillar over his wife Rachel's grave. Today, it is still the custom
to erect a tombstone on the grave of the deceased

In addition to including the name of the deceased in both
English and Hebrew and the date of birth and death, there are
some tombstones that have pictorial symbols on them. Here
are several of the more common ones.

STAR OF DAVID
a symbol of divine
protection.

THE MENORAH
an ancient symbol
of Judaism.

THE EWER OR LEVI PITCHER
a symbol associated with
the Levites, who wash
priests' hands prior to
religious services.

THE YAHRZEIT
the symbol of a
traditional
commemoration ritual
of the Jewish people.

THE MOSAIC DECALOGUE
the Ten Commandments
inscribed in abbreviated
form on two tablets.

COHANIM HANDS
a symbol of the "Cohanim,"
a Jewish caste, by
inheritance the true priests.
Used by the Cohns,
Cohen, Cahns, Cowens,
Cahans, and so on.

SCROLL OF THE
PENTATEUCH
a symbol of the Divine Law.
Represents the first five
books of the Old Testament.

THE LION
a symbol of the
strength of Judaism—
an attribute of David,
Hosea, Samson,
and Daniel.

Some Traditional Thoughts on Prayer

Daily prayer has always been an important part of a traditional Jewish day. Here is a sampling of some thoughts about prayer from rabbinic sources:

Whoever performs God's will and directs their thoughts to God, that person's prayer is heard (*Exodus Rabbah* 21:3).

Whoever has it in their power to pray on behalf of their neighbor and does not do so, that person is called a sinner (*Berakhot* 12b).

If it is impossible to pray in the synagogue, pray in the field. If that is impossible, pray in your house. If that is impossible, pray on your bed. And if that is impossible, pray in your heart (*Midrash Tehillim* 4:5).

Any person whose mind is not at rest should not pray (*Eruvin* 65a)

When you pray, always know before whom you stand (*Berakhot* 28b).

If a person can concentrate, let that person pray; not otherwise (*Berakhot* 30b).

Do not let your prayer become mechanical and unenthusiastic (*Pirke Avot* 2:13).

Let your prayer be a window to heaven (Baal Shem Tov).

Music in the Synagogue

Music, dancing, and singing have always been an integral part of the culture of the Jewish people. Throughout Jewish history we find references to music. Jubal (Genesis, chap. 4) invented the first musical instrument. Miriam and the women danced and played their timbrels after the crossing of the Red Sea (Exodus, chap. 15). King David was a master of the harp. Psalm 150 calls attention to some of the instruments used in the Jerusalem Temple.

With the destruction of the Temple, a period of national mourning set in and instrumental music ceased to be used in the worship service. Since that time it has not returned to the Orthodox synagogue, but many Reform and Reconstructionist and some Conservative synagogues use instruments during their worship services.

Here is a sampling of some of the instruments used during biblical and Temple times:

Wind Instruments
Chalil: flute or reed instrument
Oogav: similar to a bagpipe
Shofar: ram's horn
Chatzotzrah: trumpet

String Instruments
Kinor: harp
Nevel: lyre

Percussion Instruments
Metzaltim: round metal gong
Tofe: hand drum
Shalishim: triangular steel gong
Tziltzilim: castanets

Blessings

Jewish life is filled with *berakhot*—blessings. Beyond the many blessings encountered during prayer services, there are a variety of others that focus on occasions and incidents in the life of a Jew. Here are some interesting blessings for some unique occasions.

Each of the following blessings begins with the standard formula, "Blessed are You, *Adonai* Our God, Sovereign of the Universe. . . ."

Blessings for Taste

Bread

בָּרוּךְ אַתָּה יהוה אֱלֹהֵינוּ מֶלֶךְ הָעוֹלָם, הַמּוֹצִיא לֶחֶם מִן הָאָרֶץ.

Blessed are You, *Adonai* Our God, Sovereign of the Universe, who brings forth bread from the earth.

Barukh atah Adonai eloheinu melekh ha'olam hamotzi lechem min haaretz.

Food (other than bread) prepared from wheat, barley, rye, oats, or spelt:

בָּרוּךְ אַתָּה יהוה אֱלֹהֵינוּ מֶלֶךְ הָעוֹלָם, בּוֹרֵא מִינֵי מְזוֹנוֹת.

Blessed are You, *Adonai* Our God, Sovereign of the Universe, who creates different kinds of nourishment.

Barukh atah Adonai eloheinu melekh ha'olam borei meenei mezonote.

Wine

בָּרוּךְ אַתָּה יהוה אֱלֹהֵינוּ מֶלֶךְ הָעוֹלָם, בּוֹרֵא פְּרִי הַגָּפֶן.

Blessed are You, *Adonai* Our God, Sovereign of the Universe, who creates the fruit of the vine.

Barukh atah Adonai eloheinu melekh ha'olam borei pri hagafen.

Fruit

בָּרוּךְ אַתָּה יהוה אֱלֹהֵינוּ מֶלֶךְ הָעוֹלָם, בּוֹרֵא פְּרִי הָעֵץ.

Blessed are You, *Adonai* Our God, Sovereign of the Universe, who creates the fruit of the tree.

Barukh atah Adonai eloheinu melekh ha'olam borei pri ha'eitz.

Foods that grow in the ground

בָּרוּךְ אַתָּה יהוה אֱלֹהֵינוּ מֶלֶךְ הָעוֹלָם, בּוֹרֵא פְּרִי הָאֲדָמָה.

Blessed are You, *Adonai*, Our God, Sovereign of the Universe, who creates the fruit of the ground.

Barukh atah Adonai eloheinu melekh ha'olam borei pri haadamah.

Other food and drink

בָּרוּךְ אַתָּה יהוה אֱלֹהֵינוּ מֶלֶךְ הָעוֹלָם, שֶׁהַכֹּל נִהְיָה בִּדְבָרוֹ.

Blessed are You, *Adonai* Our God, Sovereign of the Universe, at whose word all things come into existence.

Barukh atah Adonai eloheinu melekh ha'olam shehakol ni- hiyeh bidvaro.

Blessings for Smell

Upon smelling fragrant spices

בָּרוּךְ אַתָּה יהוה אֱלֹהֵינוּ מֶלֶךְ הָעוֹלָם, בּוֹרֵא מִינֵי בְשָׂמִים.

Blessed are You, *Adonai* Our God, Sovereign of the Universe, who creates different kinds of spices.

Barukh atah Adonai eloheinu melekh ha'olam borei minei vesamim.

Upon smelling the fragrance of shrubs and trees

בָּרוּךְ אַתָּה יהוה אֱלֹהֵינוּ מֶלֶךְ הָעוֹלָם, בּוֹרֵא עֲצֵי בְשָׂמִים.

Blessed are You, *Adonai* Our God, Sovereign of the Universe, who creates fragrant trees.

Barukh atah Adonai eloheinu melekh ha'olam borei atzei vesamim.

Upon smelling the fragrance of plants and herbs

בָּרוּךְ אַתָּה יהוה אֱלֹהֵינוּ מֶלֶךְ הָעוֹלָם, בּוֹרֵא עִשְׂבֵי בְשָׂמִים.

Blessed are You, *Adonai* Our God, Sovereign of the Universe, who creates fragrant plants.

Barukh atah Adonai eloheinu melekh ha'olam borei isvei vesamim.

Upon smelling fragrant fruit

בָּרוּךְ אַתָּה יהוה אֱלֹהֵינוּ מֶלֶךְ הָעוֹלָם, הַנּוֹתֵן רֵיחַ טוֹב בַּפֵּרוֹת.

Blessed are You, *Adonai* Our God, Sovereign of the Universe, who gives a pleasant fragrance to fruits.

Barukh atah Adonai eloheinu melekh ha'olam hanotein rei'ach tov bapeirot.

Upon smelling fragrant oils

בָּרוּךְ אַתָּה יהוה אֱלֹהֵינוּ מֶלֶךְ הָעוֹלָם, בּוֹרֵא שֶׁמֶן עָרֵב.

Blessed are You, *Adonai* Our God, Sovereign of the Universe, who creates fragrant oil.

Barukh atah Adonai eloheinu melekh ha'olam borei shemen areiv.

Blessings for Sight

Upon seeing a rainbow

בָּרוּךְ אַתָּה יהוה אֱלֹהֵינוּ מֶלֶךְ הָעוֹלָם, זוֹכֵר הַבְּרִית וְנֶאֱמָן בִּבְרִיתוֹ וְקַיָּם בְּמַאֲמָרוֹ.

Blessed are You, *Adonai* Our God, Sovereign of the Universe, who remembers the covenant and is faithful to all promises.

Barukh atah Adonai eloheinu melekh ha'olam zokher haberit vene'eman bivrito vekayam bemaamaro.

Upon seeing trees blossoming for the first time in the year

בָּרוּךְ אַתָּה יהוה אֱלֹהֵינוּ מֶלֶךְ הָעוֹלָם, שֶׁלֹּא חִסַּר בְּעוֹלָמוֹ דָּבָר, וּבָרָא בוֹ בְּרִיּוֹת טוֹבוֹת וְאִילָנוֹת טוֹבִים לְהַנּוֹת בָּהֶם בְּנֵי אָדָם.

Blessed are You, *Adonai* Our God, Sovereign of the Universe, who has withheld nothing from the world and who has created lovely creatures and beautiful trees for people to enjoy.

Barukh atah Adonai eloheinu melekh ha'olam shelo chisar be'olamo davar uvara vo briyot tovot ve'ilanot tovim lehanot bahem benei adam.

Upon seeing the ocean

בָּרוּךְ אַתָּה יהוה אֱלֹהֵינוּ מֶלֶךְ הָעוֹלָם, שֶׁעָשָׂה אֶת־הַיָּם הַגָּדוֹל.

Blessed are You, *Adonai* Our God, Sovereign of the Universe, who has made the great sea.

Barukh atah Adonai eloheinu melekh ha'olam she'asah et hayam hagadol.

Upon seeing trees or creatures of unusual beauty

בָּרוּךְ אַתָּה יהוה אֱלֹהֵינוּ מֶלֶךְ הָעוֹלָם, שֶׁכָּכָה לוֹ בְּעוֹלָמוֹ.

Blessed are You, *Adonai* Our God, Sovereign of the Universe, who has such beauty in the world.

Barukh atah Adonai eloheinu melekh ha'olam shekakhah lo be'olamo.

Upon seeing someone of abnormal appearance

בָּרוּךְ אַתָּה יהוה אֱלֹהֵינוּ מֶלֶךְ הָעוֹלָם, מְשַׁנֶּה הַבְּרִיּוֹת.

Blessed are You, *Adonai* Our God, Sovereign of the Universe, who makes people different.

Barukh atah Adonai eloheinu melekh ha'olam meshaneh habriyot.

Upon seeing lightning, shooting stars, mountains, or a sunrise

בָּרוּךְ אַתָּה יהוה אֱלֹהֵינוּ מֶלֶךְ הָעוֹלָם, עֹשֶׂה מַעֲשֵׂה בְרֵאשִׁית.

Blessed are You, *Adonai* Our God, Sovereign of the Universe, Source of creation.

Barukh atah Adonai eloheinu melekh ha'olam oseh maaseh vereshit.

Upon seeing synagogues restored

בָּרוּךְ אַתָּה יהוה אֱלֹהֵינוּ מֶלֶךְ הָעוֹלָם, מַצִּיב גְּבוּל אַלְמָנָה.

Blessed are You, *Adonai* Our God, Sovereign of the Universe, who restores the borders of the widow. (Zion)

Barukh atah Adonai eloheinu melekh ha'olam matziv gevul almanah.

Upon seeing a person distinguished in knowledge of Torah

בָּרוּךְ אַתָּה יהוה אֱלֹהֵינוּ מֶלֶךְ הָעוֹלָם, שֶׁחָלַק מֵחָכְמָתוֹ לִירֵאָיו.

Blessed are You, *Adonai* Our God, Sovereign of the Universe, who has given wisdom to those who revere God.

Barukh atah Adonai eloheinu melekh ha'olam shechalak meichokhmato lirei'av.

Upon seeing a person distinguished in secular knowledge

בָּרוּךְ אַתָּה יהוה אֱלֹהֵינוּ מֶלֶךְ הָעוֹלָם, שֶׁנָּתַן מֵחָכְמָתוֹ לְבָשָׂר וָדָם.

Blessed are You, *Adonai* Our God, Sovereign of the Universe, who has given wisdom to mortals.

Barukh atah Adonai eloheinu melekh ha'olam shenatan mechokhmato levasar vadam.

Upon seeing a head of state

בָּרוּךְ אַתָּה יהוה אֱלֹהֵינוּ מֶלֶךְ הָעוֹלָם, שֶׁנָּתַן מִכְּבוֹדוֹ לְבָשָׂר וָדָם.

Blessed are You, *Adonai* Our God, Sovereign of the Universe, who has given glory to mortals.

Barukh atah Adonai eloheinu melekh ha'olam shenatan mikvodo levasar vadam.

Upon seeing a friend after a long separation

בָּרוּךְ אַתָּה יהוה אֱלֹהֵינוּ מֶלֶךְ הָעוֹלָם, מְחַיֵּה הַמֵּתִים.

Blessed are You, *Adonai* Our God, Sovereign of the Universe, who brings the dead back to life.

Barukh atah Adonai eloheinu melekh ha'olam mechayeh hameiteem.

Blessings Upon Hearing

Upon hearing thunder

בָּרוּךְ אַתָּה יהוה אֱלֹהֵינוּ מֶלֶךְ הָעוֹלָם, שֶׁכֹּחוֹ וּגְבוּרָתוֹ מָלֵא עוֹלָם.

Blessed are You, *Adonai* Our God, Sovereign of the Universe, whose might and power fill the entire world.

Barukh atah Adonai eloheinu melekh ha'olam shekocho ugevarato malei olam.

Upon hearing good news

בָּרוּךְ אַתָּה יהוה אֱלֹהֵינוּ מֶלֶךְ הָעוֹלָם, הַטּוֹב וְהַמֵּטִיב.

Blessed are You, *Adonai* Our God, Sovereign of the Universe, who is good and causes good things.

Barukh atah Adonai eloheinu melekh ha'olam hatov veha-metiv.

Upon hearing tragic news

בָּרוּךְ אַתָּה יהוה אֱלֹהֵינוּ מֶלֶךְ הָעוֹלָם, דַּיַּן הָאֱמֶת.

Blessed are You, *Adonai* Our God, Sovereign of the Universe, who is the true Judge.

Barukh atah Adonai eloheinu melekh ha'olam dayan ha'emet.

Other Blessings of Gratitude

After leaving the bathroom

בָּרוּךְ אַתָּה יהוה אֱלֹהֵינוּ מֶלֶךְ הָעוֹלָם, אֲשֶׁר יָצַר אֶת הָאָדָם בְּחָכְמָה וּבָרָא בּוֹ נְקָבִים נְקָבִים חֲלוּלִים חֲלוּלִים. גָּלוּי וְיָדוּעַ לִפְנֵי כִסֵּא כְבוֹדֶךָ שֶׁאִם יִפָּתֵחַ אֶחָד מֵהֶם אוֹ יִסָּתֵם אֶחָד מֵהֶם אִי אֶפְשַׁר לְהִתְקַיֵּם וְלַעֲמוֹד לְפָנֶיךָ. בָּרוּךְ אַתָּה יהוה רוֹפֵא כָל בָּשָׂר וּמַפְלִיא לַעֲשׂוֹת.

Blessed are You, *Adonai* Our God, Sovereign of the Universe, who has formed people in wisdom and created in them many orifices and hollow tubes. It is well known that if one of them be obstructed or broken, it would be impossible to stay alive. Blessed are You, Healer of all flesh, who does wondrous things.

Barukh atah Adonai eloheinu melekh ha'olam asher yatzar et haadam bechakhmah uvara vo nikavim nikavim chalulim chalulim galui veyadua lifnei kisei kevodekha she'im yipate'ach echad meihem oh yisatem echad meihem ee'efshar lehitkayem velaamod lifanekha. Barukh atah Adonai rofei kol basar umaflee laasot.

Upon affixing a mezuzah to the doorpost

בָּרוּךְ אַתָּה יהוה אֱלֹהֵינוּ מֶלֶךְ הָעוֹלָם, אֲשֶׁר קִדְּשָׁנוּ בְּמִצְוֹתָיו וְצִוָּנוּ לִקְבּוֹעַ מְזוּזָה.

Blessed are You, *Adonai* Our God, Sovereign of the Universe, who has made us distinct with commandments and commanded us to attach the *mezuzah*.

Barukh atah Adonai eloheinu melekh ha'olam asher kidshanu bemitzvotav vetzivanu likboah mezuzah.

Upon obtaining a new item, tasting a new good for the first time, entering a new home, and many other new and special occasions

בָּרוּךְ אַתָּה יהוה אֱלֹהֵינוּ מֶלֶךְ הָעוֹלָם, שֶׁהֶחֱיָנוּ וְקִיְּמָנוּ וְהִגִּיעָנוּ לַזְמַן הַזֶּה.

Blessed are You, *Adonai* Our God, Sovereign of the Universe, who has given us life, sustained us, and helped us to reach this day.

Barukh atah Adonai eloheinu melekh ha'olam shehecheyanu vikimanu vihigiyanu lazman hazeh.

INDEX

About the Author

Rabbi Ronald H. Isaacs is the spiritual leader of Temple Sholom in Bridgewater, New Jersey. He holds a doctorate from Columbia University in Instructional Technology. He is the author of several books, including *Reflections: A Jewish Grandparents' Gift of Memories* and *Loving Companions: Our Jewish Wedding Album*, both of which he co-authored with his wife, Leora, and *A Glossary of Jewish Life*, co-authored with Kerry M. Olitzky.